EYEWITNESS TRAVEL

BARCELONA
& CATALONIA

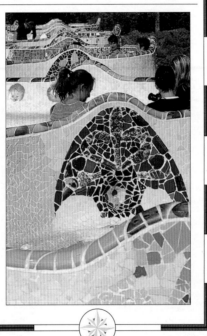

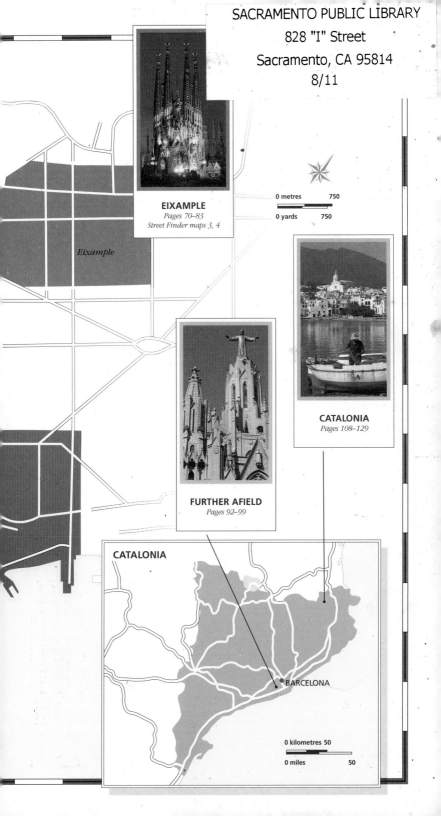

EIXAMPLE
Pages 70–83
Street Finder maps 3, 4

Eixample

0 metres 750

0 yards 750

CATALONIA
Pages 108–129

FURTHER AFIELD
Pages 92–99

CATALONIA

BARCELONA

0 kilometres 50

0 miles 50

EYEWITNESS TRAVEL

BARCELONA
& CATALONIA

MAIN CONTRIBUTOR: ROGER WILLIAMS

LONDON, NEW YORK,
MELBOURNE, MUNICH AND DELHI
www.dk.com

PROJECT EDITOR Catherine Day
ART EDITORS Carolyn Hewitson, Marisa Renzullo
EDITORS Elizabeth Atherton, Felicity Crowe
DESIGNER Suzanne Metcalfe-Megginson
MAP CO-ORDINATOR David Pugh
PICTURE RESEARCH Monica Allende
DTP DESIGNERS Samantha Borland, Lee Redmond,
Pamela Shiels

MAIN CONTRIBUTOR
Roger Williams

MAPS
Jane Hanson, Phil Rose, Jennifer Skelley (Lovell Jones Ltd),
Gary Bowes, Richard Toomey (ERA-Maptec Ltd)

PHOTOGRAPHERS
Max Alexander, Mike Dunning, Heidi Grassley, Alan Keohane

ILLUSTRATORS
Stephen Conlin, Isidoro González-Adalid Cabezas
(Acanto Arquitectura y Urbanismo S.L.), Claire Littlejohn,
Maltings Partnership, John Woodcock

Reproduced by Colourscan, Singapore
Printed and bound in China by South China Printing Co. Ltd.

First American Edition, 1999
11 12 13 14 10 9 8 7 6 5 4 3 2 1

Published in the United States by DK Publishing,
375 Hudson Street, New York, New York 10014

**Reprinted with revisions 2000, 2001, 2002,
2003, 2004, 2005, 2006, 2008, 2009, 2010, 2011**

Copyright 1999, 2011 © Dorling Kindersley Limited, London

Published in Great Britain by Dorling Kindersley Limited.

A catalog record for this book is available from the Library of Congress.

ISSN 1542-1554
ISBN 978-0-7566-6936-2

THROUGHOUT THIS BOOK, FLOORS ARE NUMBERED IN ACCORDANCE
WITH LOCAL CATALAN USAGE.

Front cover main image: Roof terrace of Gaudí's Casa Batlló

MIX
Paper from
responsible sources
FSC
www.fsc.org   FSC™ C018179

**The information in this
DK Eyewitness Travel Guide is checked regularly.**

Every effort has been made to ensure that this book is as up-to-date
as possible at the time of going to press. Some details, however,
such as telephone numbers, opening hours, prices, gallery hanging
arrangements and travel information are liable to change. The pub-
lishers cannot accept responsibility for any consequences arising
from the use of this book, nor for any material on third party websites, and cannot guarantee that any website address in this book
will be a suitable source of travel information. We value the views
and suggestions of our readers very highly. Please write to: Publisher, DK Eyewitness Travel Guides, Dorling Kindersley, 80 Strand,
London, WC2R 0RL, Great Britain, or email travelguides@dk.com.

CONTENTS

INTRODUCING
BARCELONA AND
CATALONIA

**Jaume I, "El Conquistador",
ruler of Catalonia 1213–76**

**One of the many popular cafés in
Barcelona's redeveloped Old Port**

BARCELONA
AREA BY AREA

The small, whitewashed town of Cadaqués on the Costa Brava

Spectacular stained-glass roof of
the Palau de la Música Catalana

CATALONIA

TRAVELLERS'
NEEDS

SURVIVAL GUIDE

Pa amb tomàquet – bread rubbed
with tomato, garlic and olive oil

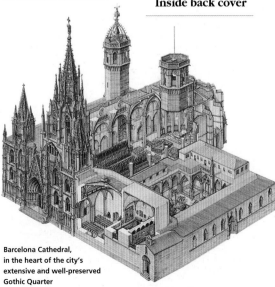
Barcelona Cathedral,
in the heart of the city's
extensive and well-preserved
Gothic Quarter

HOW TO USE THIS GUIDE

This guide has expert recommendations and detailed practical information to enrich any visit to Barcelona and Catalonia. *Introducing Barcelona and Catalonia* puts the area in geographical, historical and cultural context. *Barcelona and Catalonia* is a six-chapter guide to important sights: *Barcelona at a Glance* highlights the city's top attractions; *Old Town, Eixample* and *Montjuïc* explore Barcelona's central districts in more detail; *Further Afield* views sights outside the city centre; and *Catalonia* delves into the region's four provinces. *Travellers' Needs* covers hotels, restaurants and entertainment. The *Survival Guide* provides vital practical information.

BARCELONA AND CATALONIA

The region is divided into five sightseeing areas – the central districts of Barcelona, sights outside the centre, and those beyond the city. Each area chapter opens with an introduction and a list of sights covered. Central districts have a Street-by-Street map of a particularly interesting part of the area. The sights further afield have a regional map.

Sights at a Glance lists the area's key sights (great buildings, art galleries, museums and churches) by category.

2 Street-by-Street map
The area shaded pink on the Area Map is shown here in greater detail with accurate drawings of all the buildings.

A suggested route for a walk covers the more interesting streets in the area.

Each chapter of *Barcelona and Catalonia* has a different colour-coded thumb tab.

Locator maps show where you are in relation to other parts of Barcelona or Spain.

1 Area Map of the city
Sights are numbered and located on a map, with Metro stations where helpful. The sights are also shown on the Barcelona Street Finder on pp188–97.

A list of star sights recommends places no visitor should miss.

3 Detailed information on each sight
The sights listed at the start of the section are described individually and follow the numbering on the Area Map. A key to symbols summarizing practical information is shown on the back flap.

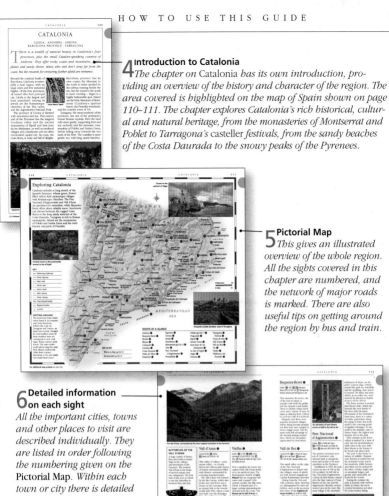

4 Introduction to Catalonia

The chapter on Catalonia has its own introduction, providing an overview of the history and character of the region. The area covered is highlighted on the map of Spain shown on page 110–111. The chapter explores Catalonia's rich historical, cultural and natural heritage, from the monasteries of Montserrat and Poblet to Tarragona's casteller festivals, from the sandy beaches of the Costa Daurada to the snowy peaks of the Pyrenees.

5 Pictorial Map

This gives an illustrated overview of the whole region. All the sights covered in this chapter are numbered, and the network of major roads is marked. There are also useful tips on getting around the region by bus and train.

6 Detailed information on each sight

All the important cities, towns and other places to visit are described individually. They are listed in order following the numbering given on the Pictorial Map. Within each town or city there is detailed information on important buildings and other sights.

Stars indicate the best features and works of art.

The Visitors' Checklist
provides a summary of the practical information you will need to plan your visit.

7 The top sights

These are given two or more full pages. Historic buildings are dissected to reveal their interiors. For larger historic sites, all the important buildings are labelled to help you locate those that most interest you.

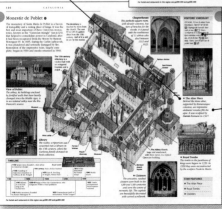

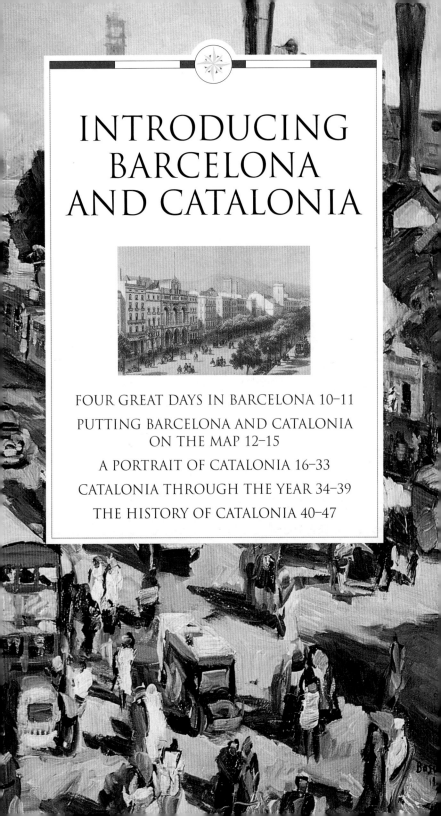

INTRODUCING BARCELONA AND CATALONIA

FOUR GREAT DAYS IN BARCELONA

Sagrada Familia

Days are long in Barcelona. The morning extends until well after midday, with lunch often starting around 2pm, and the late opening hours mean that afternoon merges into evening. With so much time at your disposal you'll want to make the most of your visit with a bit of planning. Each of these four itineraries follows a theme and sights are reachable using public transport. Prices include travel, food and admission. Family prices are for two adults and two children.

La Rambla, an exciting avenue for a stroll at any time

HISTORIC TREASURES

- **A stroll round the Gothic quarter and museums**
- **A Modernista concert hall**
- **Non-stop life on Spain's most famous street**

TWO ADULTS allow at least €40

Morning

Barcelona's preserved medieval centre is the **Barri Gòtic** *(see pp54–5)*, a warren of streets where it is easy to get lost. You can happily spend the morning here without walking great distances. The focal point is the **Cathedral** *(see pp58–9)*. Next to it is the **Palau Reial** (Royal Palace), part of which is now the **Museu d'Història de la Ciutat** *(see pp56–7)*, where you can take a fascinating subterranean stroll over the excavated ruins of Roman Barcelona. The palace also houses what is perhaps Barcelona's most fascinating museum, the eclectic **Museu Frederic Marès** *(see p56)*. There are plenty of places for a budget lunch in this area.

Afternoon

After lunch, take a guided tour of the **Palau de la Música Catalana** *(see pp62–3)* and its dazzling Modernista interior. After that, plunge into the atmospheric **Born district** *(see pp102–3)*, with its trendy shops. Take a look in the **Museu Picasso** *(see pp64–5)*, then wander to **La Rambla**, a busy street where there is always plenty of activity.

Richly ornamental interior of Palau de la Musica Catalana

GAUDÍ GREATS

- **Casa Batlló's organic forms**
- **Gaudí's extraordinary church, Sagrada Familia**
- **An evening's shopping in style in Passeig de Gràcia**

TWO ADULTS allow at least €60

Morning

For many visitors, Barcelona is synonymous with the unique architecture of Antoni Gaudí. He created many great buildings, all of which are worth visiting, but here are two places to make a start. Begin your day with a visit to Gaudí's most colourful and eccentric house, **Casa Batlló** *(see pp76–7)*. Discover its fantastic organic forms and pay the extra fee to extend your tour to see the roof with its remarkable chimneys and "dragon's back". A little further up the road is the equally renowned **Casa Milà**, also known as *La Pedrera (see p79)*. This can also be visited, but if you're short of time its remarkable façade can be admired from the outside. For lunch, you'll find there are several budget-priced restaurants in the streets near and parallel to Passeig de Gràcia.

Afternoon/Evening

Visit Gaudí's greatest, unfinished work, the **Sagrada Família** *(see pp80–3)*. Allow plenty of time to make sense of the dense detail on the two façades of this extraordinary church – the Passion façade and the Nativity façade – and also to explore the

---

◁ **El Paralelo 1930**, a portrait of one of Barcelona's main avenues in 1930 by Emili Bosch Roger (1894–1980)

Casa Batlló, a house in an alternative architectural universe

vertigo-inducing fantasy towers (you go up by lift and return by stairs). Coming back down to reality, return to the **Passeig de Gràcia** and browse in its stylish shops. Look out for the design emporium, **Vinçon** *(see p155)*.

Museu d'Art Contemporani façade

ART FOR ART'S SAKE

- **Romanesque marvels on Montjuïc hill**
- **Contemporary works of art**
- **Collection of Old Masters**

TWO ADULTS allow at least €50

Morning
The number of great galleries you can cram into a day depends on your appetite and stamina but here are four to give you a

taster. Start at 10am when the **Museu Nacional d'Art de Catalunya** *(see p88)* opens on Montjuïc hill (also take time to enjoy the great view). Here, you'll see what is arguably the best collection of Romanesque art in any museum. Close by is the city's latest contemporary art gallery, **CaixaForum** *(see p98)*, situated in a Modernista factory. Lunch in a local café.

Afternoon
For a change of pace, make your way to the **Monestir de Pedralbes** *(see p95)*, a lovely 14th-century monastery with numerous religious objects and works of art on display. Back in the city centre, visit the **Museu d'Art Contemporani** *(see pp62–3)*, where you can be sure of something surprising.

FAMILY FUN

- **A trip to the funfair**
- **A harbour cruise**
- **Sharks at the aquarium**
- **IMAX cinema experience**

FAMILY OF 4 allow at least €100

Morning
Tibidabo Amusement Park *(see pp98–9)*, on the highest hill behind Barcelona, is a family day out in itself, with getting there by tram and funicular half the fun. But if you don't want to go that far, stroll down Las Ramblas and take the lift up the **Monument a Colom** *(see pp68–9)* for a good view of this part of the city. From the nearby quayside, board a **Golondrina** *(see p69)* for a cruise round the harbour. Then cross the wavy footbridge for the Maremagnum shopping centre, also the best place to grab a bite to eat.

Afternoon/Evening
Attractions that are specifically for children can, if you want to extend the day, be saved until after dark. The **Aquarium** *(see p68)* offers several activities for kids, as well as tanks full of sharks and other fascinating creatures. Next to it, watch the hugely realistic (and stomach-churning) show at the **IMAX Cinema** *(see p164)*. A short walk away is the relaxing, child-friendly **Museu d'Historia de Catalunya** *(see pp68–9)* with exhibits on daily life in earlier times.

Barcelona's Aquarium, a wonderful experience for children

Putting Barcelona and Catalonia on the Map

Catalonia lies in the northeastern corner of the Iberian
Peninsula and occupies six per cent of Spain. Barcelona,
its capital, lies almost exactly halfway along its
coastline, which in turn stretches a quarter of the way
down Spain's Mediterranean seaboard. Barcelona is
the main bridging point to
the Catalan-speaking
Balearic Islands.

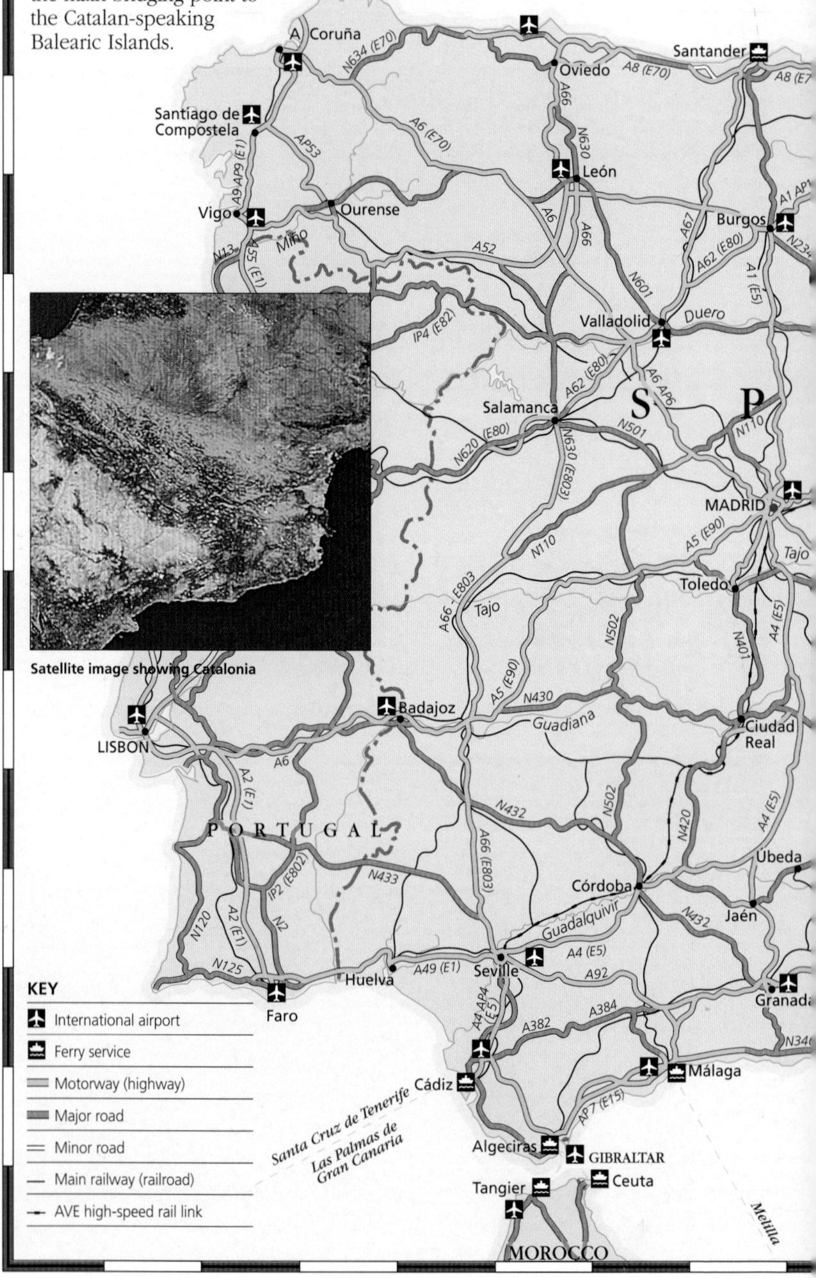

Bay
of Biscay

A Coruña

N634 (E70)

Oviedo   A8 (E70)   Santander   A8 (E7

Santiago de
Compostela

AP53

A6 (E70)

León

A6

N630

A67   Burgos   A1 AP\

Vigo   A9 AP9 (E1)

Ourense   MI80   A52   A66   A62 (E80)   A1 (E5)   N23

N-13   A55 (E1)   IP4 (E82)

Valladolid   Duero

A62 (E80)   A6 AP6

S   **P**

Salamanca   N501   N110

N620 (E80)   N630 (E803)

MADRID

A66 (E803)   N110   A5 (E90)   Tajo

Tajo   Toledo   N401   N4 (E5)

N110   N502   A4 (E5)

Satellite image showing Catalonia

LISBON   Badajoz   N430   Ciudad
Real

A6   Guadiana

A2 (E1)   N432   N502   N420   A4 (E5)

P O R T U G A L

N433   A66 (E803)   Ubeda

N120   Córdoba   Jaén

A2 (E1)   P2 (E802)   Guadalquivir   N432

N2   A4 (E5)

N125   Huelva   A49 (E1)   Seville   A92   Granada

A4 A4   A382   A384   N34

Faro   Santa Cruz de Tenerife   Cádiz   A7 (E15)   Málaga

Las Palmas de
Gran Canaria

Algeciras   GIBRALTAR

Tangier   Ceuta

Melilla

MOROCCO

KEY

✈ International airport

⛴ Ferry service

▬ Motorway (highway)

▬ Major road

= Minor road

— Main railway (railroad)

→ AVE high-speed rail link

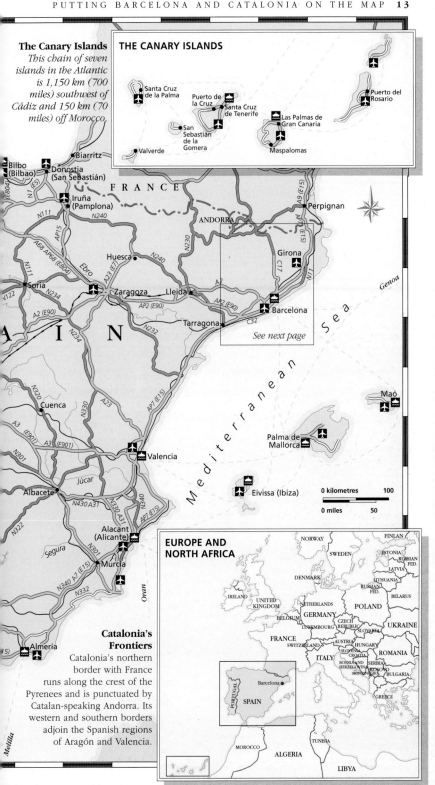

The Canary Islands

This chain of seven islands in the Atlantic is 1,150 km (700 miles) southwest of Cádiz and 150 km (70 miles) off Morocco.

THE CANARY ISLANDS

Santa Cruz de la Palma

Puerto de la Cruz

Santa Cruz de Tenerife

San Sebastián de la Gomera

Valverde

Las Palmas de Gran Canaria

Maspalomas

Puerto del Rosario

See next page

Maó

Palma de Mallorca

Eivissa (Ibiza)

| 0 kilometres | 100 |
| 0 miles | 50 |

EUROPE AND NORTH AFRICA

Catalonia's Frontiers

Catalonia's northern border with France runs along the crest of the Pyrenees and is punctuated by Catalan-speaking Andorra. Its western and southern borders adjoin the Spanish regions of Aragón and Valencia.

Barcelona City Centre

Set between the mountains and the sea, which still play an integral part in city life, Barcelona is a rare city, a patchwork of distinctive districts telling the story of its growth from a medieval core to the 19th-century expansion and today's ultra-modern showpieces. The three main sightseeing areas described in this guide illustrate this startling diversity. The hill of Montjuïc, abutting the sea, forms the southwestern end of an arc of steep hills that almost completely encloses the city. It is a district of monumental buildings and open spaces. The Old Town has a superb Gothic heart with a myriad of narrow streets twisting among ancient houses. The densely populated Eixample, in contrast, is a district of immensely long, straight streets and superb Modernista architecture.

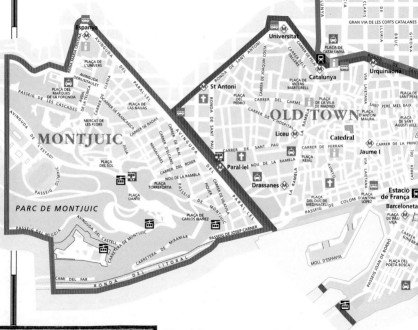

Montjuïc
There are wonderful views from the top of this large hill. Several of Barcelona's best museums are here, including the Archaeological Museum (see p88) which displays this Roman mosaic.

0 kilometres   1

0 miles   0.5

KEY

▢	Major sight
Ⓜ	Metro station
🚆	Train station
🚌	Bus stop
🚠	Cable car
🚡	Funicular
🚋	Tramway stop
🚓	Police station
ℹ	Tourist information
✚	Church

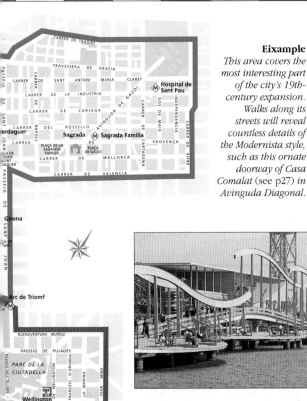

Eixample

This area covers the most interesting part of the city's 19th-century expansion. Walks along its streets will reveal countless details of the Modernista style, such as this ornate doorway of Casa Comalat (see p27) in Avinguda Diagonal.

Old Town

This area includes all the oldest districts of Barcelona and its port, the 18th-century fishing "village" of Barceloneta and the new waterside developments. This new swing bridge is in the Old Port (see p67).

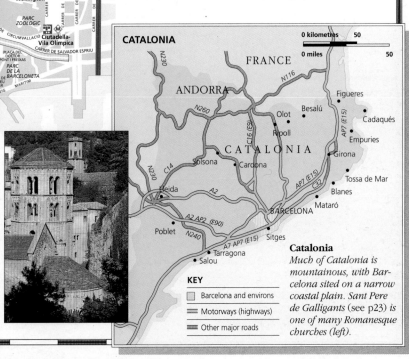

Catalonia

Much of Catalonia is mountainous, with Barcelona sited on a narrow coastal plain. Sant Pere de Galligants (see p23) is one of many Romanesque churches (left).

A PORTRAIT OF CATALONIA

Barcelona is one of the great Mediterranean cities. Few places are so redolent with history, few so boldly modern. Animated and inspired, it is a city that sparkles as much at night-time as in the full light of day. It is famous for its main avenue, La Rambla, for its bars, its museums and its enthusiasm for life.

Barcelona is the capital of the autonomous region of Catalonia, the most northeasterly corner of Spain, bordering France. The region is divided into four provinces, named after their provincial capitals: Barcelona, Girona, Lleida and Tarragona.

The city of Barcelona lies between two rivers, the Llobregat and the Besòs, and is backed by the Collserola hills which rise to a 512-m (1,680-ft) peak at the Tibidabo amusement park. The city grew up as the industrial sweatshop of Spain, though the shunting yards and seaside warehouses have now gone. Around four million people live in Barcelona and its suburbs – about half the population of Catalonia. It is Spain's second city after its old rival, Madrid.

La dama del paraigua

POLITICS AND SOCIETY

Catalonia is governed by the Generalitat, housed in the Palau de la Generalitat in the heart of the Old Town and on the site of the Roman forum. The region's parliament is located in the Parc de la Ciutadella. The city of Barcelona has a separate administration, and its town hall, the Casa de la Ciutat, faces the Generalitat across the Plaça de Sant Jaume. Catalonia has developed its own police force, which has now taken over from Spain's national police in most of Catalonia.

Catalans are progressive but, as in many other countries, people in rural areas are more conservative than those in the cities. For 23 years after Franco's death, the Generalitat was

Strollers and shoppers on La Rambla enjoying Barcelona's plentiful winter sunshine

◁ Stunning floral mosaic pillars at the Palau de la Música Catalana in Barcelona

St George's Day in April – the day for giving books

Catalans are not burdened with self doubt. The vigour with which they have rebuilt parts of their capital since the early 1980s shows flair and a firm hand. Places of great sentimental value, such as Barceloneta's beachside restaurant shacks, were torn down. Stunning new buildings such as the Museu d'Art Contemporani were put up in the Old Town, and old buildings such as the Café Zurich, a famous rendezvous for writers, artists and intellectuals on La Rambla, were restored without hesitation.

run by the conservative Convergència i Unió under the presidency of Jordi Pujol, while the city council was run by a socialist party. In 2003, however, Catalans elected a socialist Generalitat to power under Pascual Maragall, who was replaced by José Montilla, also a socialist, in 2006.

Catalans, who have no taste for bullfighting and whose sedate national dance, the *sardana*, is unruffled by passion, are a serious, hardworking people. Some would rather be associated with northern Europeans than with other Spaniards, whom they regard as indolent. Part of their complaint against Madrid has been that, as one of the richest regions of Spain, they put more into the national coffers than they take out.

Two emotions are said to guide Catalans: *seny*, which means solid common sense, and *rauxa*, a creative chaos. A bourgeois, conservative element of Barcelona society can be seen at concerts and in pastry shops, but a certain surreal air is often evident, on La Rambla, for instance, where sometimes it seems that anything goes. The two elements are mixed in each person, and even the most staid may have the occasional *cop de rauxa*, or moment of chaotic ecstasy.

Street performer on La Rambla

LANGUAGE AND CULTURE

A Romance language similar to the old Langue d'Oc, or Provençal, once used in France, Catalan is Catalonia's official language, spoken by some eight million people. It has always been a living language and it continued to be spoken in the home even when it was banned by Franco. Catalans do not think it rude to talk to each other in Catalan in front of

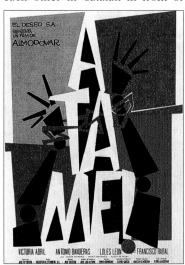
Poster for a Pedro Almodóvar film

Beach at Tossa de Mar on the Costa Brava

anywhere in the world. New Catalan writing has burgeoned since the 1970s and there are many literary prizes, but few Catalan writers of any era have been translated into English.

WORK AND LEISURE

Catalans stay true to their traditions and their families. Sunday lunch is a time to get together, although even during the week, most people who can do so return home for lunch. This creates a rush hour four times a day, with a lull in the early afternoon. Shops close around 8:30pm, and between 6pm and 8:30pm the streets are crowded. Dinner or entertainment starts around 9pm, but there is increasing pressure for business hours to conform with the rest of Europe.

Allegiance to the local football team, Barça, is a matter of national pride for its supporters. Meals out, concerts and the cinema are popular activities. The week begins quietly but, as the weekend approaches, streets fill and visitors leaving La Rambla at midnight to go to bed may feel they are leaving a good party too soon.

someone who speaks only Spanish. All public signs and official documents in Catalonia are in Spanish and Catalan.

If *rauxa* is responsible for the creative spirit as claimed, then Catalonia has been blessed with an abundance. Modernisme, led by Antoni Gaudí, is the region's gift to world architecture. Painters Joan Miró, Salvador Dalí and Antoni Tàpies were born here, while Pablo Picasso spent his formative years in Barcelona. Designs by Javier Mariscal, creator of the 1992 Olympic motifs and Cobi, the mascot, furniture by Oscar Tusquets and fashion by Toni Miró help make Barcelona a city of great style. Bigas Luna, locally-born director of *Jamón Jamón*, Pedro Almodóvar, whose film *All About My Mother* was shot in Barcelona and Woody Allen's *Vicky, Cristina, Barcelona* have raised the area's profile in the cinema.

Montserrat Caballé

Over the last 150 years, some outstanding musicians have emerged from Catalonia. The composers Isaac Albéniz (1860–1909), Enric Granados (1867–1916) and Frederic Mompou (1893–1987) brought music imbued with a true Iberian idiom into the classical mainstream. Pau Casals (1876– 1973) was considered one of the greatest of all cellists, and Montserrat Caballé and Josep Carreras can fill opera houses

Demonstration for Catalan independence

Flowers of the Matollar

The Matollar is the distinctive landscape of Spain's eastern Mediterranean coast. This scrubland rich in wild flowers is the result of centuries of woodland clearance, during which the native holm oak was felled for timber and to provide land for grazing and cultivation. Many colourful plants have adapted to the extremes of climate here. Most flower in spring, when hillsides are daubed with yellow broom and pink and white cistuses, and the air is perfumed by aromatic herbs such as rosemary, lavender and thyme. Buzzing insects feed on the abundance of nectar and pollen.

Yellow bee orchid

Spanish broom *is a small bush with yellow flowers on slender branches. The black seed pods split when dry, scattering the seeds on the ground.*

The century plant's flower stalk can reach 10 m (32 ft).

Aleppo pine **Rosemary**

Jerusalem sage, *an attractive shrub which is often grown in gardens, has tall stems surrounded by bunches of showy yellow flowers. Its leaves are greyish-white and woolly.*

Rose garlic *has round clusters of violet or pink flowers at the end of a single stalk. It survives the summer as the bulb familiar to all cooks.*

FOREIGN INVADERS

Several plants from the New World have managed to colonize the bare ground of the *matollar*. The prickly pear, thought to have been brought back by Christopher Columbus, produces a delicious fruit which can be picked only with thickly gloved hands. The rapidly growing century plant, a native of Mexico which has tough, spiny leaves, sends up a tall flower shoot only when it is 10–15 years old, after which it dies.

Prickly pear in bloom

Flowering shoots of the century plant

Common thyme *is a low-growing aromatic herb which is widely cultivated for use in the kitchen.*

The mirror orchid, *a small plant which grows on grassy sites, is easily distinguished from other orchids by the brilliant metallic blue patch inside the lip, fringed by brown hairs.*

CLIMATE CHART

Temp (°C) — Temperature
Rainfall (mm) — Rainfall

J F M A M J J A S O N D

Most plants found in the *matollar* come into bloom in the warm, moist spring. The plants protect themselves from losing water during the dry summer heat with thick leaves or waxy secretions, or by storing moisture in bulbs or tubers.

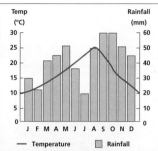

Holm oaks *are very common in eastern Spain. The leaves are tough and rubbery to prevent water loss.*

The strawberry tree *is an evergreen shrub with glossy serrated leaves. Its inedible strawberry-like fruit turns red when ripe.*

Tree heather

Grey-leaved cistus, *growing on sunny sites, has crumpled petals and bright yellow anthers.*

Narrow-leaved cistus *exudes a sticky aromatic gum used in perfumes.*

Star clover *is a low-growing annual whose fruit develops into a star-shaped seed head. Its flowers are often pale pink.*

WILDLIFE OF THE MATOLLAR

The animals which live in the *matollar* are most often seen early in the morning, before the temperature is high. Countless insects fly from flower to flower, providing a source of food for birds. Smaller mammals, such as mice and voles, are active only at night when it is cooler and there are few predators around.

Ladder snakes *feed on small mammals, birds and insects. The young are identified by a black pattern like the rungs of a ladder, but adults are marked with two simple stripes.*

Scorpions *hide under rocks or wood by day. When disturbed, the tail is curled quickly over the body in a threatening gesture. The sting, lethal to small animals, can cause some irritation to humans.*

The Dartford warbler, *a skulking bird which has a dark plumage and a cocked tail, sings melodiously during its mating display. Males are more vividly coloured than females.*

The swallow-tail butterfly *is one of the most conspicuous of the great many insects living in the matollar. Bees, ants and grasshoppers are also extremely common.*

Romanesque Art and Architecture

Catalonia has an exceptional collection of medieval buildings constructed between the 11th and 13th centuries in a distinctive local Romanesque style. There are more than 2,000 examples, most of them churches. Those in the Pyrenees, which have largely escaped both attack and modernization, have survived particularly well. Churches had lofty bell towers, barrel-vaulted naves, rounded arches and imaginative sculpture, as well as remarkable wall paintings. Some frescoes and furniture have come to rest in the Museu Nacional d'Art de Catalunya (*see p88*) in Barcelona, which has the largest Romanesque collection in the world.

Sant Jaume de Frontanyà (see p114) *is a former Augustinian canonry with typical 11th-century features, such as the Lombard bands below the roofs of the three apses. The large octagonal central lantern is, however, unusual.*

Vielha

Pont de Suert

Sort

Andorra-la Vella

La Seu d'Urgell

Puigcerdà

Berga

Sant Climent de Taüll, *an exemplary church in the Vall de Boí (see p113), was consecrated in 1123. Its frescoes, including a* Christ in Majesty *(see p88), are replicas, but the originals, which are now in Barcelona, are among the best in Catalonia.*

0 kilometres   30

0 miles   15

MONESTIR DE SANTA MARIA DE RIPOLL

The saints

The story of Solomon

The Old Testament

David and his musicians

The story of Moses

Christ with historical figures

The visions of Daniel

Plinth with patterns

The portal of the church of the former Benedictine monastery at Ripoll is known as "The Ripoll Bible" for its allegorical carvings. Although the church was founded in 879 and rebuilt under Abbot Oliva in 1032, the portal was added only in the late 12th century. In this fine piece of Romanesque decoration Christ sits above the doorway amid the beasts symbolizing the Apostles, and the monthly agricultural occupations are represented on the doorway pillars. There are seven biblical friezes running the length of the wall. The top frieze (*see p114*) over the tympanum represents the old men of the Apocalypse; the others are described in the captions above.

Sant Pere de Camprodon (see p115), *consecrated in 1169, is a monastery church in mature Romanesque style with five square apses. The slightly pointed barrel vault over the nave hints at the Gothic style to come.*

AREA OF MAJOR ROMANESQUE INTEREST

BARCELONA

Sant Cristòfol de Beget (see p115) *is a beautiful church in a picturesque hamlet hidden deep in a valley. It has a uniquely preserved interior which includes a Romanesque baptismal font and this famous 12th-century crucifix –* the Majestat.

Sant Pere de Rodes, *situated at 600 m (1,968 ft) above sea level, was a Benedictine monastery. In its church's nave are the pillars of a Roman temple once on this site.*

Ripoll

Olot

Vic

Figueres

Roses

Girona

Sant Feliu de Guíxols

Sant Pere de Besalú (see p115) *is the 12th-century church of an earlier Benedictine monastery. Stone lions guard this window over the portal. Inside, the ambulatory has finely carved capitals.*

The Museu Episcopal de Vic (see p124) *adjacent to the cathedral has an exquisite collection of Romanesque art. It includes this richly coloured and moving portrayal of the Visitation which was originally an altar decoration in Lluçà monastery.*

Sant Pere de Galligants (see p116), *a former Benedictine abbey, captures the very essence of Romanesque style. It has an 11th-century portal with a rose window, three naves and an octagonal bell tower. The cloister capitals are carved with biblical scenes. It now houses Girona's archaeology museum.*

Gaudí and Modernisme

Chimney, Casa Vicens

Towards the end of the 19th century a new style of art and architecture, Modernisme, a variant of Art Nouveau, was born in Barcelona. It became a means of expression for Catalan nationalism and counted Josep Puig i Cadafalch, Lluís Domènech i Montaner and, above all, Antoni Gaudí i Cornet *(see p78)* among its major exponents. Barcelona's Eixample district *(see pp70–83)* is full of the highly original buildings that they created for their wealthy clients.

All aspects of decoration *in a Modernista building, even interior design, were planned by the architect. This door and its tiled surround are in Gaudí's 1906 Casa Batlló (see p78).*

A dramatic cupola *covers the central salon, which rises through three floors. It is pierced by small round holes, inspired by Islamic architecture, giving the illusion of stars.*

Upper galleries are richly decorated with carved wood and cofferwork.

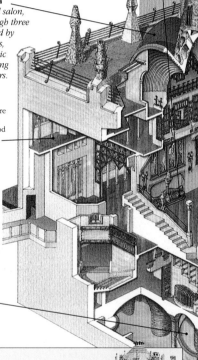

The spiral carriage ramp *is an early sign of Gaudí's predilection for curved lines. He would later exploit this to the full in the wavy façade of his masterpiece, the Casa Milà (see p79).*

THE EVOLUTION OF MODERNISME

1859 Civil engineer Ildefons Cerdà i Sunyer submits proposals for expansion of Barcelona

1878 Gaudí graduates as an architect

1900 Josep Puig i Cadafalch builds Casa Amatller *(see p78)*

1903 Lluís Domènech i Montaner builds Hospital de la Santa Creu i de Sant Pau *(see p79)*

Hospital detail

1850	1865	1880	1895	1910	1925

1883 Gaudí takes over design of Neo-Gothic Sagrada Família *(see pp80–1)*

Detail of Sagrada Família

1888 Barcelona Universal Exhibition gives impetus to Modernisme

1910 Casa Milà completed

1905 Domènech i Montaner builds Casa Lleó Morera *(see p78)*. Puig i Cadafalch builds Casa Terrades *(see p79)*

1926 Gaudí dies

Bizarrely decorated chimneys *became one of the trademarks of Gaudí's later work. They reach a fantastic extreme on the gleaming, hump-backed roof of the Casa Batlló.*

Elaborate wrought iron lamps light the grand hall.

Ceramic tiles decorate the chimneys.

GAUDÍ'S MATERIALS

Gaudí designed, or collaborated on designs, for almost every known media. He combined bare, undecorated materials – wood, rough-hewn stone, rubble and brickwork – with meticulous craftwork in wrought iron and stained glass. Mosaics of ceramic tiles were used to cover his fluid, uneven forms.

Stained-glass window in the Sagrada Família

Mosaic of ceramic tiles, Park Güell *(see p96)*

Detail of iron gate, Casa Vicens *(see pp26-7)*

Tiles on El Capricho in Comillas, Cantabria

Parabolic arches, *used extensively by Gaudí, beginning in the Palau Güell, show his interest in Gothic architecture. These arches form a corridor in his 1890 Col.legi de les Teresianes, a convent school in the west of Barcelona.*

Escutcheon alludes to the Catalan coat of arms.

PALAU GÜELL

Gaudí's first major building in the centre of the city, on La Rambla *(see p60),* established his international reputation for outstanding, original architecture. Built in 1889 for his life-long patron, the industrialist Eusebi Güell, the mansion stands on a small plot of land in a narrow street, making the façade difficult to see. Inside, Gaudí creates a sense of space by using carved screens, recesses and galleries.

Organic forms *inspired the wrought iron around the gates to the palace. Gaudí's later work teems with wildlife, such as this dragon, covered with brightly coloured tiles, which guards the steps in the Park Güell.*

La Ruta del Modernisme

The examples of Modernista architecture in Barcelona, mapped here, lie along a route designed by the city's tourist office. A *Guidebook*, available from Catalunya's tourist office *(see p175)*, the Hospital de Sant Pau, the Güell Pavillions on Avinguda Pedralbes *(see p79)* and some bookshops, provides up to 50 per cent discount on admission charges and gives you the freedom to plan your own itinerary. The Casa Batlló, Palau Güell and Palau de la Música Catalana all have guided tours, and entry is discounted at the selected museums. Many of the other premises, however, are privately owned houses, shops, cafés and hotels.

Casa Vicens
This bright, angular, turreted building by Antoni Gaudí, with ceramic mosaics and patterned brickwork, shows Moorish influence. The iron gate and fencing are hallmarks of his work ㊽

Palau Baró de Quadras
Built in 1906, this handsome house is by Josep Puig i Cadafalch. The intricate, sculptured frieze above the first-floor windows has close affinities to Spanish early Renaissance Plateresque style ㊶

Casa Lleó Morera
The first-floor dining room of this house is one of Barcelona's most stunning interiors. The stained-glass windows are by Lluís Rigalt and the eight ceramic mosaic wall panels, depicting idyllic country scenes, are by Gaspar Homar ⑲

Antiga Casa Figueres
The mosaic, stained-glass and wrought iron decoration of this, the most famous of the city's Modernista stores, was carried out in 1902 by Antoni Ros i Güell. It is today the elegant Pastisseria Escribà ⑦

KEY

– – –	Walking route
▬ ▬	Bus route
▬ ▬	Metro route
Ⓜ	Metro station

0 metres	500
0 yards	500

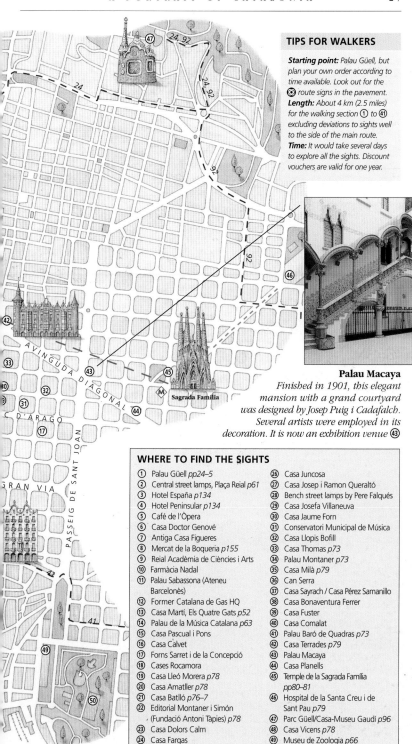

TIPS FOR WALKERS

Starting point: Palau Güell, but plan your own order according to time available. Look out for the ✪ route signs in the pavement.
Length: About 4 km (2.5 miles) for the walking section ① to ㊶ excluding deviations to sights well to the side of the main route.
Time: It would take several days to explore all the sights. Discount vouchers are valid for one year.

Palau Macaya
Finished in 1901, this elegant mansion with a grand courtyard was designed by Josep Puig i Cadafalch. Several artists were employed in its decoration. It is now an exhibition venue ㊸

Sagrada Família

WHERE TO FIND THE SIGHTS

① Palau Güell *pp24–5*
② Central street lamps, Plaça Reial *p61*
③ Hotel España *p134*
④ Hotel Peninsular *p134*
⑤ Café de l'Òpera
⑥ Casa Doctor Genové
⑦ Antiga Casa Figueres
⑧ Mercat de la Boqueria *p155*
⑨ Reial Acadèmia de Ciències i Arts
⑩ Farmàcia Nadal
⑪ Palau Sabassona (Ateneu Barcelonès)
⑫ Former Catalana de Gas HQ
⑬ Casa Martí, Els Quatre Gats *p52*
⑭ Palau de la Música Catalana *p63*
⑮ Casa Pascual i Pons
⑯ Casa Calvet
⑰ Forns Sarret i de la Concepció
⑱ Cases Rocamora
⑲ Casa Lleó Morera *p78*
⑳ Casa Amatller *p78*
㉑ Casa Batlló *p76–7*
㉒ Editorial Montaner i Simón (Fundació Antoni Tàpies) *p78*
㉓ Casa Dolors Calm
㉔ Casa Fargas
㉕ Farmàcia Bolós
㉖ Casa Juncosa
㉗ Casa Josep i Ramon Queraltó
㉘ Bench street lamps by Pere Falqués
㉙ Casa Josefa Villanueva
㉚ Casa Jaume Forn
㉛ Conservatori Municipal de Música
㉜ Casa Llopis Bofill
㉝ Casa Thomas *p73*
㉞ Palau Montaner *p73*
㉟ Casa Milà *p79*
㊱ Can Serra
㊲ Casa Sayrach / Casa Pérez Samanillo
㊳ Casa Bonaventura Ferrer
㊴ Casa Fuster
㊵ Casa Comalat
㊶ Palau Baró de Quadras *p73*
㊷ Casa Terrades *p79*
㊸ Palau Macaya
㊹ Casa Planells
㊺ Temple de la Sagrada Família *pp80–81*
㊻ Hospital de la Santa Creu i de Sant Pau *p79*
㊼ Parc Güell/Casa-Museu Gaudí *p96*
㊽ Casa Vicens *p78*
㊾ Museu de Zoologia *p66*
㊿ Parlament de Catalunya

Catalan Painting

Catalonia has a fine, if uneven, painterly tradition. It began where Spanish medieval painting was born – in the Pyrenees, where Romanesque churches were brightened by bold frescoes full of imagination (see pp22-3). The subsequent Gothic period, which represented Catalonia at the height of its powers, was followed by a long period of lesser artistic achievement until the wealth of the 19th century revived the creative spirit. This fostered some of Europe's great 20th-century painters, all of whom, as Catalans, felt a close affinity to the spirit of Catalonia's incomparable Romanesque art.

of their works can be seen at the Museu Nacional d'Art de Catalunya alongside Catalonia's only two distinguished artists of the period – Francesc Pla and Antoni Viladomat.

Procession outside Santa Maria del Mar (c.1898) by Ramon Casas

St George and the Princess (late 15th century) by Jaume Huguet

GOTHIC

One of the first-named artists in Catalonia was Ferrer Bassa (1285–1348), court painter to Jaume II. Bassa's exquisite decoration in the chapel of the Monastery of Pedralbes (see p95) constitutes the first-known example of oil-painted murals, a style undoubtedly influenced by contemporary Italian painting.

In sculpture, Catalan Gothic begins with the work of Mestre Bartomeu (1250–1300), whose extraordinary, Oriental-looking *Calvary* is in the fine Gothic collection of Girona's Museu d'Art (see p117).

There are also Gothic collections in Vic and Solsona (see p124) and particularly Barcelona, where the Museu Nacional d'Art de Catalunya (see p88) has the most impressive. Important works include those by Lluís Borrassà (1365–

1425), who painted Tarragona cathedral's altarpiece, and Lluís Dalmau (d.1463), who visited Bruges and studied under Jan van Eyck. A feature of Catalan Gothic is *esgrafiat*, a process of gilding haloes, garments and backgrounds, which was favoured by one of the greatest Catalan Gothic artists, Jaume Huguet (1415–92). His *St George and the Princess* seems to capture the full majesty of a cultured and prosperous nation.

RENAISSANCE TO NEO-CLASSICAL

Artistically, Catalonia languished from the 16th to the 18th century, a period dominated by great masters from elsewhere in Spain: El Greco in Toledo, Murillo and Zurbarán in Seville, Ribera in Valencia, and Velázquez and later Goya in Madrid. A few

THE 19TH CENTURY

Barcelona's art school opened above La Llotja (see p63) in 1849 and new patrons of the arts appeared with wealth generated by the industrial revolution. Industry had, however, already begun to train its own artists. In 1783 a school was founded in Olot (see p115) to train designers for local textile firms. An Olot School of artists developed; its main figures were Josep Berga i Boix (1837–1914) and Joaquim Vayreda i Vila (1843–94), who also founded the Art Cristià (Christian Art) workshops which today still produce church statuary.

The greens and browns of the Olot landscape artists were countered by the pale

The Gardens at Aranjuez (1907) by Santiago Rusiñol

Waiting for Soup (1899) by Isidre Nonell

blues and pinks of the Sitges Luminists – Arcadi Mas i Fontdevila (1852–1943) and Joan Roig i Soler (1852–1909). They were influenced by Marià Fortuny, who was born in Reus in 1838 and had lived in Rome and Paris. He was commissioned by Barcelona's city council to paint a vast canvas of the Spanish victory at Tetuán, Spanish Morocco, in which 500 Catalan volunteers had taken part. It is now in the Museu d'Art Modern.

In 1892, 18 years after the first Impressionist exhibition in Paris, Mas i Fontdevila staged an exhibition in Sitges bringing together the Olot School and the Luminists. It was seen as the first Modernista event and featured two other artists: Santiago Rusiñol (1861–1931) and Ramon Casas (1866–1932), the towering figures of Modernista painting. Rusiñol, the son of a textile magnate, bought a house in Sitges, Cau Ferrat (see p128), which became a Modernista haunt. Casas, the first man in Barcelona to own a car, drew all the famous people of the day and also painted large, powerful canvases such as *The Charge* and *Vile Garroting*. Rusiñol and Casas were founding members of Els Quatre Gats café, modelled on Le Chat Noir in Paris.

The Cathedral of the Poor (1897) by Joaquim Mir

THE 20TH CENTURY

Although Pablo Ruiz Picasso (1881–1973) lived in Barcelona for only eight years (see p63), they were extremely formative. His early work was strongly influenced by the city and its surroundings, as can be seen in the Museu Picasso (see p64), as well as by the leading Catalan artists – landscape painter Isidre Nonell (1873–1911), Joaquim Mir (1873–1940), and Rusiñol and Casas. He shared their view that Paris was essential to an artistic life and soon joined its Catalan fraternity. Despite a self-imposed exile during the Franco years, he kept in touch with Catalonia all his life.

Joan Miró (1893–1983) also attended the art school. Thrown out for poor draughtsmanship, he went on to become one of the 20th-century's most original talents, remarkable for his playful abstracts.

A sense of play was also never far from Salvador Dalí (see p117), whom Miró encouraged in the way that he himself had been encouraged by Picasso. Dalí joined them in Paris, where Miró introduced him to the Surrealists. Unlike his mentors, Dalí remained in Catalonia after the Civil War, and his house in Port Lligat (see p120) is in many ways his finest creation.

Also to remain was Josep-Maria Sert (1876–1945). He was a more traditional painter, best remembered for vast murals in Barcelona's Casa de la Ciutat (see p57), and in Rockefeller Center and the dining room of the Waldorf Astoria in New York. His startling work in Vic cathedral (see p124) was burnt out in the Civil War, but he was able to repaint it before he died.

Today, Catalonia's best-known living painter is Antoni Tàpies. A modest, uncompromising man, he is, like many before him, deeply rooted in his own culture. Though an abstract painter, he often uses the colours of the Catalan flag and admits to an influence of Romanesque art. Like Picasso and Miró, he has his own museum (see p78). Other living Catalan artists' work can be seen at Barcelona's Museu d'Art Contemporani (see p62).

Lithograph (1948) in Catalan flag colours by Antoni Tàpies

The Flavours of Catalonia

Food is central to the Catalan soul, and it's no accident that Barcelona's most famous literary creation, detective Pepe Carvalho, is a discerning gourmet. Reflecting Barcelona's status as the undisputed style capital of the Mediterranean, the culinary scene in Catalonia is now one of the most exciting in Europe, with innovative chefs like Ferran Adrià, of the legendary El Bullí restaurant *(see p151)*, taking Catalonia's venerable gastronomic traditions and transforming them with spectacular flair. But the old ways survive in small, family-run restaurants, authentic, sawdust-strewn tapas bars, and particularly in the superb local markets.

Ceps (bolets)

Barcelona café serving traditional pastries and desserts

Visit any one of Barcelona's excellent markets to see the spectacular variety of fresh produce that is available in Catalonia: stalls are heaped high with glistening fish from the Mediterranean; superb-quality meat and game from the mountains; and a quite dazzling array of fruit and vegetables from the plains. Catalan cuisine, even at its most experimental, is essentially simple, and relies on the superb quality and range of the local produce. It is also very much a seasonal cuisine, and each time of the year has its specialities, from the onion-like *calçots* which appear in the spring, and the luscious plethora of summer fruit, to the wild mushrooms, roasted meats and hearty, warming stews of the autumn and winter.

MEAT AND GAME

Catalan cured meats are justly famous throughout Spain, particularly the pungent cured sausage *fuet*. Pork finds its way onto almost every menu, with *peus de porc* (pigs' trotters) an old-fashioned favourite. Its mountain cousin, wild boar *(porc sanglar)* is popular in late autumn, along with game, especially

Xoriço picant — Fuet — Llonganissa — Xoriço — Pernil salat — Xoriço curat

Selection of Catalan cured meats, known as *embutits*

LOCAL DISHES AND SPECIALITIES

Some things are hallowed in Catalan cuisine, and none more so than the quartet of classic sauces which underpin almost everything. King of them all is *sofregit* (mentioned in the first Catalan cookbook of 1324), a reduction of caramelized onions, fresh tomatoes and herbs. *Samfaina* is made like *sofregit* but with the addition of roast aubergines (eggplant), courgettes (zucchini) and peppers. *Picada* is spicier, and ingredients vary but normally include breadcrumbs, garlic, almonds, saffron and pine nuts. *All i oli* is a garlicky, mayonnaise-like (but eggless) sauce, usually served with grilled meat and vegetables. But the classic Catalan dish is *pa amb tomàquet* – crusty bread rubbed with fresh tomatoes and garlic, then drizzled with olive oil. Simple, but utterly delicious.

Pa amb tomaquet

Escalivada *is a salad of marinated onions, peppers and aubergines (eggplant) that have been roasted until sweet.*

Summer fruits and vegetables lovingly displayed at La Bogueria market

partridge *(perdiu)*. Rabbit *(conill)* and snails *(cargols)*, come into their own in hearty winter dishes. Meat and fish are sometimes combined in dishes known as *mar i muntanya* (sea and mountain).

FISH

Barcelona excels at seafood. Tapas bars commonly serve mouthwatering sardines, and rosy prawns grilled or tossed in garlic. Restaurants and markets offer a dizzying array of fresh fish, including monkfish, bass, hake, sole, squid, octopus, and every possible variety of shellfish. Fish is often served simply grilled *(a la brasa)*, or perhaps with a simple sauce. It's especially good cooked paella-style in *fideuà*, or in a stew such as *suquet de peix*. But humble dried, salted cod *(bacallà)*, still reigns supreme in Catalan cuisine, and is at its most delicious when baked with tomatoes, garlic and wine *(a la llauna)*.

Locally caught sardines being grilled over charcoal

FRUIT AND VEGETABLES

Spring is heralded by *calçots*, a cross between leeks and onions, tiny broad (fava) beans and delicate asparagus spears. In summer, market stalls blaze with the colours of cherries, strawberries, figs, peaches and melons, gleaming aubergines (eggplants), courgettes (zucchini), tomatoes and artichokes. In autumn, Catalans head for the hills to seek out wild mushrooms *(bolets)*, and classic Catalan bean dishes appear on menus as winter approaches.

BEST FOOD SHOPPING

La Boqueria *(see p155).*

Bombones Blasi Carrer Cardenal Casanyes 16 (93 318 3523). Exquisite chocolates.

Olis Oliva Mercat de Santa Caterina (93 268 1472). A huge range of olive oils, plus salt.

La Pineda Carrer del Pi (93 302 43 93). Delightful old grocer's, specializing in hams.

Tot Formatge, Passeig del Born 13, (93 319 5375). Superb cheeses from Catalonia, Spain and elsewhere.

Botifarrería de Santa María, Carrer Santa María 4 (93 319 9123). Cured meats of all kinds.

Origens 99.9% Carrer Vidreria 6–8 (93 310 7581). Catalan products, organic where possible, including cheeses, hams, oils and conserves.

Conill amb cargols *is a hearty country stew of rabbit and snails with tomatoes, spices and a splash of wine.*

Suquet de peix, *a rich stew of firm-fleshed fish (often hake), with tomatoes, garlic and toasted almonds.*

Crema Catalana, *the Catalan version of crème brûlée, is a rich, eggy custard with a caramelized sugar topping.*

Cava Country

Cordoníu's world-famous *cava* label

Cava is one of Catalonia's most appreciated exports. This relatively inexpensive sparkling wine is made in the same way as French champagne, undergoing a second fermentation in the bottle in which it is sold. It was made commercially from the mid-19th century and, in 1872, full-scale production was begun by Josep Raventós, head of Codorníu. This famous winery is still run by his descendants in Sant Sadurní d'Anoia, *cava* capital of the Penedès wine-producing region. Today *cava* continues to be made using local grape varieties – Macabeo, Xarel·lo and Parellada – and some pleasant pink *cava* is also produced. The literal meaning of *cava* is simply "cellar".

Codorníu, *the first wine to be made using the* méthode champenoise, *brought* cava *international renown as one of the great sparkling wines.*

Freixenet *was established by the Sala family in 1914 and is now one of the leading* cava *brands. Their estate is in Sant Sadurní d'Anoia, heart of* cava *country, and Freixenet's distinctive black bottle is recognized throughout the world.*

Raïmat, *developed by the Raventós family using the Chardonnay grape, is considered by many to be the ultimate cava. Wrested from wasteland, the 3,000-hectare (7,410-acre) Raïmat estate, 14 km (9 miles) west of Lleida, has its own railway station and workers' village and has been declared a "model agricultural estate" by the Spanish government.*

THE OTHER WINES OF CATALONIA

A porró for drinking wine

Wine *(vi)* in Catalonia is *negre* (red), *rosat* (pink) or *blanc* (white). *Garnatxa* is a dessert wine named after the grape it comes from; *ranci* is a matured white wine. A tradition, now only practised at local *festes* or old-style bars, is to pour wine into the mouth from a *porró* (long-spouted wine jug). There are nine official DO *(Denominació de Origen)* regions which include: **Empordà-Costa Brava:** light wines from the northeast. They include *vi de l'any*, drunk in the year it is produced. *Cava* is made in Peralada. **Alella:** a tiny region, just north of Barcelona, with good light whites. **Penedès:** great reds as well as some whites, with names such as Torres and Codorníu. Visit the wine museum in Vilafranca del Penedès *(see p125)*. **Conca de Barberà:** small quantities of both reds and whites. **Costers del Segre:** includes the delicious reds from the Raïmat estate. **Priorat:** characterful reds and good whites (Falset) from a pretty region of small villages west of Tarragona. **Tarragona and Terra Alta:** traditionally hefty wines, but getting lighter.

The Art Nouveau *winery in Sant Sadurní d'Anoia is Codorníu's Modernista showpiece, designed by Josep Puig i Cadafalch in 1906. There are 26 km (16 miles) of cellars on five floors and visitors are taken round on a small train.*

Gold medals were awarded to Codorníu for its *cava* as early as 1888. By 1897 it was being served at state functions instead of champagne.

KEY

☐ Main *cava* districts

0 kilometres   20

0 miles   20

Map locations:
Manresa · C16 (E9) · Becos
NII A2 · Igualada · Terrassa · A7 AP7 (E15) · C32 · Sabadell
ERS DEL EGRE · Masquefa ⑥ · A7 AP7 (E15)
②① · Sant Sadurní d'Anoia · BARCELONA
A2 AP2 (E90) · ③
Montblanc · ④ · Vilafranca del Penedès · A7 AP7 (E15) · C32 · Castelldefels
Valls
El Vendrell · Vilanova i la Geltrú
eus Tarragona

BEST PRODUCERS

Codorníu
  Sant Sadurní d'Anoia ①
Freixenet
  Sant Sadurní d'Anoia ②
Gramona
  Sant Sadurní d'Anoia ③
Mascaró
  Vilafranca del Penedès ④
Raïmat
  Costers del Segre ⑤
Raventós Rosell
  Masquefa ⑥

CAVA TIPS

What to buy
As with champagne, the drier the wine, the higher the price. The driest *cavas* are *brut de brut* and *brut nature*. *Brut* and *sec* are slightly less dry. Sweet *semiseco* and *dulce* are best with desserts. Although inexpensive compared with the French equivalent, costs do vary, with small, specialist producers commanding high prices.

Visiting a winery
The main *cava* producers are open to the public during office hours (but many close in August). Sant Sadurní d'Anoia is 45 minutes by train from Barcelona's Sants station and the most impressive cellars to visit here are Freixenet's and Codorníu's. Vilafranca del Penedès tourist office (*see p125*) has details of all *cava* winery visits.

A rewarding tour *can be had by visiting the Freixenet cellars. The company sells more bottles of cava each year than the French sell champagne.*

CATALONIA THROUGH THE YEAR

Each *barri* (district) in Barcelona and every town and village in Catalonia has a saint's day to be celebrated in an annual *festa major*. The *sardana (see p129)* is danced and, on the Costa Brava, *havaneres* (habaneras) are sung. Food is central to any event, and open-air feasts and special pastries and cakes feature strongly. Many towns, including Barcelona,

Men give women a red rose on Sant Jordi's Day

have parades of giants *(gegants)*, bigheads *(capgrosses)* and dwarfs *(nans)* – papier-mâché caricatures of people once linked with local trade guilds. Demons and dragons provide drama. Catalans love pyrotechnics, and the fires at the midsummer *Revetlla de Sant Joan* are a lavish incendiary event. Many celebrations often start on the eve of the feast day proper.

Book stalls set up in Barcelona on Sant Jordi's Day, *el dia del llibre*

SPRING

Almond blossom gives way to cherry and apple as the earth warms and the melting snows swell the rivers. The fishing season for trout and other freshwater fish starts in late March. At Easter, families get together, often going out of town to visit relatives, or to picnic and search for wild asparagus. May is the best month in which to see wild flowers, which are particularly spectacular in the Pyrenees.

MARCH

Sant Medir *(3 Mar)*. In Barcelona processions distribute sweets in the district of Gràcia, and in Sants a week later.
Sant Josep *(19 Mar)*. Many Catalans are called Josep (often shortened to Pep). This is a holiday in Spain, although not in Catalonia. People celebrate their "name day" – the day of the saint they are named after – more than they

celebrate their birthday.
Terrassa Jazz Festival *(whole of Mar)*. Concerts by musicians from all over the world.
Setmana Santa (Holy Week) is the week before Easter and is filled with events.

APRIL

Diumenge de Rams (Palm Sunday). Palm leaves are blessed in church, notably at the Sagrada Família in Barcelona. Processions of Roman soldiers turn out in Girona, and *via crucis* (passion plays) are put on in several places, notably the spa town of Sant Hilari Sacalm, Girona province.
Dijous Sant (Maundy Thursday), Verges, Girona province. Men dressed as skeletons perform a death dance *(dansa de la mort)* thought to date back to times of plague in the 1300s.
Pasqua (Easter). On Good Friday *(Divendres Sant)* crucifixes are carried through the streets following the Stations of the Cross. On Easter Monday

(Dilluns de Pasqua) godparents buy their godchildren *mona* (egg cake), and bakers compete to make the most elaborate confections.
Sant Jordi *(23 Apr)*. Feast of St George, patron saint of Catalonia, and a day devoted to the memory of Cervantes *(see p43)*, who died on this day in 1616. Men and boys give single red roses to their mothers, wives and girlfriends, who give them books in return. The festival is also known as *el dia del llibre* (book day).

MAY

Fira de Sant Ponç *(11 May)*. Ancient celebration around the Carrer de l'Hospital in Barcelona, once the site of the city hospital. Aromatic and medicinal herbs and honey are sold.
Corpus Christi *(May/Jun)*. Flowers are laid in the streets of Sitges, and in Berga, Barcelona province, a monster dragon (la Patum) dances through the town's streets.

The feast of Corpus Christi, when carpets of flowers cover the streets

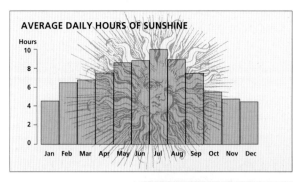

AVERAGE DAILY HOURS OF SUNSHINE

Hours

Sunshine Chart
Barcelona is a sunny city, enjoying clear blue skies for a large part of the year and often up to ten hours' sunshine a day in summer. In winter, even though it can be cold in the shade, the sun is high enough to give it warming power and it can be pleasant to sit outdoors on a sheltered, sunny terrace or patio.

SUMMER

The majority of Barcelona's inhabitants live in apartments, so they like to head out of town at weekends, either to the coast or the mountains. Motorways (highways) on Friday afternoons and Sunday evenings are best avoided. School holidays are long, starting at the end of June when the sea is warm enough for swimming. Crowds throng the marinas, the aroma of barbecued sardines fills the air, and a plethora of summer entertainment provides limitless options. Many businesses in Barcelona close in August.

JUNE

Grec Festival de Barcelona *(Jun–Jul)*. National and international performances throughout Barcelona; the main venues are the Teatre Grec, Mercat de les Flors and Poble Espanyol.
Revetlla de Sant Joan *(23, 24 Jun)*. St John's (Midsummer's) Eve is celebrated with fireworks, especially on Montjuïc in Barcelona. Bonfires are lit throughout Catalonia and lighted torches are brought down from the top of Mont Canigó, just over the border in France. *Cava* – a sparkling white wine *(see pp32–3)* – is drunk with a special *coca* (cake) sprinkled with pine nuts and crystallized fruit.
Castellers *(24 Jun)*. In Valls, Tarragona, a province famous for its *casteller* festivals, teams of men stand on each other's shoulders hoping to take the prize for building the highest human tower *(see p125)*.

Holidaymakers at Platja d'Aro, a popular Costa Brava resort

Concert season *(Jun/Jul)*. Classical music concerts, held at different parks in Barcelona, are organized by the Institut Municipal de Parcs i Jardins.

JULY

Cantada d'havaneres *(first Sun in Jul)*. Drinking *cremat* (coffee and rum), musicians and singers belt out *havaneres* in towns along the coast, most famously at Calella de Palafrugell on the Costa Brava.

A team of *castellers* in action

Virgen del Carmen *(16 Jul)*. A maritime festival that takes place around Barcelona's port. As well as processions, there are bands playing *havaneres*.
Santa Cristina *(24 Jul)*. The biggest festival of Lloret de Mar, Costa Brava, when a statue of the Virgin is brought ashore by a decorated flotilla.

AUGUST

Festa major de Gràcia *(one week beginning around 15 Aug)*. Each district of Barcelona hosts its own *festa* in which streets try to outdo each other in the inventiveness of their decorations. The *festa* in the old district of Gràcia is the biggest and most spectacular and incorporates concerts, balls, music, competitions and street games.
Festa major de Sants *(around 24 Aug)*. The big annual *festa* takes place in the Sants district of Barcelona.
Festa major de Vilafranca del Penedès *(mid-Aug)*. This town's annual festival is one of the best places to see *casteller* (human tower) competitions *(see p125)*.

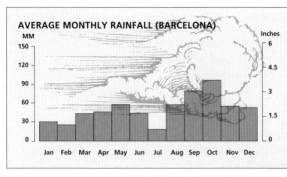

AVERAGE MONTHLY RAINFALL (BARCELONA)

Rainfall Chart
Barcelona experiences modest rainfall year round – just sufficient to maintain the city's green spaces. However, rain tends to fall in sudden, but short-lived, torrential downpours and heavy thunder storms are a feature of the summer months. Grey, drizzly weather lasting for days on end is very rare.

AUTUMN

The grape harvest *(verema)* is a highlight of the autumn, just before the vines turn red and gold. It is the season for seeking out mushrooms which swell the market stalls. From October hunters set off to bag red-legged partridge, migrating ducks and wild boar. Hardier people can be seen swimming in the sea right up until November.

SEPTEMBER

Diada de Catalunya *(11 Sep)*. Catalonia's national day marks Barcelona's fall to Felipe V in 1714 *(see p45)* when the region lost its autonomy. Political demonstrations convey strong separatist sentiment. *Sardana (see p129)* bands and people singing *Els segadors (see p44)* can be heard and Catalan flags are everywhere.
La Mercè *(24 Sep)*. This annual festival in Barcelona honours *Nostra Senyora de la Mercè* (Our Lady of Mercy) in a week of concerts, masses and dances. Look out for the

Harvesting grapes in autumn with high hopes for a successful crop

Cattle descending from the Pyrenees at the end of the summer

correfoc – a parade of fire-breathing dragons, giants and monsters; and the *piro musical* – fireworks set to music.
Sant Miquel *(29 Sep)*. Celebrations for Barceloneta's patron saint recall Napoleon's occupation of Spain *(see p45)*. Bum Bum, a Napoleonic general, parades through the streets to salvoes of gunfire. There is dancing on the beach.

OCTOBER

Festes de Sarrià i de Les Corts *(first Sun in Oct)*. Each of these Barcelona districts has a festival for its patron saint.
Día de la Hispanitat *(12 Oct)*. National holiday to mark the discovery of America in 1492 *(see p44)*, but most Catalans do not celebrate this anniversary.

NOVEMBER

Tots Sants (All Saints' Day) *(1 Nov)*. Roast chestnuts and sweet potatoes are eaten and the next day – *Dia dels difunts* (All Souls' Day) – people visit the graves of their relatives.

PUBLIC HOLIDAYS

Any Nou *(New Year's Day)* 1 Jan
Reis Mags *(Epiphany)* 6 Jan
Divendres Sant *(Good Friday)* Mar/Apr
Dilluns de Pasqua *(Easter Monday)* Mar/Apr
Festa del Treball *(Labour Day)* 1 May
Sant Joan *(Saint John's Day)* 24 Jun
Assumpció *(Assumption Day)* 15 Aug
Diada de Catalunya *(National Day)* 11 Sep
La Mercè 24 Sep
Dia de la Hispanitat *(Day of the Spanish-speaking nations)* 12 Oct
Tots Sants *(All Saints' Day)* 1 Nov
Dia de la Constitució *(Constitution Day)* 6 Dec
Immaculada Concepció *(Immaculate Conception)* 8 Dec
Nadal *(Christmas)* 25 Dec
Sant Esteve 26 Dec

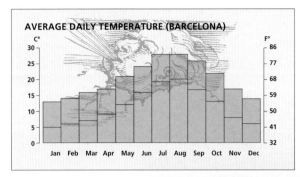

AVERAGE DAILY TEMPERATURE (BARCELONA)

Temperature Chart
This chart shows the average minimum and maximum daily temperatures recorded in Barcelona. The sunshine in winter can be deceptive, as daytime temperatures can occasionally dip to near freezing. Summer days are consistently hot. Hats and a high-factor sun screen are essential.

WINTER

Ski resorts in the Pyrenees are a popular destination at weekends. Though days can be sunny and lunches still taken alfresco, the weather is unpredictable and the nights can be chilly. Christmas is a particularly delightful time to be in Barcelona, when the city vibrates with the spirit of celebration and sharing. Crafts and decorations are on sale in the Feria de Santa Llúcia in front of the Cathedral.

A ski resort in the Pyrenees, a popular destination for weekenders

DECEMBER

Nadal and **Sant Esteve** *(25 & 26 Dec)*. Christmas is a time for people to come together. Traditional Christmas lunch consists of an *escudella* (meat stew) followed by turkey stuffed with apples, apricots, prunes, pine nuts and raisins.
Revellón *(31 Dec)*. All over Spain on New Year's Eve it has become a custom for people to eat a grape between each chime of the midnight bell. To manage the feat brings good luck all year.

JANUARY

Reis Mags *(6 Jan)*. On the eve of the Epiphany the three kings arrive in various guises throughout Catalonia giving sweets to children. The main cavalcade in Barcelona is down by the port.
Santa Eulàlia *(12 Jan)*. The feast of the ancient patron saint of Barcelona is celebrated in the old town. There is dancing and many people dress up as giants.
Els Tres Tombs *(17 Jan)*. Horsemen in top hats and tails ride three times through the city to honour St Anthony, patron saint of animals.
Pelegrí de Tossa *(20 & 21 Jan)*, Tossa de Mar. A 40-km (25-mile) pilgrimage marking the end of the plague; this town's biggest annual event.

FEBRUARY

Carnestoltes (Carnival) *(Feb/ Mar)*. King Carnival presides over the pre-Lent celebrations, children wear fancy dress and every *barri* (district) in Barcelona puts on a party. Sausage omelettes are eaten on Shrove Tuesday *(Dijous gras)*, and on Ash Wednesday *(Dimecres de cendra)* a sardine is ceremoniously buried *(Enterrament de la sardina)*. There are big celebrations in Platja d'Aro on the Costa Brava and Vilanova on the Costa Daurada. Sitges is the place to go to see the full transvestite indulgence of the feast.
De Cajón! Flamenco Festival *(early Feb–Apr)*. Concerts and classes are held in venues across Barcelona.

The winter festival of Els Tres Tombs in Vilanova i la Geltrú

Procession of *gegants* (giants) during the September festival of La Mercé in Barcelona ▷

THE HISTORY OF CATALONIA

*T*he Catalans have always been great seafarers, merchants and industrialists. Since they were united under the House of Barcelona, their nationhood has been threatened by marriages, alliances and conflicts with Madrid, and the road to their present status as a semi-autonomous region within Spain has been marked by times of power and wealth and troughs of weakness and despair.

Barcelona was not a natural site for human settlement. Its port was negligible and its heights, Montjuïc, had no water. The oldest evidence of man in Catalonia comes rather from other sites scattered across the region, notably the dolmens of the Alt (high) Empordà and passage graves of the Baix (low) Empordà and Alt Urgell.

In the first millennium BC the lands around Barcelona were settled by the agrarian Laeitani, while other parts of Catalonia were simultaneously colonized by the Iberians.

Roman mosaic floor excavated in Barcelona depicting the Three Graces

The latter were great builders in stone and remains of one of their settlements are still visible at Ullastret on the Costa Brava. Greek traders arrived on the coast around 550 BC, founding their first trading post at Empúries (Emporion, *see p120*) near Ullastret. It was the Carthaginians from New Carthage in southern Spain who put Barcelona on the map. They named the city after Hamil Barca, father of Hannibal who led his army of elephants from Catalonia over the Pyrenees and Alps to attack Rome.

In reprisal, the Romans arrived at Empúries and began the subjugation of the whole Iberian peninsula. They wiped out the Carthaginians as well as the Laeitani and established Tarraco (Tarragona, *see p128*) in the south of Catalonia as the imperial capital of Tarraconensis, one of the three administrative regions of the peninsula.

Roman Barcelona can be seen in the city gate beside the cathedral, while the 3rd-century walls that once encircled the town lie by the medieval Royal Palace (*see p56*). Foundations of the Roman city have been excavated in the basement of the Museu d'Història de la Ciutat (*see p56-7*), and pillars from the Temple of Augustus can be glimpsed inside the Centre Excursionista de Catalunya (*see p55*) behind the cathedral.

When the Roman Empire collapsed, Visigoths based in Toulouse moved in to fill the vacuum. They had been vassals of Rome, practised Roman law, spoke a similar language and in 587 their Aryan king, Reccared, converted to the Christianity of Rome.

TIMELINE

500–200 BC Fortified Iberian settlements at Ullastret. Cyclopean walls of Tarragona

550 BC Greeks establish trading settlement at Empúries

1000–500 BC Indo-Europeans invade Ter and Llobregat valleys; Iberians settle Montjuïc

Visigothic Cross

2500 BC	1500 BC	500 BC	AD 500

2000–1500 BC Megalithic monuments built throughout Catalonia

Hannibal

230 BC Barcelona founded by Hamil Barca, father of Hannibal

218 BC Romans arrive at Empúries to subjugate Spain

531 Visigoths established in Barcelona after fall of Rome

AD 258 Barcelona city walls built after a Frankish invasion

◁ **Troops fraternizing with local militia in the Baixada de la Llibreteria, Barcelona, during the 1833–9 Carlist War**

THE MOORS AND CHARLEMAGNE

The Visigoths established their capital at Toledo, just south of modern Madrid. When King Wirtzia died in 710, his son, Akhila, is said to have called on the Saracens from north Africa for help in claiming the throne. In 711, with astonishing speed, Muslim and Berber tribes began to drive up through the Iberian peninsula, reaching Barcelona in 717, then Poitiers in France in 732, where they were finally stopped by the Frankish leader, Charles Martel.

Page from a 15th-century manuscript of the *Llibre del Consolat de Mar*

The Muslims made their capital in Córdoba in southern Spain, while the Visigothic nobles found hiding places in the Pyrenees, from which they conducted sorties against the invaders. They were aided by Charles Martel's grandson, Charles the Great (Charlemagne). In 801 Barcelona was retaken by the Franks, only to be lost and taken again. The shortness of the Muslim occupation left Catalonia, unlike the rest of Spain, unmarked by the culture and language of Islam.

Ramon Berenguer I of Barcelona (1035–76)

THE COUNTS OF BARCELONA

Charlemagne created the Hispanic Marc, a buffer state along the Pyrenees, which he entrusted to local lords. The most powerful figure in the east was Guifré el Pelós (Wilfred the Hairy), who consolidated the counties of Barcelona, Cerdanya, Conflent, Osona Urgell and Girona and founded the monastery of Ripoll *(see p114)* – *el bressol de Catalunya* (the cradle of Catalonia). Guifré died in battle against the Moors in 897, but he had started a dynasty of Counts of Barcelona which was to last, unbroken, for 500 years.

Before the end of the 11th century, under Ramon Berenguer I, Catalonia had established the first constitutional government in Europe with a bill of rights, the *Usatges*. By the early 12th century, under Ramon Berenguer III, Catalonia's boundaries had pushed south past Tarragona. Catalan influence also spread north and east when he married Dolça of Provence, linking the two regions and, more lastingly, the principality of Barcelona was united with its neighbour Aragon in 1137 by the marriage of Ramon Berenguer IV and Petronila of Aragon. In 1196 the great monastery of Poblet *(see pp126–7)* in Tarragona province took the place of Ripoll as the pantheon of Catalan royalty.

TIMELINE

	717 Catalonia occupied by Muslims	**801** Moors ejected. Charlemagne sets up buffer state	*Charlemagne (742–814)*	**1060** Constitution, *Usatges*, is drawn up around the time that the word Catalan is first recorded
700		**800**	**900**	**1000**
711 North African Muslims invade Spanish mainland	*Moorish sword*	**778** Charlemagne, leader of the Franks, begins campaign to drive Moors from Spain	**878** Guifré el Pelós (Wilfred the Hairy), Count of Cerdanya-Urgell, consolidates eastern Pyrenees and gains virtual autonomy. He starts 500-year dynasty of Counts of Barcelona	**1008–46** Abbot Oliva builds church at Ripoll and oversees Benedictine building including Vic and Monserrat

MARITIME EXPANSION

Under Jaume I the Conqueror (1213–76), Catalonia began a period of prosperity and expansion. By the end of the 13th century the Balearic islands and Sicily had been conquered; many of the ships used in the enterprise were built at the vast Drassanes shipyards in Barcelona *(see p69)*. Catalonia now ruled the seas and the *Llibre del Consolat de Mar* was a code of trading practice that held sway throughout the Mediterranean. Swashbuckling admirals included Roger de Llúria, who won a definitive victory over the French fleet in the Bay of Roses in 1285, and Roger de Flor, leader of a bunch of fierce Catalan and Aragonese mercenaries, the Almogàvers. These won battles for both the King of Sicily and the Byzantine emperor before Roger de Flor was murdered in 1305.

During Jaume I's long reign the *Corts* (parliament) was established, the city walls were rebuilt to enclose an area ten times larger than that enclosed by the old Roman walls, and noble houses arose down the new Carrer Montcada

(see p64). La Llotja (the stock exchange) was sited by what was then the main port, and the church of Santa Maria del Mar *(see p64)* was built by grateful merchants. Under Pere IV (1336–87) two great halls were built: the Royal Palace's Saló del

Ex voto in the form of a 15th-century ship

Tinell and the Casa de la Ciutat's Saló de Cent *(see pp56–7).*

Prosperity brought a flowering of Catalan literature. Jaume I wrote his own *Llibre dels Feits (Book of Deeds)*, and Pere el Gran's conquest of Sicily in 1282 was described in glowing terms in a chronicle of Catalan history written by Bernat Desclot around 1285. The great Catalan poet Ramon Lull (1232–1315), born in Mallorca, was the first to use a vernacular language in religious writing. From 1395 an annual poetry competition, the Jocs Florals, was held in the city, attracting the region's troubadours. In 1450, Joanot Martorell began writing his Catalan chivalric epic narrative *Tirant lo Blanc*, though he died in 1468, 22 years before it was published. Miguel de Cervantes, author of *Don Quijote*, described it as simply "the best book in the world".

Wall painting showing Jaume I during his campaign to conquer Mallorca

1137 Barcelona united to neighbouring Aragon by royal marriage

1258–72 *Consolat de Mar*, a code of trading practice, holds sway throughout the Mediterranean

1282 Pere el Gran takes Sicily. His exploits are recorded in Desclot's *Chronicles*

1347–8 Black death kills a quarter of the population

1359 Generalitat founded

1423 Conquest of Naples

1100	1200	1300	1400

148 Frontier with Moors pushed back to Riu Ebre

1213–35 Jaume I (The Conqueror) takes Mallorca, Ibiza and Formentera

Jaume I (1213–76)

1324 Sardinia captured

1302–5 Catalan mercenaries under Admiral Roger de Flor aid Byzantium against the Turks

1287 Conquest of Mallorca under Alfons III

FERNANDO AND ISABEL OF CASTILE

Catholic Spain was united in 1479 when Fernando II of Catalonia-Aragon married Isabel of Castile, a region which by then had absorbed the rest of northern Spain. In 1492 they drove the last of the Moors from the peninsula, then, in a fever of righteousness, also drove out the Jews, who

Baptizing Jews during the era of the Catholic Monarchs

had large and commercially important populations in Barcelona *(see p56)* and Girona. This was the same year that Columbus had set foot in America, returning in triumph to Barcelona with six Carib Indians *(see p58)*. However, the city lost out when the monopoly on New World trade was given to Seville and Cádiz. Though it still had great moments, such as its involvement in the victory over the Turks at Lepanto in 1571 *(see p69)*, Barcelona went into a period of decline.

REVOLTS AND SIEGES

During the Thirty Years War with France (1618–59), Felipe IV forced Barcelona's *Corts* to raise an army to fight the French, towards whom the Catalans bore no grudge. A viceroy was imposed on the city and unruly Spanish troops were billeted throughout the region. In June 1640 the population arose, and harvesters *(segadors)* murdered the viceroy. The *Song of the Harvesters* is still sung at Catalan gatherings. Barcelona then allied itself with France, but was besieged and defeated by Felipe. The peace of 1659 ceded Catalan lands north of the Pyrenees to France.

Wall tile for a Catalan trade guild

A second confrontation with Madrid arose during the War of the Spanish Succession when Europe's two dominant royal houses, the Habsburgs and Bourbons, both laid claim to the throne. Barcelona, with England as an ally, found itself on the losing side, supporting the Habsburgs. As a result, it was heavily

The great siege of Barcelona in 1714 during the War of the Spanish Succession

TIMELINE

1492 Columbus discovers Americas. Barcelona barred from trade with the New World. Jews expelled

1494 Supreme Council of Aragon brings Catalonia under Castilian control

The Spanish Inquisition, active from 1478

1619 Spanish capital established in Madrid

1659 Treaty of the Pyrenees at end of Thirty Years War draws new border with France; Roussillon ceded to France

1450	1500	1550	1600	1650

1479 Fernando II of Catalonia-Aragon marries Isabel of Castile, uniting all the houses of Spain

1490 *Tirant lo Blanc*, epic tale of chivalry by Martorell *(see p43)*, published in Catalan

1571 Vast fleet sets sail from Barcelona to defeat the Ottomans at sea at Lepanto

1640 Revolt of the harvesters *(segadors)* against Spanish exploitation of Catalan resources during Thirty Years War with France

Women joining in the defence of Girona against the Napoleonic French in 1809

besieged by troops of the incoming Bourbon king, Felipe V. The city fell on 11 September 1714, today celebrated as National Day *(see p36)*. Felipe then proceeded to annul all of Catalonia's privileges. Its language was banned, its universities closed and Lleida's Gothic cathedral became a barracks. Felipe tore down the Ribera district of Barcelona and, in what is now Ciutadella Park *(see p65)*, built a citadel to keep an eye on the population.

With the lifting of trade restrictions with the Americas, Catalonia began to recover economically. Progress, however, was interrupted by the 1793–95 war with France and then by the 1808–14 Peninsular War (known in Spain as the War of Independence) when Napoleon put his brother Joseph on the Spanish throne. Barcelona fell in early 1808, but Girona withstood a seven-month siege. Monasteries, including Montserrat

(see pp122–3) were sacked and pillaged. They suffered further in 1835 under a republican government when many were seen as too rich and powerful and were dissolved. This was a politically vigorous time, when a minority of largely rural reactionaries fought a rearguard action against the liberal spirit of the century in the Carlist Wars.

THE CATALAN RENAIXENÇA

Barcelona was the first city in Spain to industrialize, mainly around cotton manufacture, from imported raw material from the Americas. It brought immigrant workers and a burgeoning population, and in 1854 the city burst out of its medieval walls *(see p71)*. Inland, industrial centres such as Terrassa and Sabadell flourished and *colònies industrials* (industrial workhouses) grew up along the rivers where mills were powered by water.

Just as the wealth of the 14th century inspired Catalonia's first flowering, so the wealth from industry inspired the *Renaixença*, a renaissance of Catalan culture. Its literary rallying points were Bonaventura Aribau's *Oda a la patria* and the poems of a young monk, Jacint Verdaguer, who won poetry prizes in the revived Jocs Florals *(see p43)*.

Well-to-do *barcelonins* selecting from a wide range of locally produced calico in the early 19th century

Felipe V (1700–24)	**1808–14** Peninsular War (War of Independence): Girona besieged, Barcelona occupied, Monastery of Montserrat sacked	**1823–6** French occupy Catalonia	**1835** Monasteries dissolved	
			1833–9 First Carlist War	**1859** Revival of Jocs Florals poetry competition feeds Renaissance of Catalan culture.

1700	**1750**	**1800**		**1850**

1714 Barcelona sacked by Felipe V, first Bourbon king. Catalan universities closed. Catalan language banned

1778 Catalonia allowed to trade with the Americas, bringing new wealth

1849 Spain's first railway built to link Barcelona and Mataró

1833 Aribau's *Oda a la patria* published

Poet Bonaventura Carles Aribau i Farriols

A hall of Spanish goods at the 1888 Universal Exhibition

CATALANISM AND MODERNISME

The *Renaixença* produced a new pride in Catalonia, and "Catalanism" was at the heart of the region's accelerating move towards autonomy, a move echoed in Galicia and the Basque Country. Interruptions by the Carlist Wars came to an end in 1876 and resulted in the restoration of the Bourbon monarchy.

The first home-rule party, the *Lliga de Catalunya*, was founded in 1887, and disputes with the central government continued. It was blamed for the loss of the American colonies, and therefore lucrative transatlantic trade, and for involving Spain in unnecessary conflict in Morocco. *La setmana tràgica* (tragic week) of 1909 saw the worst of the violent protests: 116 people died and 300 were injured.

Meanwhile, on a more cultural and artistic level and to show off its increasing wealth, Barcelona held in 1888 a

Poster for 1929 Exhibition

Universal Exhibition in the Parc de la Ciutadella where Felipe V's citadel had recently been torn down. The urban expansion *(eixample)* inland was carefully ordered under a plan by Ildefons Cerdà *(see p71)* and industrial barons employed imaginative architects to show off their wealth, most successfully Eusebi Güell and Antoni Gaudí *(see pp24–5)*. The destruction of the monasteries had left spaces for sumptuous buildings such as the Palau de la Música Catalana *(see p63)*, the Liceu opera house and La Boqueria market *(see p155)*.

Spain's noninvolvement in World War I meant that Catalonia's Modernista architecture was unscathed. Barcelona's place as a showcase city was confirmed with the 1929 International

Antoni Gaudí, Modernisme's most creative architect

Exhibition on Montjuïc, many of whose buildings still remain.

CIVIL WAR

The *Mancomunitat*, a local council established in 1914, disappeared on the arrival in 1923 of the dictator Primo de Rivera, Barcelona's military governor. In 1931 Francesc Macià declared himself President of the Catalan Republic, which lasted three days. Three years later Lluís Companys was arrested and sentenced to 30 years' imprisonment for attempting to do the same.

TIMELINE

1872–6 Third and last Carlist War	**1888** Universal Exhibition held in Parc de la Ciutadella, showing off the new Modernista style	**1909** *Setmana tràgica*: violent protest against Moroccan Wars	*Primo de Rivera (1870–1930)*	**1931** Francesc Macià declares independence for Catalonia

1875	1900	1925

1893 Anarchist bombs in Liceu opera house kill 14

Carlist soldiers

1901 *Lliga Regionalista*, new Catalan party, wins elections

1929 International Exhibition on Montjuïc

1936–9 Spanish Civil War. Republican government retreats from Madrid to Valencia, then Barcelona

Refugees on the march in 1939, fleeing towards the Pyrenees to seek asylum in France

Finally, on 16 July 1936, General Francisco Franco led an army revolt against the Republican government and the fledgling autonomous states. The government fled Madrid to Valencia, then Barcelona. City and coast were bombed by German aircraft, and shelled by Italian warships. When Barcelona fell three years later, thousands escaped to camps in France and thousands, including Companys, were executed in Franco's reprisals. Catalonia lost all it had gained, and its language was outlawed once more.

The *noche negra*, the dark night that followed Franco's victory, left Barcelona short of resources and largely neglected by Madrid. The 1960s, however, brought new economic opportunities, and between 1960 and 1975 two million Spaniards came to work in the city. The arrival of the first tourists to the coast during that time, to the Costa Brava and Costa Daurada, changed the face of Spain for ever.

LIFE AFTER FRANCO
Champagne flowed freely in Barcelona's streets on the news of Franco's death in 1975. Democracy and the monarchy, under the Bourbon Juan Carlos, were restored. Catalonia has since won a large degree of autonomy, including tax-raising powers and in June 2006 a new Statute of Autonomy of Catalonia was approved, giving Catalonians a new legal framework for greater political independence.

Pasqual Maragall, Barcelona's mayor until 1997 and president of Catalonia from 2003 to 2006, steered the radical shake-up of the city for the 1992 Olympic Games. Barcelona changed dramatically, with a bold new waterfront, inspired urban spaces, new access roads, and state-of-the-art museums and galleries.

Opening ceremony, 1992 Barcelona Olympic Games

1947 Spain declared a monarchy with Franco as regent	**1975** Franco dies. King Juan Carlos restores Bourbon line		**2008** High Speed AVE train line between Barcelona and Madrid inaugurated
1953 US bases welcomed	**1979** Partial autonomy granted to Catalonia	**1992** Olympic Games held in Barcelona	
1950	**1975**	**2000**	**2025**
1939 50,000 go into exile in France. Catalan President Companys executed	**1960s** Costa Brava leads package holiday boom	**1985** Medes Islands become Spain's first marine nature reserve	**2004** Universal Forum of Cultures held in Barcelona
		1986 Spain enters European Union	*Cobi, the Olympic mascot*

BARCELONA
AND CATALONIA

Introducing Barcelona

Barcelona, one of the Mediterranean's busiest ports, is more than the capital of Catalonia. In culture, commerce and sports it not only rivals Madrid, but also considers itself on a par with the greatest European cities. The success of the 1992 Olympic Games, staged in the Parc de Montjuïc, confirmed this to the world. Although there are plenty of historical monuments in the Ciutat Vella (Old Town), Barcelona is best known for the scores of buildings in the Eixample left by the artistic explosion of Modernisme *(see pp24–5)* in the decades around 1900. Always open to outside influences because of its location on the coast, not too far from the French border, Barcelona continues to sizzle with creativity: its bars and the public parks speak more of bold contemporary design than of tradition.

Casa Milà (see p79) *is the most avant-garde of all the works of Antoni Gaudí (see p78). Barcelona has more Art Nouveau buildings than any other city in the world.*

Palau Nacional (see p88), *on the hill of Montjuïc, dominates the monumental halls and the fountain-filled avenue built for the 1929 International Exhibition. It now houses the Museu Nacional d'Art de Catalunya, with an exceptional collection of medieval art, rich in Romanesque frescoes.*

MONTJUIC
(see pp 84–91)

Christopher Columbus
surveys the waterfront from the top of a 60-m (200-ft) column (see p69) in the heart of the Port Vell (Old Port). From the top, visitors can look out over the new promenades and quays that have revitalized the area.

Montjuïc Castle (see p89) *is a massive fortification dating from the 17th century. Sited on the crest of the hill of Montjuïc, it offers panoramic views of the city and port, and forms a sharp contrast to the ultra-modern sports halls built nearby for the 1992 Olympic Games.*

0 kilometres		1
0 miles	0.5	

◁ **La Rambla de Mar crossing the water in the Old Port to the Maremàgnum leisure complex**

The Sagrada Família (see pp80–1), *Gaudí's unfinished masterpiece, begun in 1882, rises above the streets of the Eixample. Its polychrome ceramic mosaics and sculptural forms inspired by nature are typical of his work.*

EIXAMPLE (see pp70–83)

OLD TOWN (see pp52–69)

Barcelona Cathedral (see pp58–9) *is a magnificent 14th-century building in the heart of the Barri Gòtic (Gothic Quarter). It has 28 side chapels which encircle the nave and contain some splendid Baroque altarpieces. The keeping of white geese in the cloisters is a centuries-old tradition.*

Parc de la Ciutadella (see p65), *between the Old Town and the Vila Olímpica, has something for everyone. The gardens full of statuary offer relaxation, the boating lake and the zoo are fun, while the Museu de Ciències Naturals within its gates covers geology and zoology.*

La Rambla (see pp60–1) *is the most famous street in Spain, alive at all hours of the day and night. A stroll down its length to the seafront, taking in its palatial buildings, shops, cafés and street vendors, makes a perfect introduction to Barcelona life.*

OLD TOWN

The old town, traversed by the city's most famous avenue, La Rambla, is one of the most extensive medieval city centres in Europe. The Barri Gòtic contains the cathedral and a maze of streets and squares. Across from the Via Laietana, the El Born neighbourhood is dominated by the Santa Maria del Mar church and is replete with 14th-century mansions. This area is bounded by the leafy Parc de la Ciutadella, home to the city's zoo. The revitalized seafront is a stimulating mix of old and new. Trendy shops and restaurants make up the fashionable marina, contrasted with the old maritime neighbourhood of Barceloneta and the new Olympic port.

SIGHTS AT A GLANCE

Museums and Galleries
Aquarium ㉔
Museu d'Art Contemporani ❿
Museu d'Historia de Catalunya ㉕
Museu de Ciències Naturals
(Edifici Geología) ⓳
Museu de Ciències Naturals
(Edifici Zoología) ⓲
Museu Frederic Marès ❷
Museu Marítim and Drassanes ㉘
Museu Picasso ⓭
Museu de la Xocolata ⓯

Parks and Gardens
Parc de la Ciutadella ⓱
Parc Zoològic ⓴

Harbour Sights
Golondrinas ㉗
Port Olímpic ㉑
Port Vell ㉓

Streets and Districts
Barceloneta ㉒
La Rambla ❼
El Raval ❾

Churches
Basílica de Santa Maria
del Mar ⓮
Cathedral (pp58–9) ❻

Historic Buildings
Casa de l'Ardiaca ❶
Casa de la Ciutat ❹
La Llotja ⓬
Palau de la Generalitat ❺
Palau de la Música Catalana ⓫
Palau Güell ❽
Museu d'Història de
la Ciutat – Plaça del Rei ❸

Monuments
Arc del Triomf ⓰
Monument a Colom ㉖

GETTING THERE
The area is well served by Metro lines 1, 3 and 4; Jaume I station is in the heart of the Barri Gòtic. Many buses pass through the Plaça de Catalunya on the edge of the Barri Gòtic.

KEY
- Street-by-Street map *pp54–5*
- Ⓜ Metro station
- 🚆 Train station
- 🚌 Main bus stop
- 🚡 Cable car
- 🚋 Tramway stop
- ℹ Tourist information

0 metres 500
0 yards 500

◁ **Els Quatre Gats café in one of the narrow streets of Barcelona's Barri Gòtic**

Street-by-Street: Barri Gòtic

The Barri Gòtic (Gothic Quarter) is the true heart of Barcelona. The oldest part of the city, it was the site chosen by the Romans in the reign of Augustus (27 BC–AD 14) on which to found a new *colonia* (town), and has been the location of the city's administrative buildings ever since. The Roman forum was on the Plaça de Sant Jaume, where now stand the medieval Palau de la Generalitat, the seat of Catalonia's government, and the Casa de la Ciutat, the city's town hall. Close by are the Gothic cathedral and royal palace, where Columbus was received by Fernando and Isabel on his return from the New World in 1492 *(see p44).*

Wax candle, Cereria Subirà

Casa de l'Ardiaca
Built on the Roman city wall, the Gothic-Renaissance archdeacon's residence now houses Barcelona's historical archives **❶**

To Plaça de Catalunya

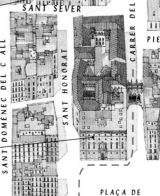

★ Cathedral
The façade and spire are 19th-century additions to the original Gothic building. Among the artistic treasures inside are medieval Catalan paintings **❻**

SANT SEVER

CARRER DEL BISBE

PIETA

SANT DOMÈNEC DEL C ALL

SANT HONORAT

Palau de la Generalitat
Catalonia's seat of government has superb Gothic features, such as the chapel and a staircase to an open-air, arcaded gallery **❺**

PLAÇA DE SANT JAUME

CARRER DE FERRAN

CARRER DE LA CIUTAT

To La Rambla

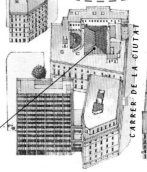

Casa de la Ciutat (*Ajuntament*)
Barcelona's town hall was built in the 14th and 15th centuries. The façade is a Neo-Classical addition. In the entrance hall stands Three Gypsy Boys *by Joan Rebull (1899–1981), a 1976 copy of a sculpture he originally created in 1946* **❹**

KEY

– – – Suggested route

Museu Frederic Marès
This medieval doorway is from an extensive display of Spanish sculpture – the mainstay of this museum's extraordinarily eclectic and high-quality collections ❷

Roman city wall

LOCATOR MAP
See Street Finder map 5

EIXAMPLE

OLD TOWN

MONTJUIC

Saló del Tinell

TAPINERIA

CARRER DELS COMTES DE BARCELONA

★ **Palau Reial**
The 14th-century Capella Reial de Santa Àgata, with a 1466 altarpiece, is one of the best surviving sections of the palace ❸

Capella Reial de
Santa Àgata

Plaça del Rei

Palau del Lloctinent

Cereria Subirà
candle shop

VIA LAIETANA

CARRER DE JAUME I

Jaume I
Metro

The Museu d'Història de la Ciutat features the
most extensive subterranean Roman ruins in the
world. Accessed through this 14th-century mansion,
visitors can view the streets and squares of Roman
Barcelona. The ruins extend underground,
through to the exit at the Palau Reial.

CARRER DEGUERIA

SOTS-TINENT NAVARRO

**The Centre Excursionista de
Catalunya,** housed in a
medieval mansion, displays
Roman columns from the Temple
of Augustus, whose site is marked
by a millstone in the street outside.

STAR SIGHTS
★ Cathedral
★ Palau Reial

0 metres   100

0 yards   100

Decorated marble mailbox, Casa de l'Ardiaca

Casa de l'Ardiaca ❶

Carrer de Santa Llúcia 1. **Map** 5 B2.
Tel *93 318 11 95.* 🚇 *Jaume I.*
⏲ *9am–8:45pm Mon–Fri,*
9am–1pm Sat. ⬤ *public hols.*
www.bcn.cat/arxiu/arxiuhistoric

Standing beside what was originally the Bishop's Gate in the Roman wall is the Archdeacon's House. It was built in the 12th century, but its present form dates from around 1500 when it was remodelled, including the addition of a colonnade. In 1870 this was extended to form the Flamboyant Gothic patio around a fountain. The Modernista architect Domènech i Montaner (1850–1923) added the fanciful marble mailbox, carved with three swallows and a tortoise, beside the Renaissance portal. Upstairs is the Arxiu Històric de la Ciutat (City Archives).

Museu Frederic Marès ❷

Plaça de Sant Iu 5. **Map** 5 B2. ***Tel*** *93 256 35 00.* 🚇 *Jaume I.* ⏲ *10am–7pm Tue–Sat, 10am–3pm Sun.* ⬤ *1 Jan, Good Fri, 1 May, 25 & 26 Dec.* 🎟 *(free to under 16s, also Wed after 3pm & 1st Sun of every month).* ♿ 🎟 *by appt.* **www**.museumares.bcn.es

The sculptor Frederic Marès i Deulovol (1893–1991) was also a traveller and collector, and this museum is a monument to his eclectic taste. As part of the Royal Palace, it was occupied by 13th-century bishops, 14th-century counts of Barcelona, 15th-century judges and 18th-

century nuns, who lived here until they were expelled in 1936. Marès, who had a small apartment in the building, opened this museum in 1948. It contains a fascinating collection of works, including some outstanding examples of Romanesque and Gothic religious art. In the crypt there are stone sculptures and two complete Romanesque portals. Exhibits on the three floors above range from clocks, crucifixes and costumes to antique cameras, pipes and postcards. There is also a room full of children's toys. Restoration work, which closed the museum, is due to end mid-2011.

Virgin, Museu Frederic Marès

Museu d'Història de la Ciutat – Plaça del Rei ❸

Plaça del Rei. **Map** 5 B2. ***Tel*** *93 256 21 00.* 🚇 *Jaume I.* ⏲ *Apr–Sep: 10am–8pm Tue–Sun; Oct–Mar: 10am–2pm, 4–7pm Tue–Sat, 10am–8pm Sun.* ⬤ *1 Jan, 1 May, 24 Jun, 25 Dec.* 🎟 *free 1st Sat afternoon of the month.* 🎟 *by appt.* **www**.museuhistoria.bcn.es

The Royal Palace was the residence of the count-kings of Barcelona from its foundation in the 13th century. The complex includes the 14th-century Gothic Saló del Tinell, a vast room with arches spanning 17 m (56 ft). This is where Isabel and Fernando *(see p44)* received Columbus after his triumphal return from America. It is also where the Holy Inquisition sat, believing the

Gothic nave of the Capella de Santa Àgata, Palau Reial

BARCELONA'S EARLY JEWISH COMMUNITY

From the 11th to the 13th centuries Jews dominated Barcelona's commerce and culture, providing doctors and founding the first seat of learning. But in 1243, 354 years after they were first documented in the city, violent anti-Semitism led to the Jews being consigned to a ghetto, El Call. Ostensibly to provide protection, the ghetto had only one entrance, which led into the Plaça de Sant Jaume. Jews were heavily taxed by the monarch, who viewed them as "royal serfs"; but in return they also received privileges, as they handled most of Catalonia's lucrative trade with North Africa. However, official and popular persecution finally led to the disappearance of the ghetto in 1401, 91 years before Judaism was fully outlawed in Spain *(see p44)*.

Originally there were three synagogues, the main one being in Carrer Sant Domènec del Call, but only the foundations are left. A 14th-century Hebrew tablet is embedded in the wall at No. 5 Carrer de Marlet, which reads: "Holy Foundation of Rabbi Samuel Hassardi. His soul will rest in Heaven".

Hebrew tablet

walls would move if lies were told. On the right, built into the Roman city wall, is the royal chapel, the Capella de Santa Àgata, with a painted wood ceiling and an altarpiece (1466) by Jaume Huguet *(see p28)*. Its bell tower is formed by part of a watchtower on the Roman wall. Stairs on the right of the altar lead to the 16th-century tower of Martí the Humanist (who reigned from 1396–1410), the last ruler of the 500-year dynasty of the count-kings of Barcelona. From the top of the tower there are fine views.

The main attraction of the Museu d'Història lies underground. Entire streets and squares of old Barcino are accessible via a lift and walkways suspended over the ruins of Roman Barcelona. The site was discovered when the Casa Clariana-Padellàs, the Gothic building from which you enter, was moved here stone by stone in 1931, as demonstrated by an extraordinary photo of the original dig towards the end of the exhibit. The water and drainage systems, baths, homes with mosaic floors, dye works, laundries and even the old forum now make up the most extensive and complete subterranean Roman ruins in the world.

Casa de la Ciutat

Plaça de Sant Jaume 1. **Map** 5 A2.
Tel 93 402 73 00. Ⓜ *Jaume I or Liceu.*
◯ *10am–1:30pm Sun (12 Feb: 10am–8pm; 23 Apr: 10am–6:30pm), or by appointment (93 402 73 64).*

The magnificent 14th-century city hall *(ajuntament)* faces the Palau de la Generalitat. Flanking the entrance are statues of Jaume I *(see p43)*, who granted the city rights to elect councillors in 1249, and Joan Fiveller, who levied taxes on court members in the 1500s. Inside is the huge council chamber, the 14th-century Saló de Cent, built for the city's 100 councillors. The Saló de les Cròniques was commissioned for the 1929 International Exhibition and decorated by Josep-Maria Sert *(see p29)* with murals of events in Catalan history.

Palau de la Generalitat ❺

Plaça de Sant Jaume 4. **Map** 5 A2.
Tel 93 402 46 00. Ⓜ *Jaume I.* ◯ *23 Apr (St Jordi's Day), Sat by appointment only (call 93 402 46 17), 2nd & 4th Sun of every month: 10:30am–1:30pm.* www.gencat.cat

Since 1403 the Generalitat has been the seat of the Catalonian Government. Above the entrance, in its Renaissance

The Italianate façade of the Palau de la Generalitat

façade, is a statue of Sant Jordi (St George) – the patron saint of Catalonia – and the Dragon. The late Catalan-Gothic courtyard is by Marc Safont (1416).

Among the fine interiors are the Gothic chapel of Sant Jordi, also by Safont, and Pere Blai's Italianate Saló de Sant Jordi. The building is open to the public only on the saint's feast day. At the back, one floor above street level, lies the *Pati dels Tarongers*, the Orange Tree Patio, by Pau Mateu, which has a bell tower built by Pere Ferrer in 1568.

The Catalan president has offices here as well as in the Casa dels Canonges. The two buildings are connected across Carrer del Bisbe by a bridge built in 1928 and modelled on the Bridge of Sighs in Venice.

The magnificent council chamber, the Saló de Cent, in the Casa de la Ciutat

Barcelona Cathedral ❻

This compact gothic cathedral, with a Romanesque chapel (the Capella de Santa Llúcia) and beautiful cloister, was begun in 1298 under Jaume II, on the foundations of a Roman temple and Moorish mosque. It was not finished until the early 20th century, when the central spire was completed. A white marble choir screen, sculpted in the 16th century, depicts the martyrdom of St Eulàlia, the city's patron. Next to the font, a plaque records the baptism of six native Caribbeans, brought back from the Americas by Columbus in 1493.

Statue of St Eulàlia

The twin octagonal bell towers date from 1386–93. The bells were installed in this tower in 1545.

The main façade was not completed until 1889, and the central spire until 1913. It was based on the original 1408 plans of the French architect Charles Galters.

Nave Interior
The Catalan-style Gothic interior has a single wide nave with 28 side chapels. These are set between the columns supporting the vaulted ceiling, which rises to 26 m (85 ft).

★ Choir Stalls
The top tier of the beautifully carved 15th-century stalls contains painted coats of arms (1518) of several European kings.

Capella del Santíssim Sagrament
This small chapel houses the 16th-century Christ of Lepanto crucifix.

Capella de Sant Benet
This chapel, dedicated to the founder of the Benedictine Order and patron saint of Europe, houses a magnificent altarpiece showing The Transfiguration *by Bernat Martorell (1452).*

VISITORS' CHECKLIST

Plaça de la Seu. **Map** 5 A2.
Tel *93 342 82 60.* Jaume I.
17, 19, 45. 8am–7:30pm daily, guided tours 1–5pm daily (2–5pm Sun). (free from 8am–12:45pm & 5:15–7:30pm daily).
Sacristy Museum 9am–1pm, 5–7pm daily. **Choir**
daily. services daily.

★ Crypt
In the crypt, beneath the main altar, is the alabaster sarcophagus (1339) of St Eulàlia, martyred for her beliefs by the Romans during the 4th century AD.

★ Cloisters
The fountain, set in a corner of the Gothic cloisters and decorated with a statue of St George, provided fresh water.

Porta de Santa Eulàlia,
entrance to cloisters

STAR SIGHTS

★ Choir Stalls

★ Crypt

★ Cloisters

The Sacristy Museum has a small treasury. Pieces include an 11th-century font, tapestries and liturgical artifacts.

Capella de Santa Llúcia

TIMELINE

	400	700	1000	1300	1600	1900
		559 Basilica dedicated to St Eulàlia and Holy Cross	**1339** St Eulàlia's relics transferred to alabaster sarcophagus		**1913** Central spire completed	
		877 St Eulàlia's remains brought here from Santa Maria del Mar	**1046–58** Romanesque cathedral built under Ramon Berenguer I		**1889** Main façade completed, based on plans dating from 1408 by architect Charles Galters	
	4th century Original Roman (paleo-Christian) basilica built	**985** Building destroyed by the Moors	**1257–68** Romanesque Capella de Santa Llúcia built	**1493** Indians brought back from the Americas are baptized		
			1298 Gothic cathedral begun under Jaume II			

Plaque of the Caribbeans' baptism

La Rambla ❼

The historic avenue of La Rambla, leading to the sea, is busy around the clock, especially in the evenings and at weekends. Newsstands, caged bird and flower stalls, tarot readers, musicians and mime artists throng the wide, tree-shaded central walkway. Among its famous buildings are the Liceu Opera House, the huge Boqueria food market and some grand mansions.

The busy, tree-lined avenue of La Rambla

Exploring La Rambla

The name of this long avenue, also known as Les Rambles, comes from the Arabic *ramla*, meaning the dried-up bed of a seasonal river. The 13th-century city wall followed the left bank of such a river that flowed from the Collserola hills to the sea. Convents, monasteries and the university were built on the other bank in the 16th century. As time passed, the riverbed was filled in and those buildings demolished, but they are remembered in the names of the five consecutive Rambles that make up the great avenue between the Port Vell and Plaça de Catalunya.

Mercat de Sant Josep Plaza de la Boqueria. **Map** 2 F3. **Tel** *93 318 20 17.* Ⓜ *Liceu.* ◻ *8am–8:30pm Mon–Sat.*
Palau de la Virreina La Rambla 99. **Map** 5 A2. **Tel** *93 316 10 00.* Ⓜ *Liceu.* ◻ *11am–2pm, 4–8:30pm Mon–Fri, 11am–8:30pm Sat, 11am–3pm Sun.*
Museu de Cera Pg de la Banca 7. **Map** 2 F4. **Tel** *93 317 26 49.* Ⓜ *Drassanes.* ◻ *10am–1:30pm & 4–7:30pm Mon–Fri, 11am–2pm & 4:30–8:30pm Sat, Sun & public hols (Jul–Aug: 10am–10pm daily).*

Mercat de Sant Josep ⑤
Popularly known as "La Boqueria", the Mercat de Sant Josep is Barcelona's most colourful food market.

Gran Teatre del Liceu ⑦
Barcelona's opera house has had to be restored twice following damage caused by fires in 1861 and 1994.

Palau Güell ⑨
This Neo-Gothic palace, completed in 1889, is considered to be one of Gaudí's most important works (*see p62*).

The monument to Columbus at the bottom of the tree-lined Rambla

Font de Canaletes ①
This 19th-century fountain has four taps from which to drink. Saying that someone "drinks the waters of Canaletes" indicates he or she is from Barcelona.

Reial Acadèmia de Ciències i Arts ②
Converted to a theatre in 1910, this building is the home of Barcelona's first official public clock.

Palau Moja ③
This Classical building dates back to 1790. The Baroque first-floor salon of Palau Moja is used for exhibitions.

Palau de la Virreina ④
The first person to live in this great palace in 1777, was the widowed *virreina* (viceroy's wife) of Spain in Peru.

Plaça de la Boqueria ⑥
This square features a colourful mosaic pavement by Joan Miró (1976) and a Modernista dragon designed for a former umbrella shop.

Plaça Reial ⑧
Barcelona's liveliest square was built in the 1850s and is adorned with palms. Its Neo-Classical carriage lamps were designed by Gaudí.

Museu de Cera ⑩
This waxwork museum is housed in an atmospheric, 19th-century stately home. The museum was established in 1973 and contains over 300 exhibits.

KEY

🔁	FGC train station
Ⓜ	Metro station
🅿	Parking
✚	Church

0 metres 100
0 yards 100

Palau Güell 8

Nou de la Rambla 3–5. **Map** 2 F3.
Tel 93 317 39 74. 🚇 Liceu.
◯ Closed for restoration from July
2010 until mid-2011. Check website
for opening times. ♿ Ground floor
only. **www**.palauguell.cat

Gaudí's first major work in
Barcelona's city centre was
commissioned by his wealthy
patron Eusebi Güell. Güell
made it known that, even
if he was investing in an
inexperienced architect, there
would be no limit to the
budget at Gaudí's disposal.
Gaudí took his patron at his
word as can be seen in the
quality of the materials used
for what was a dispropor-
tionately grand building raised
on a small plot in a narrow
street. The stone work is clad
with marble and inside, high
quality woods are employed
throughout.
As in his other buildings,
Gaudí designed furniture,
lights, stained glass, and many
other fittings, working closely
with craftsmen to realise his
ideas. The house was finished
in 1889 and was used not
only as a luxurious family
home for a wealthy man but
also a place to hold political
meetings, chamber concerts
and to put up important
guests.
From the street there is little
hint of the colour and playful-
ness to come in Gaudí's
mature work, except in the
spire-like chimneys behind
the parapet on the roof. The
austere façade of Palau Güell
is symmetrical and character-
ised mostly by straight lines,
both horizontal and vertical.
The only indication of Gaudí's
later preference for curves is
in the two doorways, each
formed by a parabolic arch –
a geometric shape that he
would subsequently employ
to great effect.
Inside, the most notable
feature of the house is its very
high central room on the main
floor. Something between a
sitting room and a covered
courtyard, this central room
rises fully three floors (of a six
floor building) and is spanned
by a cupola. The other rooms
are grouped around it.

**Palau Güell's spire-like
roof chimneys**

El Raval 9

Map 2 F3. 🚇 Catalunya, Liceu.

The district of El Raval lies
west of La Rambla and
includes the old red-light area
near the port, once known as
Barri Xinès (Chinese quarter).
From the 14th century, the
city hospital was in Carrer de
l'Hospital, which still has
several herbal and medicinal
shops. Gaudí (see p78) was
brought here after being
fatally hit by a tram in 1926.
The buildings now house
the Biblioteca de Catalunya
(Catalonian Library), but the
elegant former dissecting
room has been fully restored.

Towards the port in Carrer
Nou de la Rambla is Gaudí's
Palau Güell. At the end of
Carrer Sant Pau is the city's
most complete Romanesque
church, the 12th-century
Sant Pau del Camp, with a
charming cloister featuring
exquisitely carved capitals.

Museu d'Art
Contemporani 10

Plaça dels Angels 1. **Map** 2 F2. **Tel** 93
412 08 10. 🚇 Universitat, Catalunya.
◯ 24 Jun–24 Sep: 11am–8pm Mon,
Wed & Sat, 11am–midnight Thu–Fri,
10am–3pm Sun; 25 Sep–23 Jun:
11am–7:30pm Mon & Wed–Fri,
10am–8pm Sat, 10am–3pm Sun.
◉ 1 Jan, 25 Dec. 📷 ♿ 🎫 Tours in
English 6pm Mon. **www**.macba.cat
Centre de Cultura Contemporània
Montalegre 5. **Tel** 93 306 41 00.
www.cccb.org

This dramatic, glass-fronted
building was designed by the
American architect Richard
Meier. Its light, airy galleries act
as the city's contemporary art
mecca. The permanent collection of predominantly Spanish
painting, sculpture and install-
ation from the 1950s onwards
is complemented by temporary
exhibitions from foreign artists
such as South African photo-
journalist David Goldblatt and
US painter Susana Solano.
Next to the MACBA is the
**Centre de Cultura Contem-
porània**, a lively arts centre.

Façade of the Museu d' Art Contemporani

Glorious stained-glass dome, Palau de la Música Catalana

Palau de la Música Catalana ⓫

Carrer de Sant Pere Més Alt, s/n. **Map** 5 B1. **Tel** 90 244 28 82. Ⓜ Urquinaona. ☐ 10am–3:30pm daily; (to 6pm Easter and Aug); and for concerts. Buying tickets a week in advance online is recommended. ☑ & ☑ on the hour in English. www.palaumusica.org

This is a real palace of music, a Modernista celebration of tilework, sculpture and glorious stained glass. It is the only concert hall in Europe lit by natural light. Designed by Lluís Domènech i Montaner, it was completed in 1908. Although a few extensions have been added, the building still retains its original appearance. The elaborate red-brick façade is hard to appreciate fully in the confines of the narrow street. It is lined with mosaic-covered pillars topped by busts of the great composers Palestrina, Bach and Beethoven. The large stone sculpture of St George and other figures at the corner of the building portrays an allegory from Catalan folksong by Miquel Blay.

But it is the interior of the building that is truly inspiring. The auditorium is lit by a huge inverted dome of stained glass depicting angelic choristers. The sculptures of composers Wagner and Clavé on the proscenium arch that frames the stage area were designed by Domènech but finished by Pau Gargallo. The stunning "Muses of the Palau", the group of 18 highly stylized, instrument-playing maidens are the stage's backdrop. Made of terracotta and trencadís (broken pieces of ceramic) they have become the building's most admired feature.

The work of Josep Anselm Clavé (1824–74) in promoting Catalan song led to the creation of the Orfeó Català choral society in 1891, a focus of Catalan nationalism and the inspiration behind the Palau.

Although the Orfeó is now based at the more state-of-the-art L'Auditori in Plaça de les Glòries (see p162), there is a concert at the Palau nearly every night; it is the main venue for the city's jazz and guitar festivals and national and international symphony orchestras regularly grace its flamboyant stage.

The Palau's new era began with the completion of the work carried out by the top local architect Oscar Tusquets. An underground concert hall and an outdoor square for summer concerts were added, consolidating the Palau's reputation as Barcelona's most loved music venue.

La Llotja ⓬

Carrer del Consolat de Mar 2. **Map** 5 B3. **Tel** 93 319 24 12 or 90 244 84 48. Ⓜ Barceloneta. ◉ closed to public (except twice a year, days vary).

La Llotja (meaning commodity exchange) was built in the 1380s as the headquarters of the Consolat de Mar (see p43). It was remodelled in Neo-Classical style in 1771 and housed the city's stock exchange until 1994, the original Gothic hall acting as the main trading room. It can still be seen through the windows.

The upper floors housed the Barcelona School of Fine Arts from 1849 to 1970, attended by the young Picasso and Joan Miró (see p29). This is now occupied by local government offices.

Statue of Poseidon in the courtyard of La Llotja

A wedding service in the Gothic interior of Santa Maria del Mar

Museu Picasso ⑬

Carrer Montcada 15–23. **Map** 5 B2.
Tel *93 256 30 00.* 🚇 *Jaume I.*
⏰ *10am–8pm Tue–Sun.* ⚫ *1 Jan,*
1 May, 24 Jun, 25 & 26 Dec.
🎟 *free 1st Sun of month.* ♿
📧 *email: museupicasso_reserves@*
bcn.cat. Free tours in English
6pm Thu, noon Sat. **www.**
museupicasso.bcn.cat

The popular Picasso Museum is housed in five adjoining medieval palaces on Carrer Montcada: Berenguer d'Aguilar, Baró de Castellet, Meca, Mauri and Finestres. The museum opened in 1963 showing works

donated by Jaime Sabartes, a friend of Picasso. After Sabartes' death in 1968, Picasso himself donated paintings. He also left graphic works in his will and ceramics were donated by his widow, Jacqueline.

The strength of the 3,000-piece collection is Picasso's early works. Even at the age of 15, he was painting major works such as *The First Communion* (1896) and *Science and Charity* (1897). There are a few works from his Blue and Rose periods. Most famous is his series of 44 paintings, *Las Meninas*, inspired by Velázquez's masterpiece.

Basílica de Santa Maria del Mar ⑭

Pl Sta Maria 1. **Map** 5 B3. ***Tel*** *93 310 23 90.* 🚇 *Jaume I.* ⏰ *9am– 1:30pm & 4:30–8pm daily (10am Sun).*

This beautiful building, the city's favourite church with superb acoustics for concerts, is the only example of a church entirely in the Catalan Gothic style. It took just 55 years to build, with money donated by merchants and shipbuilders. The speed – unrivalled in the Middle Ages – gave it a unity of style both inside and out.

Pablo Picasso, *Self-Portrait* in charcoal (1899–1900)

PABLO PICASSO IN BARCELONA

Picasso (1881–1973) was 13 when he arrived in Barcelona, where his father, José Ruiz y Blasco, had found work teaching in the city art school situated above the Llotja. The city was rich, but it also possessed a large, poor working class which was becoming organized and starting to rebel. Shortly after the family's arrival, a bomb was thrown into a Corpus Christi procession. They settled at No 3 Carrer de la Mercè, a gloomy, five-storeyed house not far from the Llotja. Picasso's precocious talent gave him admittance to the upper school, where all the other pupils were aged at least 20. Here he immediately made friends with another artist, Manuel Pallarès Grau, and the two lost their virginity to the whores of Carrer d'Avinyó, who were to inspire *Les Demoiselles d'Avignon* (1906–7), considered by many art critics to be the wellspring of modern art. Picasso travelled with Pallarès to the Catalan's home town of Horta, where he painted some early landscapes, now in the Museu Picasso The two remained friends for the rest of their lives.

The west front has a 15th-century rose window of the Coronation of the Virgin. More stained glass, dating from the 15th to the 18th centuries, lights the wide nave and high aisles.

When the choir and furnishings were burned in the Civil War *(see p46)*, it added to the sense of space and simplicity.

Museu de la Xocolata **⑮**

Comerç 36. **Map** 5 C2. *Tel 93 268 78 78.* Ⓜ *Jaume I, Arc de Triomf.* ◯ *10am–7pm Mon–Sat, 10am–3pm Sun & pub hols.* ◉ *1 Jan, 1 May, 25 & 26 Dec.* 🖼 ♿ 🎫 *by appointment.* ▣ **www.**museudelaxocolata.com

Founded by Barcelona's chocolate and pastry-makers union, this museum takes you through the history of one of the most universally-loved foodstuffs: from the discovery of cocoa in South America to the invention of the first chocolate machine in Barcelona. This is done using old posters, photographs and footage. The real thing is displayed in a homage to the art of the *mona*. A Catalan invention, this was a traditional easter cake that over the centuries evolved into an edible sculpture. Every year, pastissiers compete for the most imaginative piece, decorating their chocolate versions of well-known buildings or folk figures with jewels, feathers and other materials.

Arc del Triomf **⑯**

Passeig Lluís Companys. **Map** 5 C1. Ⓜ *Arc de Triomf.*

The main gateway to the 1888 Universal Exhibition, which filled the Parc de la Ciutadella, was designed by Josep Vilaseca i Casanovas. It is built of brick in Mudéjar (Spanish Moorish) style, with sculpted allegories of crafts, industry and business. The frieze by Josep Reynés on the main façade represents the city welcoming foreign visitors.

The pink brick façade of the late 19th-century Arc del Triomf

Parc de la Ciutadella **⑰**

Avda del Marquès de l'Argentera. **Map** 6 D2. Ⓜ *Barceloneta, Ciutadella-Vila Olímpica.* ◯ *Oct–Mar: 8am–6pm daily; Apr–Sep: 8am–8pm daily.* ♿

This popular park has a boating lake, orange groves and parrots living in the palm trees. It was once the site of a massive star-shaped citadel, built for Felipe V between 1715 and 1720 following a 13-month siege of the city *(see p45)*. The fortress was intended to house soldiers to keep law and order, but was never used for this purpose. Converted into a prison, the citadel became notorious during the Napoleonic occupation *(see p45)*, and, during the 19th-century liberal repressions, it was hated as a symbol of centralized power. In 1878, under General Prim, whose statue stands in the middle of the park, the citadel was pulled down and the park given to the city, to become, in 1888, the venue of the Universal Exhibition *(see p46)*. Three buildings survived: the Governor's Palace, now a school; the chapel; and the arsenal, which continues to be occupied by the Catalan parliament.

The park offers more cultural and leisure activities than any other in the city and is particularly popular on Sunday afternoons when people gather to play instruments, dance and relax, or visit the museums and zoo. A variety of works by Catalan sculptors such as Marès, Arnau, Carbonell, Clarà, Llimona, Gargallo, Dunyach and Fuxà, can be seen in the park, alongside work by modern artists such as Tàpies and Botero.

The gardens in the Plaça de Armes boast a triumphal arch designed by architect Josep Fontseré, with the help of Antoni Gaudí, then still a young student.

Ornamental cascade in the Parc de la Ciutadella designed by Josep Fontseré and Antoni Gaudí

Museu de Ciències Naturals (Edifici Zoología) ⑱

Passeig de Picasso. **Map** 5 C2.
Tel 93 319 69 12. 🚇 Arc de
Triomf or Jaume I. 🕐 10am–6pm
Tue–Sat, 10am–2:30pm Sun.
📷 Free first Sun of month. ♿
🎫 by appointment.

At the entrance to the Parc de la Ciutadella is the fortress-like Castell dels Tres Dragons (Castle of the Three Dragons), named after a play by Frederic Soler that was popular at the time it was built.

This crenellated brick edifice was built by Lluís Domènech i Montaner for the 1888 Universal Exhibition. His inspiration was Valencia's Gothic commodities exchange. He later used the building as a workshop for Modernista design, and it became a focus of the movement. Shortly afterwards it housed the History Museum and it was not

One of the galleries inside the spacious Castell dels Tres Dragons

until 1910, when a fishing exhibition was held here, that specimens from the natural sciences began to appear. In 1917 it became the Museum of Catalonia, where flora, fauna and geological collections were displayed. It later housed the Biology Museum and since 1937 it has been home to the Zoological Museum, now the city's Museum of Natural Science. Among the thousands of specimens on display are worms, starfish, sea urchins, beetles and butterflies.

Children peering into an animal enclosure at the Parc Zoològic

Museu de Ciències Naturals (Edifici Geologia) ⑲

Parc de la Ciutadella. **Map** 5 C3.
Tel 93 319 68 95. 🚇 Arc de Triomf,
Jaume I. 🕐 10am–6pm Tue–Sat,
10am–2:30pm Sun. 🌑 1 Jan,
Good Fri, 1 May, 25 & 26 Dec.
📷 Free first Sun of month.
🎫 by appointment.

This landmark, Barcelona's oldest museum, opened in 1882, the same year the Parc de la Ciutadella became a public space. The origin of the museum goes back to the Martorell Museum, founded in 1878 to house the natural science and archaeological collection bequeathed by Francesc Martorell i Peña to the city of Barcelona. This Neo-Classical building, designed by architect Antoni Rovira i Trias, was the city's

first public museum. Today, the museum boasts a large collection of fossils and minerals, including specimens from Catalonia. Beside it is the Hivernacle, a glasshouse by Josep Amargós now used for concerts, and the Umbra-cle, a brick and wood conservatory by the park's architect, Josep Fontseré. Both date from 1884.

Parc Zoològic ⑳

Parc de la Ciutadella. **Map** 6 D3.
Tel 93 225 67 80. 🚇 Ciutadella-Vila Olímpica. 🕐 Apr–Sep:
10am–7:30pm daily; Oct–Mar:
10am–5pm daily. 📷 ♿
www.zoobarcelona.com

This zoo was laid out in the 1940s to a relatively enlightened design – the animals are separated by moats instead of bars. Roig i Soler's 1885 sculpture by the entrance,

Hivernacle glasshouse, Museu de Ciències Naturals (Edifici Geologia)

Yachts at the Port Olímpic overlooked by Barcelona's tallest skyscrapers

The Lady with the Umbrella (see p17), has become a symbol of Barcelona.

The zoo has pony rides, electric cars and a train for children. Dolphin and whale shows are currently held here but the marine animals will move to the Zoo Marí (Marine Zoo), not due for full completion until summer 2015.

Port Olímpic ㉑

Map 6 F4. Ciutadella-Vila Olímpica.

The most dramatic rebuilding for the 1992 Olympics was the demolition of the old industrial waterfront and the laying out of 4 km (2 miles) of promenade and pristine sandy beaches. At the heart of the project was a 65-ha (160-acre) new estate of 2,000 apartments and parks called Nova Icària. The area is still popularly known as the Vila Olímpica because the buildings originally housed the Olympic athletes.

The sole building of Barcelona's Old Port still standing is the former General Stores building. The Stores were designed in 1881 by the engineer Maurici Garrán and were intended for use as trading depots. They were refurbished in 1992 and today house the Museu d'Història de Catalunya (*see pp68–9*). On the sea front

there are twin 44-floor buildings, Spain's second and third tallest skyscrapers, one occupied by offices, the other by the Arts hotel (*see p135*). They stand beside the Port Olímpic, which was also built for 1992. This has shops and nightclubs as well as two levels of restaurants around the marina which have made it a popular place to eat out. The wonderful outdoor setting attracts business people at lunchtime and pleasure seekers in the evenings and at weekends.

Lunch can be walked off along the string of beaches that is edged by a palm-

Sandy, palm-fringed beach at Barcelona's Port Olímpic

fringed promenade with cafés. Behind it, the coastal road heads around a park that lies beside the last three beaches, divided by rocky breakwaters. Swimming is safe on the gently sloping, sandy strands.

Barceloneta ㉒

Map 5 B5. Barceloneta.

Barcelona's fishing "village", which lies on a triangular tongue of land jutting into the sea just below the city centre, is renowned for its little restaurants and cafés. Its beach is also the closest to the city centre and is well equipped with lifeguards, disabled access, showers and play areas for children.

The area was designed in 1753 by the architect and military engineer Juan Martín de Cermeño to rehouse people made homeless by the construction, just inland, of the Ciutadella fortress (*see p65*). Since then it has housed largely workers and fishermen. Laid out in a grid system with narrow two- and three-storey houses, in which each room has a window on the street, the area has a friendly, intimate air.

In the small Plaça de la Barceloneta, at the centre of the district, is the Baroque church of Sant Miguel del Port, also by Cermeño. A market is often held in the square here.

Today, Barceloneta's fishing fleet is still based in the nearby Moll del Rellotge (the clock dock), by a small clock tower. On the opposite side of this harbour is the Torre de Sant Sebastià, terminus of the cable car that runs right across the port, via the World Trade Centre, to Montjuïc.

Fishing boat moored in Barceloneta harbour

Maremàgnum shopping complex on the Moll d'Espanya, Port Vell

Port Vell ㉓

Map 5 A4.
Ⓜ *Barceloneta, Drassanes.*

Barcelona's marina is located at the foot of La Rambla, just beyond the old customs house. This was built in 1902 at the Portal de la Pau, the city's former maritime entrance. To the south, the Moll de Barcelona, with a new World Trade Centre, serves as the passenger pier for visiting liners. In front of the customs house, La Rambla is connected to the yacht clubs on the Moll d'Espanya by a swing bridge and a pedestrian jetty, known as La Rambla de Mar. The Moll d'Espanya boasts a vast new shopping and restaurant complex known as the Maremàgnum. Also on the Moll d'Espanya is an IMAX cinema and one of the largest aquariums in Europe.

On the shore, the Moll de Fusta (Timber Wharf), with terrace cafés, has red structures inspired by the bridge at Arles painted by Van Gogh. At the end of the wharf is *El Cap de Barcelona (Barcelona Head)*, a 20-m (66-ft) tall sculpture by Pop artist Roy Lichtenstein.

The attractive Sports Marina on the other side of the Moll d'Espanya was once lined with warehouses. The only one left, built by Elies Rogent in the 1880s, has been given a new

lease of life as the Palau de Mar. Restaurants provide alfresco dining, but the building is otherwise given over to the Museu d'Història de Catalunya.

Spectacular glass viewing tunnel at the aquarium, Port Vell

Aquarium ㉔

Moll d'Espanya. **Map** 5 B4. Ⓜ *Barceloneta, Drassanes.* **Tel** *93 221 74 74.* ◯ *9:30am–9pm daily (to 9:30pm Sat, Sun & Jun, Sep; to 11pm Jul–Aug).* ♿ www.aquariumbcn.com

Populated by over 11,000 organisms belonging to 450 different species, Barcelona's aquarium is one of the biggest in Europe. Occupying three levels of a glass building, the aquarium focusses particularly on the local Mediterranean coast. Two nature reserves, for instance, the Delta del Ebro and the Medes isles off the Costa Brava, are given a tank apiece. Tropical seas are also represented and moving

platforms ferry visitors through a glass tunnel under an "ocean" of sharks, rays and sunfish. A large hall of activities for children includes an irregularly shaped tank of rays built around an island which is reached through crawl-through glass tunnels.

Museu d'Història de Catalunya ㉕

Plaça Pau Vila 3. **Map** 5 A4.
Ⓜ *Barceloneta, Drassanes.* **Tel** *93 225 47 00.* ◯ *10am–7pm Tue, Thu–Sat, 10am–8pm Wed, 10am–2:30pm Sun & public hols.* ● *25 & 26 Dec, 1 & 6 Jan.* ♿ *except 1st Sun every month.* ♿ *noon & 1pm Sun & public hols.* www.mhcat.net

This museum charts the history of Catalonia, from Lower Palaeolithic times through to the region's heydays as a maritime power and industrial pioneer. Second floor exhibits

Café-lined façade of the Museu d'Història de Catalunya

include the Moorish invasion, Romanesque architecture, medieval monastic life and the rise of Catalan seafaring. Third floor exhibits cover the industrial revolution and the impact of steam power and electricity on the economy. There is also a glass floor laid over a relief map of Catalonia which visitors can walk over. The first floor is reserved for temporary exhibits. Some captions are in English; pick up a free guide for the rest.

The Columbus Monument lit by fireworks during La Mercè fiesta

Monument a Colom ㉖

Plaça del Portal de la Pau.
Map 2 F4. **Tel** 93 302 52 24.
🚇 Drassanes.
◯ 9am–8:30pm daily. 🎫

The Columbus monument at the bottom of La Rambla was designed by Gaietà Buigas for the 1888 Universal Exhibition (see p46). At the time Catalans considered that the great explorer had been a Catalan rather than Italian.

The 60-m (200-ft) monument marks the spot where Columbus stepped ashore in 1493 after returning from his voyage to the Caribbean, bringing with him six Caribbean Indians. He was given a state welcome by the Catholic Monarchs in the Saló del Tinell of the Plaça del Rei (see p56). The Indians' subsequent conversion to Christianity is commemorated in the cathedral (see pp58–9).

A *golondrina* tour boat departing from the Portal de la Pau

A lift leads to a viewing platform at the top of the monument. The bronze statue was designed by Rafael Arché.

Golondrinas ㉗

Plaça del Portal de la Pau.
Map 2 F5. **Tel** 93 442 31 06.
🚇 Drassanes. **Departures:** variable (phone for details). 🎫 Catamaran Orsom **Tel** 93 441 05 37.
www.lasgolondrinas.com

Sightseeing trips around Barcelona's harbour and to the Port Olímpic can be made on *golondrinas* ("swallows") – small double-decker boats that moor at Portal de la Pau in front of the Columbus Monument at the foot of La Rambla.

The half-hour harbour tours are on traditional wooden boats and go out beneath the castle-topped hill of Montjuïc towards the industrial port. There is also a one-and-a-half hour trip on modern catamarans that takes in Barcelona harbour, the local beaches and finally Port Olímpic.

Museu Marítim and Drassanes ㉘

Avinguda de les Drassanes.
Map 2 F4. **Tel** 93 342 99 20. 🚇 Drassanes. ◯ 10am–8pm Mon–Sun.
🚫 1 & 6 Jan, 25 & 26 Dec. 🎫 ♿ audioguide available.
www.museumaritimbarcelona.org

The great galleys that were instrumental in making Barcelona a major seafaring power were built in the sheds of the Drassanes (shipyards) that now house the maritime

museum. These royal dry docks are the largest and most complete surviving medieval complex of their kind in the world. They were founded in the mid-13th century, when dynastic marriages uniting the kingdoms of Sicily and Aragón meant that better maritime communications between the two became a priority. Three of the yards' four original corner towers survive.

Among the vessels to slip from the Drassanes' vaulted halls was the *Real*, flagship of Don Juan of Austria, who led the Christian fleet to the famous victory against the Turks at Lepanto in 1571. The highlight of the museum's collection is a full-scale replica decorated in red and gold.

The *Llibre del Consolat de Mar*, a book of nautical codes and practice, is a reminder that Catalonia was once the arbiter of Mediterranean maritime law (see p43). There are Pre-Columbian maps, including one from 1439 that was used by Amerigo Vespucci.

Stained-glass window in the Museu Marítim

EIXAMPLE

Barcelona claims to have the greatest collection of Art Nouveau buildings of any city in Europe. The style, known in Catalonia as Modernisme, flourished after 1854, when it was decided to tear down the medieval walls to allow the city to develop into what had previously been a construction-free military zone.

The designs of the civil engineer Ildefons Cerdà i Sunyer (1815–76) were chosen for the new expansion (*eixample*) inland. These plans called for a rigid grid system of streets, but at each intersection the corners were chamfered to allow the buildings there to overlook the junctions or squares. The few exceptions to

Jesus of the Column, Sagrada Família

this grid system include the Diagonal, a main avenue running from the wealthy area of Pedralbes down to the sea, and the Hospital de la Santa Creu i de Sant Pau by Modernista architect Domènech i Montaner (1850–1923). He hated the grid system and deliberately angled the hospital to look down the diagonal Avinguda de Gaudí towards Antoni Gaudí's church of the Sagrada Família, the city's most spectacular Modernista building (*see pp80–3*). The wealth of Barcelona's commercial elite, and their passion for all things new, allowed them to give free rein to the age's most innovative architects in designing their residences as well as public buildings.

SIGHTS AT A GLANCE

Museums and Galleries
Fundació Antoni Tàpies ❸

Churches
Sagrada Família pp80-3 ❼

Modernista Buildings
Casa Batlló ❶
Casa Milà, "La Pedrera" ❹
Casa Terrades, "Casa de les Punxes" ❺
Hospital de la Santa Creu i de Sant Pau ❻
Illa de la Discòrdia ❷

GETTING THERE
Metro line 3 has stations at either end of the Passeig de Gràcia (Catalunya and Diagonal), and one in the middle, at the Illa de la Discòrdia (Passeig de Gràcia). Metro line 5 takes you straight to the Sagrada Família and Hospital de Sant Pau (a long walk from other sights).

KEY

▨	Street-by-Street map *pp194-5*
Ⓜ	Metro station
🚆	Train station
🚌	Main bus stop
ℹ	Tourist information

0 metres 500
0 yards 500

◁ **Nativity façade of the Sagrada Família – the only façade to be more or less completed in Gaudí's lifetime**

Street-by-Street: Quadrat d'Or

The hundred or so city blocks centring on the Passeig de Gràcia are known as the Quadrat d'Or, "Golden Square", because they contain so many of the best Modernista buildings *(see pp24–5)*. This was the area within the Eixample favoured by the wealthy bourgeoisie, who embraced the new artistic and architectural style with enthusiasm, not only for their residences, but also for commercial buildings. Most remarkable is the Mansana de la Discòrdia, a single block with houses by Modernisme's most illustrious exponents. Many interiors can be visited by the public, revealing a feast of stained glass, ceramics and ornamental ironwork.

Perfume bottle, Museu del Perfum

Diagonal Metro

Vinçon home decor store *(see p155)*

Passeig de Gràcia, the Eixample's main avenue, is a showcase of highly original buildings and smart shops. The graceful street lamps are by Pere Falqués (1850–1916).

RAMBLA DE CATALUNYA

PASSEIG DE GRÀCIA

Fundació Tàpies
Topped by Antoni Tàpies' wire sculpture Cloud and Chair, *this 1879 building by Domènech i Montaner houses a wide variety of Tàpies' paintings, graphics and sculptures* **3**

Casa Amatller

Museu del Perfum

Casa Ramon Mulleras

★ **Illa de la Discòrdia**
In this city block, three of Barcelona's most famous Modernista houses vie for attention. All were created between 1900 and 1910. This ornate tower graces the Casa Lleó Morera by Domènech i Montaner **2**

To Plaça de Catalunya

Casa Batlló

Casa Lleó Morera

Passeig de Gràcia Metro

Palau Baró de Quadras was designed by Puig i Cadafalch in 1904 in a neo-Gothic style. The ornate façade is riddled with grotesque sculptures including this one, which adorns the doorway.

EIXAMPLE

OLD TOWN

LOCATOR MAP
See Street Finder map 3

AVINGUDA DIAGONAL

CARRER DE PAU CLARIS

CARRER DE PROVENÇA

CARRER DE LLÚRIA

CARRER DE ROUGER DE MALLORCA

CARRER DE VALÈNCIA

CARRER DEL BRUC

CARRER D' ARAGÓ

Casa Thomas

To Sagrada Família

Palau Ramon de Montaner

Casa Terrades "Les Punxes"
Built in red brick with carved stone ornamentation, this 1905 house by Puig i Cadafalch echoes the Gothic buildings of northern Europe ❺

★ **Casa Milà**
Gaudí put all his architectural daring into this, his most famous house. The result is a remarkable wave-like façade and a roofscape of chimneys and vents resembling abstract sculptures ❹

| 0 metres | 100 |
| 0 yards | 100 |

KEY

– – – Suggested route

STAR SIGHTS

★ Illa de la Discòrdia

★ Casa Milà

Casa Batlló ❶

Unlike Gaudí's other works, this block of flats, which was commissioned by Josep Batlló i Casanovas on the prestigious Passeig de Gràcia, involved the conversion of an existing building. With its reworked façade in stunning organic forms and its fantastic chimneys and rooftop, it remains as bold and convention-defying today as it did when it was finished in 1906. The building has been said to symbolise the legend of St George killing the dragon, whose scaly back arches above the main façade. It was designated a UNESCO World Heritage Site in 2005.

View of façade and Dragon's Back

★ The Chimneys
Extraordinary chimneys, usually the unseen and functional parts of a building, have become Gaudí's trademark. These fine examples are tightly-packed and covered in abstract patterns.

Patio and Rear Façade
This outdoor space at the back of the house allows a view of the rear façade which has cast iron balconies and superbly colourful trencadis work at the top.

Attics
The closely-packed brick arches support- ing the roof are plas- tered and painted white giving the sensation of being inside the skeleton of a large animal.

Stairs to main floor

Dining Room
The bulbous forms in the ceiling of the Batlló family's dining room are thought to represent the splash caused by a drop of water.

STAR SIGHTS

★ The Chimneys

★ The Dragon's Back

★ Main Drawing Room

◁ Casa Milà

★ The Dragon's Back

One of the most extra-ordinary innovations to the house is this steep, narrow, colourfully-tiled cap above the façade which it is difficult to see as anything other than the spine of a reptile. Inside it is a white domed room which was used as a water deposit.

VISITORS' CHECKLIST

Passeig de Gràcia 43.
Map 3 A4. **Tel** 93 216 03 06.
Ⓜ Passeig de Gràcia.
🔲 9am–8pm daily. 📷 🔲
www.casabatllo.cat

Light-well
The patio of the original building was enlarged to provide maximum light.

The cross
The ceramic cross was made in Mallorca but was damaged in transit. Gaudí liked the cracked effect and refused to send it back for repair. The arms point to the four cardinal points of the compass.

Dragon's belly room

The iron balconies have been likened to masks in carnival processions.

***Trencadis* decorations**

Façade
Salvador Dalí saw the curving walls and windows as "representing waves on a stormy day". The spindly, individually shaped columns across the first floor windows were also compared to tibias, earning Casa Batlló the nickname, "House of Bones".

Entrance

Fireplace room
Josep Batlló's former office has a mushroom-shaped fireplace tiled in earthy colours.

★ Main Drawing Room
One side of this room is formed by stained-glass windows looking out over the Passeig de Gràcia. The ceiling plaster is moulded into a spiral and the doors and window-frames undulate playfully.

Sumptuous interior of the Casa Lleó Morera, Illa de la Discòrdia

Illa de la Discòrdia ❷

Passeig de Gràcia, between Carrer d'Aragó and Carrer del Consell de Cent. **Map** 3 A4. ⊛ *Passeig de Gràcia.* **Institut Amatller d'Art Hispànic Tel** *93 487 72 17.* ⬭ *10am–8:30pm daily.* 📷 *noon Mon–Fri (by appointment only).* 🖼

Barcelona's most famous group of Modernista *(see pp24–5)* buildings illustrates the wide range of styles used by the movement's architects. They lie in an area known as the Illa de la Discòrdia (Block of Discord), after the startling visual argument between them. The three finest were remodelled in the Modernista style from existing houses early in the 20th century. No. 35 Passeig de Gràcia is Casa Lleó Morera (1902–6), the first residential work of Lluís Domènech i Montaner. A shop was installed in the ground floor in 1943, but the Modernista interiors upstairs, with their magnificent stained-glass bay windows, still exist. The house is not open to the public, however, if the door is open it is possible to see the painted ceiling of the hallway. Beyond the next two houses is Casa Amatller, designed by Puig i Cadafalch in 1898. Its façade, under a stepped gable roof, features a harmonious blend of Moorish and Gothic windows. The ground floor of the house contains a shop. The entrance patio, with its spiral columns, and the staircase covered by a

stained-glass skylight can be seen but the rest of the building, including the beautiful wood-panelled library, is occupied by the Institut Amatller d'Art Hispànic. The third house in the block is Antoni Gaudí's Casa Batlló *(see pp76–7)* with its fluid façade evoking marine or natural forms. The bizarrely decorated chimneys became a trademark of Gaudí's later work.

Fundació Antoni Tàpies ❸

Carrer d'Aragó 255. **Map** 3 A4. **Tel** *93 487 03 15.* ⊛ *Passeig de Gràcia.* ⬭ *10am–8pm Tue–Sun & public hols.* ⬛ *1 & 6 Jan, 25 & 26 Dec.* 🖼 *(free to under 16s).* 📷 *by appointment (93 207 58 62).* ♿ **www.**fundaciotapies.org

Antoni Tàpies *(see p29)*, born in 1923, is Barcelona's best-known living artist. Inspired by Surrealism, his abstract work is executed in a variety of materials, including concrete and metal *(see pp72–3)*. Although perhaps difficult to appreciate at first, the exhibits should help viewers obtain a clearer perspective of Tàpies' work. The collection is housed in Barcelona's first domestic building to be constructed with iron (1880), designed by Domènech i Montaner for his brother's publishing firm.

ANTONI GAUDÍ (1852–1926)

Born in Reus (Tarragona) into an artisan family, Antoni Gaudí i Cornet was the leading exponent of Catalan Modernisme. After a blacksmith's apprenticeship, he studied at Barcelona's School of Architecture. Inspired by a nationalistic search for a romantic medieval past, his work was supremely original. His first major achievement was the Casa Vicens (1888) at No. 24 Carrer de les Carolines *(see p26)*. But his most celebrated building is the church of the Sagrada Família *(see pp80–83)*, to which he devoted his life from 1914. When he had put all his money into the project, he went from house to house begging for more. He was killed by a tram in 1926.

Decorated chimneypot, Casa Vicens

◁ **Extraordinary sculptured and ceramic-encrusted chimneys of Gaudí's Casa Milà**

The rippled façade of Gaudí's apartment building, Casa Milà

Casa Milà ❹

Passeig de Gràcia 92. **Map** 3 B3.
Tel 90 240 09 73. Ⓜ Diagonal.
◑ Mar–Oct: 9am–8pm daily;
Nov–Feb: 9am–6:30pm daily.
◑ 1 & 6 Jan, 25 & 26 Dec.
http://obrasocial.caixacatalunya.es

Usually called *La Pedrera* (the
Stone Quarry), this is Gaudí's
greatest contribution to Barcelona's civic architecture, and his
last work before he devoted
himself entirely to the Sagrada
Família *(see pp80–83)*.

Built between 1906–10, *La
Pedrera* departed from established construction principles
and, as a result, was ridiculed
by Barcelona's intellectuals.
Gaudí designed this eight floor
apartment block around two
circular courtyards. It features
the city's first underground car
park. The ironwork balconies,
by Josep Maria Jujol, are like
seaweed against the wave-like
walls of white stone. There are
no straight walls anywhere in
the building.

The Milà family had an apartment on the first floor, which
now features a typical *Modernista* interior. The museum, "El
Espai Gaudí", on the top floor,
includes models and explana-
tions of Gaudí's work. From
here, visitors can access the
extraordinary roof. The sculptured ducts and chimneys have
such a threatening appearance
they are known as *espanta-
bruixes*, or witch-scarers.

Casa Terrades ❺

Avinguda Diagonal 416. **Map** 3 B3.
Ⓜ Diagonal. ◑ to public.

This free-standing, six-
sided apartment block by
Modernista architect
Josep Puig i Cadafalch
gets its nickname, *Casa
de les Punxes* (House
of the Points), from the
spires on its six corner
turrets. It was built be-
tween 1903 and 1905
by converting
three existing
houses on the
site and was
Puig's largest
work. It is an
eclectic mixture
of medieval and
Renaissance
styles. The towers

**Spire on the main
tower, Casa Terrades**

and gables are influenced in
particular by the Gothic architecture of northern Europe.
However, the deeply carved,
floral stone ornamentation of
the exterior, in combination
with red brick used as the
principal building material,
are typically Modernista.

Hospital de la Santa Creu i de Sant Pau ❻

Carrer de Sant Antoni Maria Claret
167, 08025 Barcelona. **Map** 4 F1.
Tel 93 177 652. Ⓜ Hospital de Sant
Pau. **Grounds** ◑ 10am–2pm daily.
Ⓗ ◪ daily at 10:15am and
12:15pm in English, call to arrange
any other time. **www**.santpau.es

Lluís Domènech i Montaner
began designing a new city
hospital in 1902. His innovative scheme consisted of 26
attractive Mudéjar-style pavilions set in large gardens, as
he believed that patients
would recover better among
fresh air and trees. All the
connecting corridors and
service areas were hidden
underground. Also believ-
ing art and colour to be
therapeutic, he decorated
the pavilions profusely.
The roofs were tiled
with ceramics,
and the reception
pavilion has
mosaic murals and
sculptures by Pau
Gargallo. After his
death, the project
was completed in
1930 by his son, Pere.

Statue of the Virgin, Hospital de la Santa Creu i de Sant Pau

Sagrada Família **❼**

A carved whelk

Europe's most unconventional church, the Temple Expiatori de la Sagrada Família, is an emblem of a city that likes to think of itself as individualistic. Crammed with symbolism inspired by nature and striving for originality, it is the greatest work of Gaudí *(see pp24–5)*. In 1883, a year after work had begun on a Neo-Gothic church on the site, the task of completing it was given to Gaudí, who changed everything, extemporizing as he went along. It became his life's work and he lived like a recluse on the site for 14 years. He is buried in the crypt. At his death only one tower on the Nativity façade had been completed, but work resumed after the Civil War and several more have since been finished to his original plans. Work continues today, financed by public subscription.

Bell Towers
Eight of the 12 spires, one for each apostle, have been built. Each is topped by Venetian mosaics.

THE FINISHED CHURCH

Gaudí's initial ambitions have been kept over the years, using various new technologies to achieve his vision. Still to come is the central tower, which is to be encircled by four large towers representing the Evangelists. Four towers on the Glory (south) façade will match the existing four on the Passion (west) and Nativity (east) façades. An ambulatory – like an inside-out cloister – will run round the outside of the building.

Tower with lift

The apse was the first part of the church Gaudí completed. Stairs lead down from here to the crypt below.

The altar canopy, designed by Gaudí, is still waiting for the altar.

Main entrance

★ Passion Façade
This bleak façade was completed between 1986 and 2000 by artist Josep Maria Subirachs. A controversial work, its sculpted figures are angular and often sinister.

Spiral Staircases
*Steep stone steps –
370 in each staircase
– allow visitors to
descend from the
towers and upper
galleries. Majestic
views can be enjoyed
from the top.*

VISITORS' CHECKLIST

C/ Mallorca 401. **Map** 4 E3.
Tel 93 208 0414. Ⓜ Sagrada
Familia. 🚌 19, 33, 34, 43, 44,
50, 51. ⬜ Apr–Sep: 9am–8pm;
Oct– Mar: 9am–6pm daily (25 &
26 Dec, 1 & 6 Jan: 9am– 2pm).
✝ numerous services daily. 🅿
🎥 ♿ except crypt & towers.
www.sagradafamilia.org

**Tower
with lift**

★ **Nativity Façade**
*The most complete part of Gaudí's
church, finished in 1930, has
doorways which represent Faith,
Hope and Charity. Scenes of the
Nativity and Christ's childhood are
embellished with symbolism, such as
doves representing the congregation.*

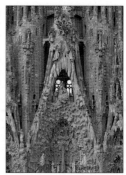

★ **Crypt**
*The crypt, where Gaudí is buried,
was begun by the original architect,
Francesc de Paula Villar i Lozano,
in 1882. This is where services are
held. On the lower floor a museum
traces the careers of both architects
and the church's history.*

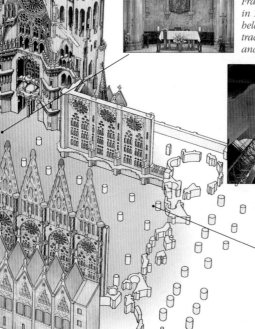

Nave
*In the nave, which is still under
construction, a forest of fluted
pillars will support four galleries
above the side aisles, while
skylights let in natural light.*

STAR FEATURES

★ Passion Façade

★ Nativity Façade

★ Crypt

Passion Façade

It has been said that the Sagrada Família is like a book in stone: meant to be read in the same way as a medieval cathedral, with each element representing a Biblical event or aspect of Christian faith. This was certainly Gaudí's intent: his architecture was inseparable from the profound Catholicism which inspired it. The temple is dedicated to the Sagrada Família, the Holy Family.

Gargoyle on Sagrada Familia

Detail on brass door of the Passion façade

The two existing façades are detailed, visual accounts of two key Bible passages. The Glory façade (yet to be built) will address the theme of judgement of sinners.

Main entrance to the Passion façade

top of a flight of three steps representing the three days of the Passion. Peter denying Christ is indicated by the cock that will crow 3 times in fulfilment of Jesus' prophecy. Behind this group of figures is a labyrinth, a metaphor for the loneliness of Jesus' path to the cross.

The sculptural group on the bottom right is in two parts. First is Ecce Homo (Christ bound with ropes and crowned with thorns). Pilate, overlooked by the Roman eagle, is shown washing his hands, freeing himself of responsibility for Jesus' death. Above, the "Three Marys" weep as Simon the Cyrene, a passer-by, is compelled by the Romans to pick up Christ's cross.

Christ's Passion

The Passion façade depicts the sufferings and execution of Jesus, and its style reflects its subject matter. The statuary by Catalan sculptor Josep Maria Subirachs has attracted much criticism for its chunky, angular, "dehumanised" carving but Gaudí would probably have approved. He is known to have favoured an Expressionist style to give the story of Christ's Passion maximum impact.

A great porch whose roof is held up by six inclined buttress-like swamp tree roots shades the 12 groups of sculptures, arranged in three tiers and to be viewed from bottom to top, left to right in an inverted "S". The first scene, bottom left-hand corner, is the Last Supper at which Jesus (standing) announces his impending betrayal. Next to this is the arrest in the Garden of Gethsemane. An olive trunk's grain mimics the shape of the high priest's servant's

ear that Peter cut off. The kiss of betrayal by Judas follows. The numbers of the cryptogram to the side of Jesus add up to 33 in every direction: his age at the time of his death.

The Flagellation

In the flagellation (between the central doors) Jesus is shown tied to a column at the

Knights sculpture on the Passion façade

The Holy Shroud

The central sculpture depicts an event not described in the Bible but added to the story of the Passion by later tradition. A woman named Veronica holds up her head cloth which she has offered to Jesus to wipe the blood and sweat from his face. It has been returned impressed with his likeness.

Next comes the solitary figure of the Roman centurion on horseback piercing the side of Jesus with his sword. Above him, three soldiers beneath the cross cast lots for Jesus' tunic. The largest sculpture (top centre) shows Christ hanging from a horizontal cross. At his feet is a skull referring to the place of the Crucifixion, Golgotha. Above him is the veil of the Temple of Jerusalem. The final scene is the burial of Jesus. The figure of Nicodemus, who is anointing the body, is thought to be a self-portrait of the sculptor Subirachs.

Nativity Façade

The northern, Nativity façade (overlooking Carrer Marina), finished according to Gaudí's personal instructions before his death, is far more subdued than the Passion façade. So much so that many of the sculptures barely rise out of the surface of the wall, making them difficult to identify. A great many natural forms are incorporated into the work, confusing interpretation further. Gaudí intended the whole work to be coloured but his wishes are unlikely ever to be carried out.

Detail of sculpture on Nativity façade

Faith, Hope and Charity

The lavish ornamentation of the façade is arranged around three doors dedicated to Hope (left), Faith (right) and Charity or Christian Love in the middle. The two columns between the doorways rest on a turtle and a tortoise signifying the permanence and stability of Christianity. In contrast, the two chameleons on either extreme of the façade, represent forces of change. The four angels on top of the columns are calling to the four winds and announcing the proximity of the end of the world.

Detail of a spire, Nativity façade

Hope Doorway

The lowest carvings of the Hope Doorway show the Flight into Egypt (left) and the Slaughter of the Innocents (right). Above the door are Joseph and the child Jesus watched over by Mary's parents (Jesus' grandparents), St Ann and St Joachim. The lintel of the door is composed of a woodcutter's two-handled saw and various other tools such as a hammer, axe, square and mallet - all indicative of Joseph's profession as a craftsman. Further above is a triangular grouping showing the betrothal of Mary and Joseph. The spire above the doorway is in the form of an elongated boulder which is an allusion to the holy Catalan mountain of Montserrat *(see pp122-3)*. At the base of this boulder sits Joseph in a boat, bearing a close resemblance to Gaudí himself and is very likely a posthumous homage by the masons who put the final touches to the façade after the master's death.

Faith Doorway

The Faith Doorway illustrates passages from the gospels and Christian theology. The heart of Jesus can be seen set into the lintel above the door. The scene on the lower left is the Visitation by Mary to Elizabeth, her cousin and mother of John the Baptist. On the right, Jesus wields a hammer and chisel in his father's workshop. Above the door is Jesus in the temple with John the Baptist (left) and John's father Zachariah (right). Higher up, the baby Jesus is presented in the temple, held by Simeon. As it rises, the stonework forms an intricate pinnacle recording the fundamentals of Catholicism including a lamp with 3 wicks for the trinity, bunches of grapes and ears of wheat for the Eucharist, and a hand set with an eye, showing God's omniscience and infinite care.

Charity Doorway

The double doors of the central Charity Doorway are separated by a column recording Jesus' genealogy. The three magi are on the lower left of the door with the shepherds opposite them. Out of nativity emerges the spiky tail of a many-pointed star (or comet). Around it are a children's choir and musicians. Above the star is the Annunciation and the Coronation of the Virgin Mary by Jesus. Above is a pelican sitting on a crown next to a glass egg bearing the JHS anagram of Jesus.

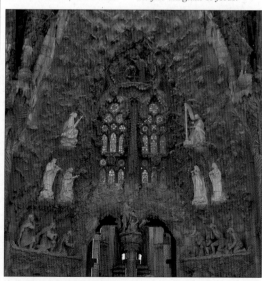

The lavish Nativity façade entrance

MONTJUÏC

The hill of Montjuïc, rising to 213 m (699 ft) above the commercial port on the south side of the city, is Barcelona's biggest recreation area. Its museums, art galleries, gardens and nightclubs make it a popular place in the evenings as well as during the day.

There was probably a Celt-Iberian settlement here before the Romans built a temple to Jupiter on their Mons Jovis, which may have given Montjuïc its name – though another theory suggests that a Jewish cemetery on the hill inspired the name Mount of the Jews.

The absence of a water supply meant that there were few buildings on Montjuïc until the castle was erected on the top in 1640.

The hill finally came into its own as the site of the 1929 International Fair. With great energy and flair, buildings were erected all over the north side, with the grand Avinguda de la Reina Maria Cristina, lined with huge exhibition halls, leading into it from the Plaça d'Espanya. In the middle of the avenue is the Font Màgica (Magic Fountain), which is regularly illuminated in colour. Above it is the Palau Nacional, home of the city's historic art collections. The Poble Espanyol is a crafts centre housed in copies of buildings from all over Spain. The last great surge of building on Montjuïc was for the 1992 Olympic Games, which left Barcelona with international-class sports facilities.

Statue, gardens of the Palau Nacional

SIGHTS AT A GLANCE

Historic Buildings
Castell de Montjuïc **7**

Modern Architecture
Estadi Olímpic de Montjuïc **8**
Pavelló Mies van der Rohe **4**

Museums and Galleries
Fundació Joan Miró **1**
Museu Arqueològic **2**
Museu Nacional d'Art de Catalunya **3**

Squares
Plaça d'Espanya **6**

Theme Parks
Poble Espanyol **5**

GETTING THERE

Apart from the exhibition halls near Espanya Metro station, reaching Montjuïc's attractions on foot involves a steep climb. Buses 61 and 50 will take you up the hill from Plaça d'Espanya. For the castle, take the funicular (9am–8pm daily in winter, to 10pm in spring and summer) from Metro Paral.lel, then the cable car (10am–6pm daily in winter, to 7pm in spring and to 9pm in summer).

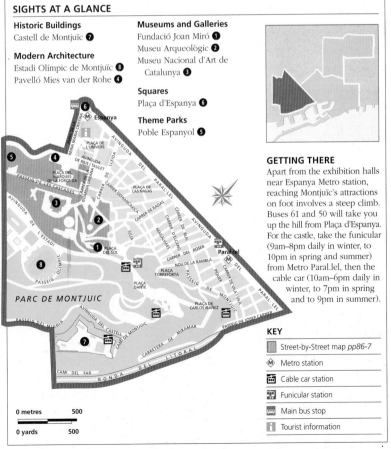

KEY

	Street-by-Street map *pp86–7*
Ⓜ	Metro station
	Cable car station
	Funicular station
	Main bus stop
ℹ	Tourist information

◁ Changing colours of the Font Màgica (Magic Fountain) on the grand avenue leading up to Montjuïc

Street-by-Street: Montjuïc

Montjuïc is a spectacular vantage point from which to view the city. It has a wealth of art galleries and museums, as well as theatres. Many of the buildings were designed for the 1929 International Exhibition, and the 1992 Olympics were held on its southern slopes. Montjuïc is approached from the Plaça d'Espanya between brick pillars based on the campanile of St Mark's in Venice. They give a foretaste of the eclecticism of building styles from the Palau Nacional, which houses magnificent Romanesque art, to the Poble Espanyol, which illustrates the architecture of Spain's regions.

Pavelló Mies van der Rohe
This elegant statue by Georg Kolbe stands serenely in the steel, glass, stone and onyx pavilion built in the Bauhaus style as the German contribution to the 1929 International Exhibition ➍

AVINGUDA DEL MARQUÈS DE COMILLAS

AVINGUDA DELS MONTANYANS

PASSEIG DE LES CASC

AVINGUDA DE L'ESTADI

★ Poble Espanyol
Containing replicas of buildings from many regions of Spain, this "village" provides a fascinating glimpse of vernacular styles ➎

★ Museu Nacional d'Art de Catalunya
On show in the Palau Nacional (National Palace), the main building of the 1929 International Exhibition, is Europe's finest collection of Romanesque frescoes. These were a great source of inspiration for Joan Miró ➌

To Montjuïc castle and Olympic stadium

STAR SIGHTS

- ★ Museu Nacional d'Art de Catalunya
- ★ Poble Espanyol
- ★ Fundació Joan Miró

Fountains and cascades
descend in terraces from the Palau Nacional. Below is the Font Màgica (Magic Fountain), whose jets are programmed to a music and light show on Thursday to Sunday evenings from May to September, and Fridays and Saturdays in winter (except 7 Jan–mid Feb). This marvel of engineering was built by Carles Buigas (1898–1979) for the 1929 International Exhibition.

LOCATOR MAP
See Street Finder map 1

To Plaça d'Espanya

RUIS I TAULET

Museu Etnològic
displays artifacts from Oceania, Africa, Asia and Latin America.

Museu Arqueològic
The museum displays important finds from prehistoric cultures in Catalonia and the Balearic Islands. The Dama d'Evissa, *a 4th-century sculpture, was found in Ibiza's Carthaginian necropolis* ❷

AVINGUDA DE LA TÈCNICA

CARRER DE LLEIDA

Mercat de les Flors theatre
(see p162)

Teatre Lliure
is a prestigious Catalan theatre.

PASSEIG DE LA SANTA MADRONA

Teatre Grec is an open-air theatre set among gardens.

PASSEIG DE LA SANTA MADRONA

PASSEIG DE SANTA MADRONA

PASSEIG DE LA SANTA MADRONA

★ Fundació Joan Miró
This tapestry by Joan Miró hangs in the centre he created for the study of modern art. In addition to Miró's works in various media, the modern building by Josep Lluís Sert is of architectural interest ❶

AVINGUDA DE MIRAMAR

To Montjuïc castle and cable car

KEY

– – – Suggested route

0 metres	100
0 yards	100

Flame in Space and Naked Woman (1932) by Joan Miró

Fundació Joan Miró **❶**

Parc de Montjuïc. **Map** 1 B3. ***Tel*** *93 443 94 70.* Ⓜ *Pl. Espanya, then bus 50 or 55; or Paral.lel, then funicular to Montjuïc.* ◯ *Jul–Sep: 10am–8pm Tue–Sat (till 9:30pm Thu); Oct– Jun: 10am–7pm Tue–Sat (till 9:30pm Thu), 10am–2:30pm Sun & public hols.* ⬤ *1 Jan, 25 & 26 Dec.* 🎫 ♿ **http://**fundaciomiro-bcn.org

Joan Miró (1893–1983) went to La Llotja's art school *(see p63)*, but from 1919 spent much time in Paris. Though opposed to Franco, he returned to Spain in 1940 and lived mainly in Mallorca, where he died. An admirer of Catalan art and Modernisme *(see p24–5)*, Miró remained a Catalan painter *(see p29)* but invented and developed a Surrealistic style, with vivid colours and fantastical forms. During the 1950s he concentrated on ceramics.

In 1975, after the return of democracy to Spain, his friend, the architect Josep Lluís Sert, designed this stark, white

building to house a permanent collection of graphics, paintings, sculptures and tapestries lit by natural light. Miró himself donated the works and some of the best pieces on display include his *Barcelona Series* (1939–44), a set of 50 black-and-white lithographs. Exhibitions of other artists' work are also held regularly.

Museu Arqueològic **❷**

Passeig Santa Madrona 39–41. **Map** 1 B3. ***Tel*** *93 423 21 49.* Ⓜ *Espanya, Poble Sec.* ◯ *9:30am–7pm Tue–Sat, 10am–2:30pm Sun & public hols.* ⬤ *1 Jan, 25, 26 Dec.* 🎫 *except 11 Feb, 23 Apr, 18 May, 11 & 24 Sep.* ♿ 🎫 **www**.mac.es

Housed in the 1929 Palace of Graphic Arts, the museum has artifacts from prehistory to the Visigothic period (AD 415–711). Highlights are finds from the Greco-Roman town of Empúries *(see p120)*, Hellenistic Mallorcan and Visigothic jewellery and Iberian silver treasure.

Museu Nacional d'Art de Catalunya **❸**

Parc de Montjuïc, Palau Nacional. **Map** 1 A2. ***Tel*** *93 622 03 76.* Ⓜ *Espanya.* 🚌 *PM, 55.* ◯ *10am–7pm Tue–Sat, 10am–2:30pm Sun & public hols.* ⬤ *1 Jan, 1 May, 25 Dec.* 🎫 *(free 1st Sun of month).* 📷 ♿ 🎫 *by appointment (93 622 03 75). Audio guides available.* **www**.mnac.cat

The austere Palau Nacional was built for the 1929 International Exhibition, but since 1934, it has housed the city's most important art collection.

The museum has probably the greatest display of Romanesque *(see pp22–3)* items in the world, centred around a series of magnificent 12th-century frescoes. The most remarkable are the wall paintings from Sant Climent de Taüll and La Seu d'Urgell *(see p144)*.

There is also an expanding Gothic collection. Notable artists include the 15th-century Spanish artists Lluís Dalmau and Jaume Huguet *(see p28)*.

Works by El Greco, Zurbarán and Velázquez are displayed in the Cambó Rooms in a collection of notable Baroque and Renaissance pieces from across Europe. The museum houses the entire body of 20th-century art, furniture and sculpture previously at the Museu d'Art Modern in the Parc de la Ciutadella. It also houses part of the Thyssen-Bornemisza collection, with works by Tiepolo, Titian, Lotto, Canaletto and Velázquez.

12th-century *Christ in Majesty*, **Museu Nacional d'Art de Catalunya**

Morning by Georg Kolbe (1877–1945), Pavelló Mies van der Rohe

Pavelló Mies van der Rohe ❹

Avinguda del Marquès de Comillas. **Map** 1 B2. **Tel** 93 423 40 16. Espanya. 50. 10am–8pm daily. 1 Jan, 25 Dec. free to under 18s. 5–7pm Wed & Fri (in English). **www**.miesbcn.com

If the simple lines of this glass and polished stone pavilion look modern today, they must have shocked visitors to the 1929 International Exhibition. Designed by Ludwig Mies van der Rohe (1886–1969), director of the Bauhaus school, it included his world famous *Barcelona Chair*. The building was demolished after the exhibition, but an exact replica was built for the centenary of his birth.

Poble Espanyol ❺

Avinguda del Marquès de Comillas. **Map** 1 A2. **Tel** 93 508 63 30. Espanya. 9am–8pm Mon, 9am–2pm Tue–Thu, 9am–4pm Fri, 9am–5pm Sat, 9am–midnight Sun. (free 24th Sep for the Fiesta Mayor). **www**.poble-espanyol.com

The idea behind the Poble Espanyol (Spanish Village) was to illustrate and display local Spanish architectural styles and crafts. It was laid out for the 1929 International Exhibition, but has proved to be enduringly popular. Building styles from all over Spain are illustrated

by 116 houses created by many well-known architects and artists of the time. The village was refurbished at the end of the 1980s.

Resident artisans produce crafts including hand-blown glass, ceramics Toledo damascene and Catalan sandals (*espardenyes*). The Torres de Ávila, which form the main entrance, have been converted into a nightspot, with an interior by designers Alfredo Arribas and Javier Mariscal (*see p19*). There is plenty more to entertain visitors including handicraft shops, bars and a children's theatre.

Looking down from the Palau Nacional towards Plaça d'Espanya

Plaça d'Espanya ❻

Avinguda de la Gran Via de les Corts Catalanes. **Map** 1 B1. Espanya. **Magic Fountain Music and Light Show** May–Sep: 9–11pm Thu–Sun; Oct–Apr: 7–9pm Fri–Sat; every half hour (except 7 Jan–mid-Feb).

The fountain in the middle of this junction, the site of public gallows until they were moved to Ciutadella in 1715, is by Josep Maria Jujol, one of Gaudí's followers. The 1899 bullring to one side is by Font i Carreras and has been converted into Las Arenas, a spectacular shopping and entertainment centre by Richard Rogers.

On the Montjuïc side is the Avinguda de la Reina Maria Cristina. This is flanked by two 47-m (154-ft) high brick campaniles, modelled on the bell towers of St Mark's in Venice and built as the entrance way to the 1929 International Exhibition. The avenue leads up to Carles Buïgas's illuminated *Font Màgica* (Magic Fountain) in front of the Palau Nacional.

Castell de Montjuïc ❼

Parc de Montjuïc. **Map** 1 B5. **Tel** 93 256 44 45. Paral·lel, then funicular & cable car. PM from Plaça Espanya. 9am–7pm Tue–Sun (until 9pm Apr–Sep).

At the summit of Montjuïc is a huge, 18th-century castle. The first was built in 1640, but destroyed by Felipe V in 1705. The current star-shaped fortress was built for the Bourbon family. During the War of Independence it was taken by French troops. After the Civil War it became a prison where Catalan leader Lluís Companys (*see p47*) was executed in 1940.

Visitors can explore the ramparts and views. There is also a Centre for Peace here.

Estadi Olímpic de Montjuïc ❽

Passeig Olímpic, S/N. **Map** 1 A3. **Tel** 93 426 20 89. Espanya, Poble Sec. 50, 61. for concerts & football matches. **Museum** 10am–6pm (to 8pm Apr–Sep) Tue–Sat, 10am–3:30pm Sun.

The original Neo-Classical façade has been preserved from the stadium built by Pere Domènech i Roura for the 1936 Olympics, cancelled at the onset of the Spanish Civil War. The arena's capacity was raised to 70,000 for the 1992 Olympics. Next door is the Museu Olímpic i de l'Esport with interactive exhibits dedicated to sport. Nearby are the steel-and-glass Palau Sant Jordi stadium by Japanese architect Arata Isozaki, and swimming pools by Ricard Bofill.

Entrance to the Olympic Stadium, refurbished in 1992

FURTHER AFIELD

Radical redevelopments throughout Barcelona in the late 1980s and 1990s have given it a wealth of new buildings, parks and squares. Sants, the city's main station, was rebuilt and the neighbouring Parc de l'Espanya Industrial and Parc de Joan Miró were created containing futuristic sculpture and architecture. In the east, close to the revitalized area of Poblenou, the city now has a new national theatre and concert hall. In the

Park Güell gateway sign

west, where the streets climb steeply, are the historic royal palace and monastery of Pedralbes, and Gaudí's Torre Bellesguard an Park Güell. Beyond, the Serra de Collserola, the city's closest rural area, is reached by two funiculars. Tibidabo, the highest point, has an amusement park, the Neo-Gothic church of the Sagrat Cor and a nearby steel-and-glass communications tower. It is a popular place among *barcelonins* for a day out.

SIGHTS AT A GLANCE

Museums and Galleries
CaixaForum ⑫
CosmoCaixa ⑨
Museu del Futbol Club
  Barcelona ③

Historic Buildings
Monestir de Pedralbes ⑤
Palau Reial de Pedralbes ④
Torre Bellesguard ⑩

Modern Buildings
Torre de Collserola ⑥

Parks and Gardens
Parc de l'Espanya Industrial ②
Park Güell ⑦
Parc de Joan Miró ①
Parc del Laberint d'Horta ⑪

Squares and Districts
Estació del Nord ⑬
Plaça de les Glòries Catalanes ⑭
Poblenou ⑮

Theme Parks
Tibidabo ⑧

KEY

▨	Street-by-Street maps
▢	Built-up area
🚉	Train station
🚟	Funicular station
═══	Motorway (highway)
──	Major road
──	Minor road

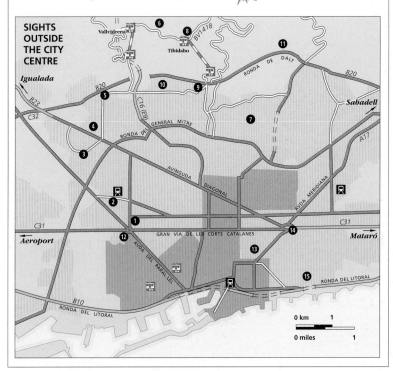

SIGHTS OUTSIDE THE CITY CENTRE

Igualada
Vallvidrera
Tibidabo
Sabadell
Aeroport
Mataró

0 km   1
0 miles   1

◁ The Neo-Gothic Temple Expiatori del Sagrat Cor dominating the summit of Tibidabo

Dona i Ocell (1983) by Joan Miró in the Parc de Joan Miró

Parc de Joan Miró ❶

Carrer d'Aragó 1. 🚇 *Tarragona.*

Barcelona's 19th-century slaughterhouse (*escorxador*) was transformed in the 1980s into this unusual park, hence its alternative name, Parc de l'Escorxador.

It is constructed on two levels; the lower is devoted to football pitches interspersed with landscaped areas of palms, pines, eucalyptus trees and flowers; the upper level is completely paved and dominated by a magnificent 1983 sculpture by the Catalan artist Joan Miró (*see p29*) entitled *Dona i Ocell* (*Woman and Bird*). Standing 22 m (72 ft) high, its surface is covered with colourful glazed tiles. The park has several play areas for children.

Parc de l'Espanya Industrial ❷

Plaça de Joan Peiró. 🚇 *Sants-Estació.*

This modern park, designed by the Basque architect Luis Peña Ganchegui, owes its name to the textile mill that used to stand on the 5-hectare (12-acre) site.

Laid out in 1986 as part of Barcelona's policy to provide more open spaces within the city, the park has canals and a rowing lake – with a Classical statue of Neptune at its centre. Tiers of steps rise around the lake like an amphitheatre and on one side a row of ten futuristic watchtowers dominates the entire area. Their only function is to serve as public viewing platforms and lamp standards.

Six contemporary sculptors are represented in the park, among them Andrés Nagel, whose enormous metal dragon incorporates a children's slide.

Museu del Fútbol Club Barcelona ❸

Avda de Arístides Maillol (7, 9). **Tel** 90 218 99 00. 🚇 *Maria Cristina, Collblanc.* ☐ *10am–6:30pm Mon–Sat (to 8pm Apr–early Oct), 10am–2:30pm Sun & public hols.* ◐ *1 & 6 Jan, 25 Dec.* 🎫♿🎫 *of the stadium only (no tours on Champions League match days and museum closes at 3pm).* **www**.fcbarcelona.com

Camp Nou, Europe's largest football stadium, is home to the city's famous football club, Barcelona FC (known as Barça). Founded in 1899, it is one of the world's richest soccer clubs, with some 100,000 members.

Line of watchtowers in the Parc de l'Espanya Industrial

The stadium is a magnificent, sweeping structure, built in 1957 to a design by Francesc Mijans. An extension was added in 1982 and it can now comfortably seat 100,000 fans.

The club's popular museum displays club memorabilia and trophies, and has a souvenir shop. There are also paintings and sculptures of famous club footballers commissioned for the Blaugrana Biennial, an exhibition held in celebration of the club in 1985 and 1987, and others donated by Catalan artists. *Blau-grana* (blue-burgundy) are the colours of Barça's strip. The club's flags were used as an expression of local nationalist feelings when the Catalan flag was banned during the Franco dictatorship.

As well as hosting its own high-profile matches (mainly at weekends), Camp Nou also accommodates affiliated local soccer clubs and promotes other sports in its sports centre, ice rink and mini-stadium.

View across Camp Nou stadium, prestigious home of the Fútbol Club Barcelona

Palau Reial de Pedralbes ❹

Avinguda Diagonal 686. ◈ *Palau Reial.* **Museu de Ceràmica, Museu de Arts Decoratives & Museu Tèxtil i d'Indumentària** *Tel 93 256 34 65.* ◯ *10am–6pm Tue–Sat, 10am–3pm Sun & public hols.* ● *1 & 6 Jan, 24 Jun, 25 & 26 Dec.* ▨ *(free Sun from 3pm).* ♿ 📷 *by appointment* **www**.dhub-bcn.cat

The Palace was once the main house on the estate of Count Eusebi Güell. In 1919 he offered it to the Spanish royal family. The first visit was from Alfonso XIII in 1926.

Three fascinating museums and the gardens are open to the public. The Museu de Arts Decoratives, opened in 1937, displays period furniture and fine household items from the Middle Ages to the present. A genealogical tree traces the 500-year dynasty of the count-kings of Barcelona *(see p42).*

The Museu de Ceràmica has displays of old Catalan and Moorish pottery and modern ceramics, including works by Miró and Picasso. The permanent collection of the Museu Tèxtil i d'Indumentària moved here in 2008 (temporary exhibitions are still held in Montcada street in the Born).

The gardens are laid out with small ponds and paths. Behind them in Avinguda de Pedralbes is the entrance to the original Güell estate. It is guarded by a black wrought-iron gate, its top forged into a great, open-jawed dragon, and two gate houses, all by Gaudí *(see pp24–5).*

Madonna of Humility, Monestir de Santa Maria de Pedralbes

Monestir de Santa Maria de Pedralbes ❺

Baixada del Monestir 9. *Tel 93 203 92 08.* ▨ *Reina Elisenda.* ◯ *Oct–Mar: 10am–2pm Tue–Sat, 10am–8pm Sun; Apr–Sep: 10am–5pm Tue–Sat, 10am–8pm Sun.* ▨ *(free Sun from 3pm).* 📷 *by appointment (Tel 93 256 21 22).* **www**.museuhistoria.bcn.es

Approached through an arch in its ancient walls, the lovely monastery of Pedralbes retains the air of an enclosed community. This is heightened by the good state of preservation of its furnished kitchens, cells, infirmary and refectory.

But the nuns of the Order of St Clare moved to an adjoining building back in 1983, when the building was opened to the public. The monastery was founded in 1326 by Elisenda de Montcada de Piños, fourth wife of Jaume II of Catalonia and Aragón. Her alabaster tomb lies in the wall between the church and the cloister. On the church side her effigy is dressed in royal robes; on the other, in a nun's habit.

The monastery is built around a spacious, three storey cloister. The main rooms encircling the cloister include a dormitory, a refectory, a chapterhouse, an abbey and day cells. Numerous works of art, as well as liturgical ornaments, pottery, furniture, altar cloths and gold and silver work, are on display here.

The most important room in the monastery is the Capella (chapel) de Sant Miquel, with murals of the *Passion* and the *Life of the Virgin,* both painted by Ferrer Bassa in 1346.

Torre de Collserola ❻

Carretera de Vallvidrera al Tibidabo. *Tel 93 211 79 42.* ▨ *Peu del Funicular, then Funicular de Vallvidrera & bus 211.* ◯ *check the website or phone to confirm opening times.* ● *1 & 6 Jan, 25 Dec, 26 Dec, 31 Dec.* ▨ ♿ **www**.torredecollserola.com

In a city that enjoys thrills, the ultimate ride is offered by the communications tower near Tibidabo mountain *(see p98).* A glass-sided lift swiftly reaches the top of this 288-m (944-ft) tall structure standing on the summit of a 445-m (1,460-ft) hill. The tower was designed by English architect Norman Foster for the 1992 Olympic Games. Needle-like in form, it is a tubular steel mast on a concrete pillar, anchored by 12 huge steel cables. There are 13 levels. The top one has an observatory with a telescope and a public viewing platform with a 360° view of the city, the sea and the mountain chain on which Tibidabo sits.

BARCELONA V REAL MADRID

FC Barcelona

Més que un club is the motto of Barcelona FC: "More than a club". It has above all, however, been a symbol of the struggle of Catalan nationalism against the central government in Madrid. To fail to win the league is one thing. To come in behind Real Madrid is a complete disaster. Each season the big question is which of the two teams will win the title. Under the Franco regime in a memorable episode in 1941, Barça won 3–0 at home. At the return match in Madrid, the crowd was so hostile that the police and referee "advised" Barça to prevent trouble. Demoralized by the intimidation, they lost 11–1. Loyalty is paramount: one Barça player who left to join Real Madrid received death threats.

Real Madrid

Park Güell ❼

In 1910 the industrialist Eusebio Güell commissioned Gaudí to lay out a private housing estate on a hillside above Barcelona. The plan was to create a mini-garden city with common amenities, leisure areas and decorative structures, but only two of the houses were ever built. What was left after the project fell through, however, was one of the most original public spaces ever conceived. The layout is loosely based on the Sanctuary of Apollo at Delhi and Gaudí makes ingenious use of the contours to create arcades and viaducts all of natural stone. The most striking features of the park, however, are those covered with *trencadís* – mosaics made up of broken tiles – which are largely the work of the architect Josep Maria Jujol.

Hypostyle Hall
A total of 86 Classical columns – unusually conventional in style for Gaudí's work – support the weight of the square above. Set into the ceiling are four mosaic representations of the sun.

Hill of the Crosses
A serpentine path leads up to this stone tower from which there is a panoramic view over the city from the port to the heights of Tibidabo and Collserola.

Güell
House

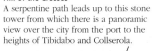

Entrance

★ **Double Staircase**
Water trickles from the mouth of the park's emblematic multicoloured dragon that presides over this monumental flight of steps. Above is an ornamental brown tripod and below another fountain, this time the head of a snake.

★ **Entrance Pavilions**
The two fairy-tale like gatehouses have oval ground plans and intri-cately tiled trencadís *exteriors. Inside are irregular rooms, odd shaped windows and narrow staircases.*

★ The Square

A serpentine bench covered in trencadis – the world's first collage – curves all the way around the edge of this square intended for markets and public events. From here are impressive views over Barcelona.

VISITORS' CHECKLIST

Olot 7, Vallcarca. *Tel* 010 (from Barcelona). ⓜ 1.3 km (1 mile) walk from Lesseps, along a main road and uphill. 🚌 24. ⭘ Nov–Feb: 10am–6pm; Mar & Oct: 10am–7pm; Apr & Sep: 10am–8pm; May–Aug: 10am–9pm; daily. ♿ **Casa-Museu Gaudí** *Tel* 93 219 38 11. ⭘ Oct–Mar: 10am–6pm daily; Apr–Sep: 10am–8pm daily. 🎫 (combined ticket with **Sagrada Família**). **www**.sagradafamilia.org

The Trias house is one of only two houses to have been built in the would-be housing estate.

Upper Viaduct

This is one of three viaducts that carry snaking pathways on the east side of the park.

The perimeter wall follows the contours around the park. The Carretera El Carmel entry is formed by a swivelling section of wall executed in wrought iron.

| 0 meters | 40 |
| 0 yards | 40 |

Casa Museu Gaudí

This house, which Gaudí lived in until he moved to the Sagrada Família, contains furniture designed by the architect, including benches and cupboards from Casa Mila.

STAR SIGHTS

★ Entrance Pavilions

★ Double Staircase

★ The Square

Merry-go-round, Tibidabo

Tibidabo ❽

Plaça del Tibidabo 3–4. **Tel** *93 211 79 42.* 🚇 *Avda Tibidabo, then Tramvia Blau & Funicular; or Peu del Funicular, then Funicular & bus 111; or Tibi Bus from Plaça Catalunya.* **Amusement Park** ◯ *ring to confirm.* ⬤ *Oct–Apr: Mon–Fri.* ♿ **Temple Expiatori del Sagrat Cor Tel** *93 417 56 86.* ◯ *10am–8pm daily.* ♿ **www**.tibidabo.es

The heights of Tibidabo can be reached by Barcelona's last surviving tram. The name, inspired by Tibidabo's views of the city, comes from the Latin *tibi dabo* (I shall give you) – a reference to the Temptation of Christ when Satan took Him up a mountain and offered Him the world spread at His feet.

The hugely popular Parc d'Atraccions (Amusement Park, *see p163*) first opened in 1908. The rides were renovated in the 1980s. While the old ones retain their charm, the newer ones provide the latest in vertiginous experiences. Their location at 517 m (1,696 ft) adds to the thrill. Also in the park is the Museu d'Autòmats, displaying automated toys, juke boxes and slot machines.

Tibidabo is crowned by the Temple Expiatori del Sagrat Cor (Church of the Sacred Heart), built with religious zeal but little taste by Enric Sagnier between 1902 and 1911. A lift takes you up to the feet of an enormous figure of Christ.

Just a short bus ride away is another viewpoint – the Torre de Collserola (*see p95*).

CosmoCaixa ❾

Teodor Roviralta 47–51. **Tel** *93 212 60 50.* 🚇 *Avinguda del Tibidabo.* 🚌 *17, 22, 58, 73.* ◯ *10am–8pm Tue–Sun.* ⬤ *1 & 6 Jan, 25 Dec.* 🎫 *(free 1st Sun of month).* ♿ **www**.cosmocaixa.com

Barcelona's revamped science museum is even more stimulating and interactive than its popular predecessor which was housed in the Modernista building that still stands on site. Beside it now is a new wing on nine levels, six of them are underground. Its particular boast is a glasshouse containing a recreated section of a flooded Amazon forest inhabited by fish, amphibians, insects, reptiles, mammals, birds and plant species. Other exhibition spaces include the Matter Room, which takes a look at the big-bang theory, a Geological Wall, which examines different types of rock, and a planetarium.

Torre Bellesguard ❿

Carrer de Bellesguard 16. 🚇 *Avda del Tibidabo.* ⬤ *closed to public.*

Bellesguard means "beautiful spot" and here, halfway up the Collserola hills, is the place chosen by the medieval Catalan kings as their summer home. Their castle, built in 1408, was in particular a favourite residence of Barcelona's Martí the Humanist (*see p57*).

The surrounding district of Sant Gervasi was developed in the 19th century after the

Wrought-iron entrance door at Antoni Gaudí's Torre Bellesguard

coming of the railway. In 1900 Gaudí built the present house on the site of the castle, which had fallen badly into ruin. Its castellated look and the elongated, Gothic-inspired windows refer clearly to the original castle. Gaudí kept the vestiges of its walls in his structure. The roof, with a walkway behind the parapet, is topped by a distinctive Gaudí tower. Ceramic fish mosaics by the main door symbolize Catalonia's past sea power.

Parc del Laberint d'Horta ⓫

Germans Desvalls, Passeig Castanyers. **Tel** *010 (from Barcelona).* 🚇 *Mundet.* ◯ *10am–6pm daily (winter); 10am–9pm daily (summer).* 🎫 *(free Wed & Sun).* ♿ **www**.bcn.es/parcsijardins

As its name suggests, the centrepiece of the city's oldest public park, created in the 18th century for Joan Antoni Desvalls, Marqués de Llúpia i d'Alfarràs, is a cypress maze. Even without this Horta would be an agreeable place.

The semi-wild garden slopes steeply uphill from the entrance beside the marquis' semi-derelict palace which now houses a gardening school. It is a veritable compendium of aristocratic Baroque fantasies. Classical temples dedicated to Ariadne (who helped Theseus escape the Minotaur's labyrinth) and Danae (mother of Perseus) stand at either side of a broad paseo, which oversees the maze. From here a monumental flight of steps leads up to a Neo-Classical temple. Elsewhere there is a "romantic garden", a faux cemetery and, in the woodland into which the garden eventually leads, a hermit's cave.

CaixaForum ⓬

Avinguda del Marquès de Comillas 6–8, Montjuïc. **Tel** *93 476 86 00.* 🚇 *Espanya.* 🚌 *13, 50.* ◯ *10am–8pm daily (to 10pm Sat).* 🎫 ♿

Barcelona is growing ever stronger in the field of contemporary art and this exhibition centre can only

Catalonia's new National Theatre near the Plaça de les Glòries Catalanes

enhance its reputation further. The "la Caixa" Foundation's collection of 700 works by Spanish and international artists, is housed in the Antiga Fàbrica Casaramona, a restored textile mill in Modernista style. The mill was built by Josep Puig i Cadafalch after he had completed the Casa de les Punxes. Opened in 1911, it was intended to be a model factory – light, clean and airy – but had only a short working life until the business closed down in 1920. The building then became a storehouse and later, after the Civil War, stables for police horses. The collection is displayed according to changing themes but one permanent exhibit is Joseph Beuys' *Espai de Dolor (Chamber of Pain)*. There are also temporary exhibitions.

Estació del Nord ⓭

Avinguda de Vilanova. **Map** 6 D1. Ⓜ *Arc de Triomf.*

Only the 1861 façade overlooking a park and the grand 1915 entrance remain of this former railway station. The rest

has been remodelled as a sports centre, a police headquarters, and the city's bus station. Two elegant, blue-tiled sculptures, *Espiral arbrada (Branched Spiral)* and *Cel obert (Open Sky)* by Beverley Pepper (1992) sweep through the pleasant park. In front of the station, at Avinguda de Vilanova 12, is a carefully restored building occupied by Catalonia's power generating company. It was built as a power station in 1897 by the architect Pere Falqués. Though the great machinery inside is not visible, the exterior of this iron and brick structure is unmistakably Modernista.

Plaça de les Glòries Catalanes ⓮

Gran Via de les Corts Catalanes. **Map** 4 F5. Ⓜ *Glòries.*

This whole area, where the Diagonal crosses the Gran Via de les Corts Catalanes, continues to be redeveloped as the city expands northeastwards and the Diagonal is extended down to the sea, completing the vision of the

Eixample's planner Ildefons Cerdà *(see p71)*. On the north side, a new shopping centre contrasts with the Encants Vells flea market *(see p155)*, which sprawls beside the highway heading north out of town. It is open 8am–8pm four days a week, and much of the merchandise of furniture, clothes, and bric-à-brac is simply laid out on the ground. It is busiest early in the day and bartering is all part of the fun.

To the south of the *plaça* is the new Teatre Nacional de Catalunya, a vast temple to culture by the Barcelona architect Ricard Bofill. Beside it is the Auditori de Barcelona, with two concert halls by Rafael Moneo that were inaugurated in 1999. The Museu de la Música is located here.

La Rambla del Poblenou, a good place for a stroll and a cup of coffee

Poblenou ⓯

Rambla del Poblenou. Ⓜ *Poblenou.*

Poblenou is the trendy part of town where artists have built their studios in the defunct warehouses of the city's former industrial heartland. The area is centred on the Rambla del Poblenou, a quiet avenue, that extends from Avinguda Diagonal down to the sea. Here palm trees back a stretch of sandy beach. A walk around the quiet streets leading from the Rambla will reveal a few protected pieces of industrial architecture, legacies from the time Barcelona was known as "the Manchester of Spain".

Along the parallel Carrer del Ferrocarril is the Plaça de Prim with low, whitewashed houses reminiscent of a small country town. See pages 106–7 for a guided walk through Poblenou.

Blue-tiled sculpture by Beverley Pepper, Parc de l'Estació del Nord

THREE GUIDED WALKS

There is no shortage of good places to take a stroll in Barcelona. Each of the Street-by-Street maps in the book (the Old Town, the Eixample and Montjuïc) has a short walk marked on it which takes in the well-known sights in the area. Other classic walks are down La Rambla *(see pp60–61)* and around Park Güell *(see pp96–7)*. The walks described on the next six pages, however, take you to three less-explored districts, each with a distinct flavour.

The first walk is around the Born, once a run-down area to stay clear of but now an appealing quarter mixing old streets and fashionable shops. Next comes Gràcia, which could be thought of as "village Barcelona": a proud working-class area of low-rise houses, tiny boutiques and charming

Trueta memorial, Poblenou walk

squares that host a busy nightlife. The final walk is around the post-industrial heartland of Poblenou whose buildings are being restored and put to new uses, and whose skyline is punctuated by a few surviving slender brick chimneys. Each route avoids heavy traffic as far as possible and makes the most of quiet or pedestrianized streets and squares. While there are monuments to be seen along the way, the appeal here is as much in the atmosphere of the areas and the unusual shops, characterful cafés and architectural oddities encountered. All three walks begin and end with a metro station. As in any big city, care should be taken with personal belongings and although it is safe to walk at any time, be aware that the character of areas can change when the bars open.

CHOOSING A WALK

The Three Walks
This map shows the location of the three guided walks in relation to the main sightseeing areas of Barcelona.

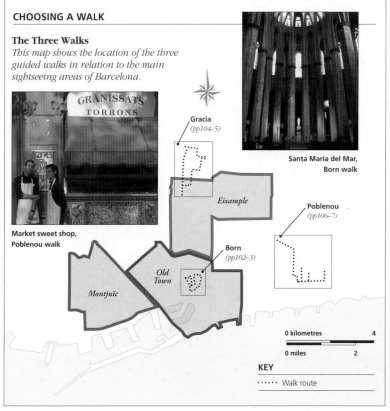

Gracia *(pp104–5)*

Santa Maria del Mar, Born walk

Eixample

Poblenou *(pp106–7)*

Market sweet shop, Poblenou walk

Born *(pp102–3)*

Old Town

Montjuïc

| 0 kilometres | 4 |
| 0 miles | 2 |

KEY

······ Walk route

◁ Plaça del Sol Café, Gràcia walk

A One-Hour Walk Around the Born

The tiny district of El Born, across the Via Laietana from the Barrí Gotic, has made a comeback after long years of neglect. Close to the waterfront, this area flourished in Catalonia's mercantile heyday from the 13th century. The narrow streets still bear the names of the craftsmen and guilds that set up here, for instance, hatters in Carrer dels Sombrerers, mirror-makers in Carrer dels Mirallers, silversmiths in Carrer de la Argentaria. While it still has something of a medieval air, El Born has become the hip and arty place to be.

left into Placeta de Montcada which becomes Carrer Montcada (see p64), an immaculate collection of Gothic mansions dating from the 14th century with later Renaissance refurbishments. Most of the buildings are now museums and galleries. The Casa Cervelló-Guidice at 25 ⑥ is the only

Passeig del Born, the main street of El Born area ⑮

The Carrer de Montcada
From Jaume I metro station in Plaça de l'Angel ① set off down Carrer de la Argenteria but turn left almost at once at the tobacconist's (marked "Tabac") into Carrer del Vigatans. After passing the youth hostel on your left, note the carved head protruding from the wall on the right at the corner of Carrer dels Mirallers ②. At the end of the street you have no choice but to turn sharp left into Carrer de la Carassa to meet Carrer de Barra de

Ferro. Turn right and right again into Carrer de Banys Vells. Halfway down this street on the left at 7 is an enticing little chocolate shop, L'Ametller ③, which sells all kinds of locally produced sweet treats. At the end of the street you meet the side wall of the church of Santa Maria del Mar ④. Turn left along Carrer Sombrerers. On your left at 23 is Casa Gispert ⑤, a famous old shop selling coffee roasted on the premises, nuts and dried fruit. When you can go no further, turn

building on the street still with its original façade. Opposite it, at 20 ⑦, is the Palau Dalmases, whose patio has an ornately carved staircase. Its neighbour at 22 is El Xampanyet (see p152) ⑧, the city's best known bar for *cava* (Catalan sparkling wine) and tapas. Much of the right-hand side of Montcada is taken up by five palaces including the Museu Picasso ⑨ (see pp64). Opposite this are two more museums. The first you come to at 14 is the Museu Barbier-Mueller ⑩, in the Palau Nadal. This collection of pre-Columbian sculptures, fabrics, ceramics and ritual

TIPS FOR WALKERS

Starting point: *Plaça de l'Angel*
Length: *1.5 km (1 mile)*
Getting there: *Go to Jaume I metro station in the Plaça de l'Angel on Line 4.*
Stopping off points: *There are many bars and eateries along the route including the Café del Born (Plaça Comercial) and Origens 99,9% (Carrer Vidrieria 6–8), a Catalan restaurant and shop. You'll find lots on Carrer de la Argenteria, notably Xocolateria Xador (for hot chocolate; 61–3), and Taller de Tapas (51).*

Visitors flocking to the popular Museu Picasso ⑨

Enjoying the café culture in Plaça de Comercial in front of Mercat del Born ⑯

into the arch at the start of Carrer de l'Hostal de Sant Antoni (on your right) ⑭ to see an unusual hieroglyphic-like frieze. Carrer Triangle leads you into Carrer del Rec and before long you meet the Passeig del Born ⑮. It was the jousts held in this broad avenue from the 13th to 17th centuries that gave the name to the Born quarter of which it forms the heart. To the left, the Passeig opens out into the Plaça de Comercial, which is dominated by the Mercat del Born ⑯, the former wholesale market. This old iron and glass building was modelled on Les Halles in Paris but is now being converted into a cultural centre. Excavations on the site have helped archaeologists piece together a clear picture of life in 18th-century Barcelona. Continue on Carrer del Rec on the other side of the Passeig del Born and turn right at the next junction into Carrer de l'Esparteria. Turn left at Carrer de Vidriera to reach Plaça de les Olles. Turn right here and follow the wide pavement which skirts the Plaça del Palau. It also passes an old ironmonger's with giant paella pans.

When you reach the Café La Bolsa – across the road from La Llotja (see p63) ⑰ – turn right into Carrer dels Canvis Vells. Bear right into the Carrer de l'Anisadeta, which is so short that it is over almost as soon as it is begun, and you find yourself back in the charming Plaça de Santa Maria ⑱, facing the church of the same name (see pp64–5). Pop inside to admire the beautiful Catalan Gothic interior. Bear left across the square to the start of Carrer de la Argenteria, the busiest street in El Born, lined with bars and shops. Follow this back to your starting point at the metro in Plaça de l'Angel.

KEY

• • • Walk route

Ⓜ Metro station

objects was assembled by the great Swiss art collector, Josef Mueller (1887–1977) with the aid of his son-in-law Jean Paul Barbier, who felt that "primitive" art deserved to be more admired and appreciated. The courtyard is dominated by a reproduction of a giant Olmec head from Mexico. Just after is the temporary

exhibition space of Barcelona's Disseny Hub in Palau del Marquès de Llió (or Mora) ⑪, which usually features exhibitions on textiles or fashion. At the end of Montcada turn right along Carrer de la Princesa, where you'll find several tempting shops. First you pass the windows of Brunells pastry shop at 22 ⑫, then the *turrón* and sweet shop of La Campana (founded in 1890) at 36 ⑬.

The Passeig del Born

Take the next small street to the right, Carrer del Corretger, which turns a sharp corner. Turn right at the cake shop into Carrer Triangle. Look up

Brunells chocolate shop ⑫

A 90-Minute Walk Through Gràcia

When you cross the Avinguda Diagonal and plunge into the maze of sinuous streets and small squares on the other side, it is easy to get the impression that you have left the city behind and entered a village. Since Gràcia became part of Barcelona in 1897 it has never lost its sense of independence and identity. During the day, it feels calmly removed from the pace of modern metropolitan life just a few blocks away. In August and in the evening, however, expect a hullabaloo as the district draws crowds to its exotic shops and nightlife.

façade, Carrer Gràcia. Turn left and quickly right down Carrer Domènech. Turn left at the end up Carrer de Francisco Giner and this will lead you into Plaça de la Vila de Gràcia ⑤, where a 33-m (108-ft) clock tower is overlooked by the sky blue façade of Gràcia's local government

The façade of Casa Fuster, a Modernista building, now a hotel ③

The Passeig de Gràcia

From Plaça Joan Carles I ① the famous Passeig de Gràcia continues briefly as a modest, plane tree-shaded avenue. On your left, almost immediately, you come to Casa Bonaventura Ferrer ②, a Modernista building by Pere Falqués I Urpi, with stonework sculpted into swirling leaves and a façade finished off with an iron crown. A short way along, the road narrows to go round another Modernista building (although its inspiration is

clearly Neo-Gothic). The last work of architect Lluís Domènech i Montaner, Casa Fuster ③ has been converted into a hotel. The Café Vienés on the ground floor is open to non-residents.

The squares of Gràcia

A few steps beyond Casa Fuster up the Passeig de Gràcia's well-to-do continuation, Gran de Gràcia, you can see the handsome stained-glass *miradores* (upper-floor bay windows) above La Colmena *patisseria* at 15 ④. Then go back to Casa Fuster and turn down the road behind its rear

TIPS FOR WALKERS

Starting point: *Plaça Joan Carles I*

Length: *2.5 km (1.5 miles)*

Getting there: *Diagonal metro station in Plaça Joan Carles I is on Line 3 or reached by FCG train.*

Stopping-off points: *Most of Gràcia's squares have bars and restaurants. Try Bo Restaurant (tapas) in Plaça de la Vila de Gràcia; Café del Sol (drinks and music) or Mirasol (classic bar) in Plaça de Sol; Niu Toc (fish) on Plaça Revolució de Setembre de 1868 or Virreina Bar (sandwiches and beer) in Plaça de la Virreina.*

A performance of *castellers* at fiesta time in Gràcia ⑤

Nightlife at the Plaça del Sol ⑥

0 metres 125

0 yards 125

KEY

• • • Walk route

Ⓜ Metro station

streets, and stroll along Carrer Xiquets de Valls, named after a renowned team of *castellers*. This brings you into the Plaça del Sol ⑥, a nightlife hub popularly known as Plaça dels Encants. Turn left to leave by Carrer Maspons. Straight ahead, on the other side of Carrer del Torrent l'Olla, is the Plaça Revolució de Setembre de 1868 ⑦. The name commemorates the *coup d'état* led by General Prim, which unseated Spain's ruling Bourbon dynasty, who were so antagonistic to the Catalans they ushered in the first republican government in Spain's history. Turn left into the square and leave by Carrer de Verdi that sprouts from the top of it. This is a busy but pleasant street of modern shops. After passing Cinemes Verdi (on your right), which often shows original-version foreign films, turn right down Carrer de l'Or. You soon arrive in one of

Stained-glass windows in *miradores* ④

Gràcia's most agreeable squares, the Plaça Virreina ⑧, where the church of Sant Joan faces downhill towards two fine buildings: one is a residence with a tower and the other a redbrick house in Modernista style with a graphic red and cream façade and wrought iron balconies.

Casa Vincens

Leave Virreina by the shady Carrer de Astúries and stay on

it across the top of Plaça Diamant ⑨. This is where a civil war air-raid shelter has been discovered – now open to the public by appointment (call 93 219 61 34). Turn right up Carrer Torrent l'Olla and left down Santa Agata. When you reach Gran de Gràcia cross over it into Carrer de les Carolines. At the bottom of this street at 24 is one of Antoni Gaudí's early works, Casa Vicens ⑩. It is privately owned but well worth admiring from the outside. Commissioned as a summer house by a brick and tile maker, it took the inexperienced Gaudí five years to build (1883–8). Inspired by Moorish architecture, the house was a bold break with tradition and the lavish use of colour and ornament clearly indicate where Gaudí's interests lay. The exterior of the house is a checkerboard of green and white tiles and other tiles with a marigold motif. The riotous ironwork shows off with extravagant loops and intriguing beasts. Now retrace your steps to Gran de Gràcia. If you are in the mood for more Gaudí, go uphill to Plaça Lesseps and from there follow the signs to Park Güell (*see pp96–7*). If not, go downhill past pretty Plaça Trilla ⑪. You can either finish the walk at Fontana metro station or continue on back to your starting point.

headquarters. A plaque on the wall commemorates the achievements of Catalonia's *castellers*, teams of amateur gymnasts who can often be seen building human towers up to eight people high on fiesta days in Gràcia. Cross the square and leave by Carrer Mariana Pineda. Cross Travessera de Gràcia, one of the district's main shopping

The interior and stained-glass windows at Casa Vicens ⑩

A Two-hour Walk Through Poblenou

It's hard to believe today but the trendy district of Poblenou once had the highest concentration of smoke-belching factories in Catalonia. By the 1960s these had gone out of business or moved to the outskirts, leaving their old buildings to decay. With the 1992 Olympic Games came an impetus for recovery and since then Poblenou's warehouses have been spruced up and converted into chic studios for artists and photographers. New developments brought hotels, discos and restaurants, creating a fascinating mix of industrial archaeology and contemporary culture.

The controversial Torre Agbar ③

The Avinguda Diagonal

Leave the metro station in Plaça de les Glòries Catalanes ① (an area of ongoing redevelopment; *see p99*) by the Carrer Badajoz exit, which will lead you on to the wide seaward extension of Avinguda Diagonal ②. This takes you directly beneath a tall, unusual and much-criticised building that breaks up the city skyline, the Torre Agbar ③. A domed cylindrical tower of 33 floors, unkindly

TIPS FOR WALKERS

Starting point: *Plaça de Les Glòries Catalanes*
Length: *3.5 km (2 miles)*
Getting there: *Glòries metro station is on metro line 1.*
Stopping off points: *There are bars on Rambla de Poble Nou, swish restaurants on Carrer Taulat and a few cheaper bars on Carrer Maria Aguilo. Go for an ice cream at El Tio Che.*

described as an upended blue cigar, it was built by French architect Jean Nouvel for the local water company, Aigües de Barcelona.
Continue on down Diagonal, which has a wide *paseo* in the middle flanked by traffic lanes, tramways that link Glòries with Sant Adrià del Besòs as well as cycle tracks. About 700 m (half a mile) down Diagonal turn right into Rambla del Poblenou ④, the main street of Poblenou that leads eventually to the sea. After crossing Carrer de Pere IV, the Rambla narrows and becomes more attractive. In the middle is a memorial to Doctor Josep Trueta ⑤. This pioneering surgeon was born in Poblenou in 1897 and, after working to save lives during the bombardments of the Civil War, went into a 30-year exile in England on the fall of democracy in 1939.

Rambla del Poblenou

Keep straight on down the Rambla over the next three circular road junctions. Along the way are several buildings worth stopping to look at, such as 51 (on the

right) ⑥, a handsome salmon-coloured building by Josep Masdeu dating from 1914, which is decorated with Modernista floral motifs.
At the next junction with Carrer Joncar, turn left between El Tio Che ⑦, a well-known shop founded in 1912, selling ice cream and *turrón* (a typical Spanish sweet made of almonds) and, opposite it, the Casino de l'Alliança de Poblenou ⑧, a concert hall (not a gambling enterprise as its name might suggest). Turn right at the

Memorial to civil-war hero, Dr Josep Trueta ⑤

El Tio Che, the renowned ice cream and *turrón* parlour ⑦

first junction you come to down Carrer Maria Aguilo, a lively but humanly-scaled pedestrianized shopping street. On the left, up a short street, is the district's market, the Mercat de la Unió ⑨. Beside it is a handsome building, 24 Plaça de la Unió, with Art Nouveau white and green ceramic festoons draped over the windows.

On the right of Maria Aguilo, at 120 ⑩, is the shop of the artist Chema Vidal who makes scale models of monuments in Poblenou, both existing and demolished. Cross over Carrer del Taulat (the junction is slightly staggered) into Carrer del Ferrocarril and turn left into the old square of Plaça del Prim ⑪. Here, you'll see gnarled, leaning, fat-rooted ombu trees (an Argentinian species) and low whitewashed houses. Now somewhat lost amid the modernity around it, this square is the original heart of Poblenou, from which all else grew.

It is said that among the fishermen and workers who lived on this square were many followers of the mid-19th century Icaria Utopian movement, which militated against capitalism and attempted to create a world of "universal brotherhood". Return to Carrer del Taulat and turn right. If you wish to end your walk here, turn left up Carrer de Bilbao to reach Poblenou

metro station. Otherwise, continue along Taulat, a strip of gardens through modern residential developments.

A short detour to the corner of Carrer de Ramon Turró and Espronceda takes you to a garden ⑫ dedicated to the Indian social reformer and philosopher Mahatma Gandhi, with a sculpture of him by the Nobel Peace Prize winner Adolfo Pérez Esquivel.

Returning to Passeig del Taulat, ahead of you all the while rises the most characteristic surviving industrial building in Poblenou, the Torre de les Aigües ⑬. Turn left into Carrer de la Selva to get to the base of this structure, which stands in the

Torre de les Aigües ⑬

middle of Plaça Ramon Calsina. This round, red-brick tower, 63 m (207 ft) high, was built to raise and store water from the nearby Besos river. Near the top of it is a vertigo-inducing metal staircase that leads round the brickwork to a balcony.

From here continue up Carrer de la Selva to Selva de Mar metro station on the corner of Carrer de Pujades. On the way you might like to wander a few steps to your left along Carrer de Llull. On the corner with Carrer de Provençals rises the highest chimney in Barcelona ⑭. This graceful flat-topped 65-m (213-ft) spire used to form part of the now-defunct Macosa steelworks. Return to Carrer de la Selva and end your walk at the Selva de Mar metro stop.

0 metres   250
0 yards   250

KEY

• • • Walk route

Ⓜ Metro station

The unusual ombu trees in the village-like Plaça del Prim ⑪

CATALONIA

LLEIDA · ANDORRA · GIRONA
BARCELONA PROVINCE · TARRAGONA

There is a wealth of natural beauty in Catalonia's four provinces, plus the small Catalan-speaking country of Andorra. They offer rocky coasts and mountains, fertile plains and sandy shores. Many who visit don't stray far from the coast, but the rewards for venturing further afield are immense.

Beyond the constant bustle of Barcelona, Catalonia is essentially a rural region, with no large cities and few industrial blights. Of the four provinces, all named after their principal city, Lleida is the largest and least populated. Among its jewels are the Romanesque churches of the Boí valley and the Aigüestortes National Park.

Santa Maria, Ripoll

The province of Girona is blessed with mountains and sea. This eastern end of the Pyrenees has the magical Cerdanya valley and the ancient monasteries of Ripoll and Sant Joan de les Abadesses, as well as medieval villages and a handsome and too-often overlooked capital city. Its coast, the Costa Brava, is rocky and full of delights.

Barcelona province has its own coasts; the Maresme to the north is rather spoiled by the railway running beside the sea, but the Garraf to the south is more exciting – Sitges is a highly fashionable spot. Inland are the Holy Mountain of Montserrat (Catalonia's spiritual heart), the Penedès winelands, and the country town of Vic.

Tarragona, the most southerly of the provinces, has one of the peninsula's former Roman capitals. Here the land rolls more gently, supporting fruit and nut orchards and the monastic communities of Poblet and Santes Creus, before falling away towards the rice lands of the Ebre. The coastline is more gentle, too, with long, sandy beaches.

Aigüestortes y E. Sant Maurici National Park in the central Pyrenees, in the province of Lleida

◁ A fisherman inspects his nets in Cadaqués on the Costa Brava

Exploring Catalonia

Catalonia includes a long stretch of the Spanish Pyrenees, whose green, flower-filled valleys hide picturesque villages with Romanesque churches. The Parc Nacional d'Aigüestortes and Vall d'Aran are paradises for naturalists, while Baqueira-Beret offers skiers reliable snow. Sun-lovers can choose between the rugged Costa Brava or the long sandy stretches of the Costa Daurada. Tarragona is rich in Roman monuments. Inland are the monasteries of Poblet and Santes Creus and the well-known vineyards of Penedès.

Isolated houses in the countryside around La Seu d'Urgell

KEY

▭▭▭	Motorway (highway)
▭▭	Other highway
▬	Main road
▭▭▭	Minor road
▬	Scenic route
▬▬	Main railway
▬	Minor railway
▬▬▬	International border
▬▬▬	Regional border
△	Summit

GETTING AROUND

The motorway from France enters Spain at La Jonquera and, from Barcelona, follows the coast via Tarragona and Tortosa. Buses connect most towns. The main north–south railway hugs the coast from Blanes southwards. Other lines connect Barcelona to Vic and Lleida (*see inside back cover*).

SEE ALSO

- *Where to Stay* pp134–41
- *Restaurants* pp146–51

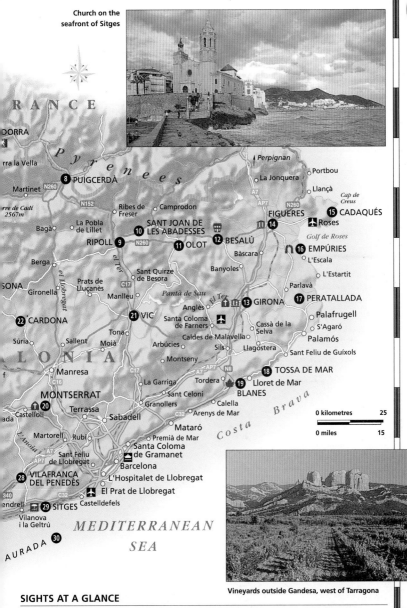

Church on the seafront of Sitges

FRANCE

ANDORRA

Andorra la Vella

Pyrenees

Martinet · **N260**

Serre de Cadí
2567m · **N152**

8 PUIGCERDÀ

Ribes de Freser · Camprodon

Bagà · La Pobla de Lillet

SANT JOAN DE LES ABADESSES · **10**

RIPOLL · **9** · **N260** · **11** OLOT · **12** BESALÚ

Berga

el Ter

Bàscara

Banyoles

Perpignan

La Jonquera · Portbou

Llançà

Cap de Creus

FIGUERES · **15** CADAQUÉS

14 · Roses

Golf de Roses

16 EMPÚRIES · L'Escala

L'Estartit

Gironella · GIRONA · Sant Quirze de Besora

Prats de Lluçanès · Manlleu

CARDONA · **22**

Súria · Sallent · Tona

Manresa

MONTSERRAT · **20**

Castellolí · **20**

Terrassa · Sabadell

Martorell · Rubí

Sant Feliu de Llobregat

28 VILAFRANCA DEL PENEDÈS

el Llobregat

el Ter

Pantà de Sau

21 VIC

Santa Coloma de Farners

Arbúcies

Caldes de Malavella

Sils · Montseny

La Garriga

Sant Celoni

Granollers · Calella

Arenys de Mar

Premià de Mar

Santa Coloma de Gramanet

Barcelona

L'Hospitalet de Llobregat

El Prat de Llobregat

Castelldefels

Parlavà

Anglès · **13** GIRONA

Cassà de la Selva

Sant Feliu de Guíxols

Tordera · **19** Lloret de Mar

BLANES

17 PERATALLADA

Palafrugell

S'Agaró

Palamós

18 TOSSA DE MAR

Costa Brava

CATALONIA

El Vendrell · **29** SITGES

Vilanova i la Geltrú · **30**

COSTA DAURADA

MEDITERRANEAN SEA

0 kilometres   25

0 miles   15

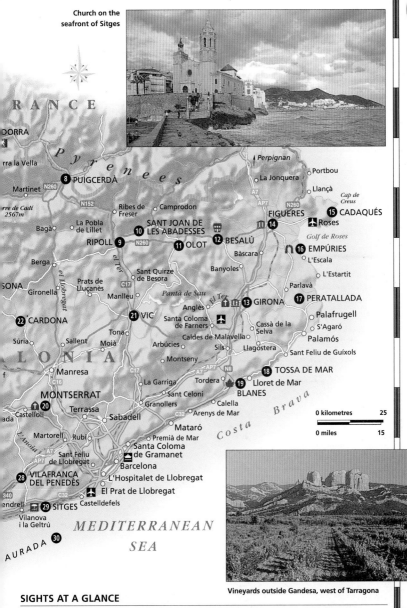

Vineyards outside Gandesa, west of Tarragona

SIGHTS AT A GLANCE

The Vall d'Aran, surrounded by the snow-capped mountains of the Pyrenees

BUTTERFLIES OF THE VALL D'ARAN

A huge variety of butterflies and moths is found high in the valleys and mountains of the Pyrenees. The isolated Vall d'Aran is the home of several unique and rare subspecies. The best time of the year in which to see the butterflies is between May and July.

Chequered Skipper
(Carterocephalus palemon)

Clouded Apollo
(Parnassins mnemosyne)

Grizzled Skipper (underside)
(Pyrgus malvae)

Vall d'Aran ❶

Lleida N230. 🚌 *Vielha.*
ℹ️ *Vielha (973 64 06 88).*

This valley of valleys – *aran* means valley – is a lovely 600-sq km (230-sq mile) haven of forests and meadows filled with flowers, surrounded by towering mountain peaks.

The Vall d'Aran was formed by the Riu Garona, which rises in the area and flows out to France as the Garonne. With no proper link to the outside world until 1924, when a road was built over the Bonaigua Pass, the valley was cut off from the rest of Spain for most of the winter. Snow blocks the narrow pass from November to April, but today access is easy through the Túnel de Vielha from El Pont de Suert.

The fact that the Vall d'Aran faces north means that it has a climate similar to that on the Atlantic coast. Many rare wild flowers and butterflies flourish in the perfect conditions that are created by the shady slopes and damp breezes. It is also a famous habitat for many species of narcissus.

Tiny villages have grown up beside the Riu Garona, often around Romanesque churches, notably at **Bossòst, Salardú, Escunhau** and **Arties**. The valley is also ideal for outdoor sports such as skiing and is popular with walkers.

Vielha ❷

Lleida. 👥 *2,000.* 🚌 ℹ️ *Carrer Sarriulera 10 (973 64 01 10).* 🚌 *Thu.* 🎉 *Festa de Vielha (8 Sep), Feria de Vielha (8 Oct).*

Now a modern ski resort, the capital of the Vall d'Aran retains its medieval past. The Romanesque church of **Sant Miquel** has an octagonal bell tower and a 12th-century crucifix, the *Mig Aran Christ*. It formed part of a larger carving representing the Descent from the Cross. The **Museu de la Vall d'Aran** is devoted to Aranese culture.

🏛 **Museu de la Vall d'Aran**
Carrer Major 26. **Tel** *973 64 18 15.*
🕐 *10am–1pm (mid-Jun–mid-Sep only), 5–8pm Tue–Sat, 10am–1pm Sun.* ⚫ *bank hols.* 📷

Mig Aran Christ (12th-century), Sant Miquel church, Vielha

Baqueira-Beret ❸

Lleida. 🏘 100. 🚉 ❗ *Baqueira-Beret (973 63 90 10).* 🎭 *Romeria de Nostra Senyora de Montgarri (2 Jul).*

This extensive ski resort, one of the best in Spain, is popular with both the public and the Spanish royal family. There is reliable winter snow cover and a choice of over 40 pistes at altitudes from 1,520 m to 2,470 m (4,987 ft to 8,104 ft).

Baqueira and Beret were separate mountain villages before skiing became popular, but they have now merged to form a single resort. The Romans took full advantage of the thermal springs located here, which are nowadays appreciated by tired skiers.

Vall de Boí ❹

Lleida N230. 🚉 *La Pobla de Segur.* 🚌 *Pont de Suert.* ❗ *Barruera (973 69 40 00).* **www**.vallboi.com

This small valley on the edge of the Parc Nacional d'Aigüestortes is dotted with tiny villages, many of which are built around magnificent Catalan Romanesque churches.

Dating from the 11th and 12th centuries, these churches are distinguished by their tall belfries, such as the six-storey bell tower of the **Església de Santa Eulàlia** at Erill-la-Vall.

The two churches at Taüll, **Sant Climent** *(see pp22–3)* and **Santa Maria**, have superb frescoes. Between 1919 and 1923 the originals were taken for safekeeping to the Museu Nacional d'Art de Catalunya in Barcelona *(see p88).* Replicas now stand in their place. You can climb the towers of Sant Climent for superb views of the surrounding countryside.

Other churches in the area worth visiting include those at **Coll**, for its fine ironwork, **Barruera**, and **Durro**, which has another massive bell tower.

At the head of the valley is the hamlet of **Caldes de Boí**, popular for its thermal springs and ski facilities. It is also a good base for exploring the Parc Nacional d'Aigüestortes, the entrance to which is only 5 km (3 miles) from here.

The tall belfry of Sant Climent church at Taüll in the Vall de Boí

Parc Nacional d'Aigüestortes ❺

Lleida. 🚉 *La Pobla de Segur.* 🚌 *Pont de Suert, La Pobla de Segur.* ❗ *Boí (973 69 61 89); Espot (973 62 40 36).*

The pristine mountain scenery of Catalonia's only national park is among the most spectacular to be seen anywhere in the Pyrenees.

Established in 1955, the park covers an area of 102 sq km (40 sq miles). Its full title is Parc Nacional d'Aigüestortes i Estany de Sant Maurici, named after the lake *(estany)* of Sant Maurici in the east and the Aigüestortes (literally, twisted waters) area in the west. The main village is the mountain settlement of Espot, on the park's eastern edge, although you can access the park from Boí in the west. Around the park are waterfalls and some 150 lakes and tarns which, in an earlier era, were scoured by glaciers to depths of up to 50 m (164 ft).

The finest scenery is around Sant Maurici lake, which lies beneath the twin shards of the Serra dels Encantats, (Mountains of the Enchanted). From here, there is a variety of walks, particularly along the string of lakes that leads north to the towering peaks of Agulles d'Amitges. To the south is the dramatic vista of Estany Negre, the highest and deepest tarn in the park.

Early summer in the lower valleys is marked by rhododendrons, while later on wild lilies bloom in the forests of fir, beech and silver birch.

The park is also home to a variety of wildlife. Chamois (also known as izards) live on the mountain screes and in the meadows, while beavers and otters can be spotted by the lakes. Golden eagles nest on mountain ledges, and grouse and capercaillie are found in the woods.

During the summer the park is popular with walkers, while in winter, the snow-covered mountains are ideal for cross-country skiing.

A crystal-clear stream, Parc Nacional d'Aigüestortes

LES QUATRE BARRES

The four red bars on the *senyera*, the Catalan flag, are said to represent the four provinces: Barcelona, Girona, Lleida and Tarragona. The design derives from a legend of Guifré el Pelós, first Count of Barcelona *(see p42)*. It relates how he received a call for help from Charles the Bald, who was King of the West Franks and grandson of Charlemagne. Guifré went to his aid and turned the tide of battle, but was mortally wounded. As he lay dying, Charles dipped his fingers in Guifré's blood and dragged them across his plain gold shield, giving him a grant of arms.

Catalonia's national emblem

Andorra ❻

Principality of Andorra. 🏛 *77,000.*
🚊 *Andorra la Vella.* 🛈 *Plaça de la Rotonda, Andorra la Vella (376 87 31 03).* **www**.andorra.ad

Andorra occupies 464 sq km (179 sq miles) of the Pyrenees between France and Spain. In 1993, it became fully independent and held its first ever democratic elections. Since 1278, it had been an autonomous feudal state under the jurisdiction of the Spanish bishop of La Seu d'Urgell and the French Count of Foix (a title adopted by the President of France). These are still the ceremonial joint heads of state.

Andorra's official language is Catalan, though French and Castilian are also spoken by most residents.

For many years Andorra has been a tax-free paradise for shoppers, a fact reflected in the crowded shops and super-markets of the capital **Andorra la Vella**. Les Escaldes (near the capital), as well as Sant Julià de Lòria and El Pas de la Casa (the towns nearest the Spanish and French borders), have also become shopping centres.

Most visitors never see Andorra's rural charms, which match those of other parts of the Pyrenees. The region is excellent for walkers. One of the main routes leads to the **Cercle de Pessons**, a bowl of lakes in the east, and past Romanesque chapels such as **Sant Martí** at La Cortinada. In the north is the picturesque Sorteny valley where traditional farmhouses have been converted into snug restaurants.

La Seu d'Urgell ❼

Lleida. 🏛 *13,000.* 🚊 🛈 *Avenida Valles de Andorra 33 (973 35 15 11).* 🚊 *Tue & Sat.* 🎉 *Festa major (last week of Aug).* **www**.turismeseu.com

This Pyrenean town was made a bishopric in the 6th century. Feuds between the bishops of Urgell and the Counts of Foix over land, gave rise to Andorra in the 13th century. The **cathedral** has a Romanesque statue of Santa Maria d'Urgell. The **Museu Diocesà** contains a 10th-century copy of St Beatus of Liébana's *Commentary on the Apocalypse.*

🏛 Museu Diocesà
Plaça del Deganat. **Tel** *973 35 32 42.* ⏰ *10am–1pm, 4–7pm Mon–Sat (to 6pm Oct–May), 10am–1pm Sun.* 🚫 *1 Jan, 25 Dec & public hols.* 🈲 🚻

Carving, La Seu d'Urgell cathedral

Puigcerdà ❽

Girona. 🏛 *9,000.* 🚊 🚊 🛈 *Carrer Querol 1 (972 88 05 42).* 🚊 *Sun.* 🎉 *Festa de l'Estany (third Sun of Aug); Festa del Roser (mid-Jul).* **www**.puigcerda.com

Puig is Catalan for hill. Despite sitting on a relatively small hill compared with the encircling mountains, which rise to 2,900 m (9,500 ft), Puigcerdà nevertheless has a fine view down the beautiful Cerdanya valley.

Puigcerdà was founded in 1177 by Alfons II as the capital of Cerdanya, an important agricultural region, which shares a past and its culture with the French Cerdagne. The Spanish enclave of **Llívia**, an attractive little town with a medieval pharmacy, lies 6 km (3.75 miles) inside France.

Cerdanya is the largest valley in the Pyrenees. At its edge is the **Cadí-Moixeró** nature reserve *(see p170)*, a place for ambitious walks.

Portal of Monestir de Santa Maria

Ripoll ❾

Girona. 🏛 *11,000.* 🚊 🚊 🛈 *Plaça del Abat Oliba (972 70 23 51).* 🚊 *Sat.* 🎉 *Festa major (11–12 May), La Llana y Casament a Pagès (Sun after Festa major).* **www**.elripolles.com

Once a tiny mountain base from which raids against the Moors were made, Ripoll is now best known for the **Monestir de Santa Maria** *(see p22)*, founded in 879. The town is called the "cradle of Catalonia" as the monastery was the power base of Guifré el Pelós (Wilfred the Hairy), founder of the House of Barcelona *(see p42)*. He is also buried here. In the later 12th century, the west portal was decorated with what are regarded as the finest Romanesque carvings in Spain. This and the cloister are the only parts of the medieval monastery to have survived.

Environs
In the mountains to the west is **Sant Jaume de Frontanyà** *(see p22)*, another superb Romanesque church.

The medieval town of Besalú on the banks of the Riu Fluvià

Sant Joan de les Abadesses ⑩

Girona. 🏠 *3,600.* 🚌 ℹ️ *Plaça de Abadia 9 (972 72 05 99).* 🚆 *Sun.* 📷 *Festa major (second week of Sep).* 📷
www.santjoandelesabadesses.cat

A fine, 12th-century Gothic bridge arches over the Riu Ter to this unassuming market town, whose main attraction is its **monastery**.

Founded in 885, it was a gift from Guifré, first count of Barcelona, to his daughter, the first abbess. The church has little decoration except for a wooden calvary, *The Descent from the Cross.* Though made in 1150, it looks modern. The figure of a thief on the left was burnt in the Civil War and replaced so skilfully that it is hard to tell it is new. The museum has Baroque and Renaissance altarpieces.

12th-century calvary, Sant Joan de les Abadesses monastery

Environs
To the north are **Camprodon** and **Beget**, both with Romanesque churches *(see p23).* Camprodon also has some grand houses, and its region is noted for sausages.

Olot ⑪

Girona. 🏠 *30,000.* 🚌 ℹ️ *Carrer Hospici 8 (972 26 01 41).* 🚆 *Mon.* 📷 *Feria de mayo (1 May), Corpus Christi (Jun), Festa del Tura (8 Sep), Feria de Sant Lluc (18 Oct).*
www.turismeolot.cat

This small market town is at the centre of a landscape pockmarked with extinct volcanoes. But it was an earthquake in 1474 that destroyed its medieval past.

During the 18th century the town's textile industry spawned the "Olot School" of art *(see p28):* cotton fabrics were printed with drawings. In 1783 the Public School of Drawing was founded. Much of the school's work, which includes paintings such as Joaquim Vayreda's *Les Falgueres,* is in the **Museu Comarcal de la Garrotxa**. *Modernista* sculptor Miquel Blay's damsels support the balcony at No. 38 Passeig Miquel Blay.

🏛 **Museu Comarcal de la Garrotxa**
Carrer Hospici 8. **Tel** *972 27 11 66.*
⬜ *Sep–May: 10am–1pm, 3–6pm Mon–Fri; Jun–Aug: 11am–2pm, 4–7pm Mon–Fri; all year: 11am–2pm & 4–7pm Sat, 11am–2pm Sun.* 📷 ♿

Besalú ⑫

Girona. 🏠 *2,000.* 🚌 ℹ️ *Plaça de la Llibertat 1 (972 59 12 40).* 🚆 *Tue.* 📷 *Sant Vicenç (22 Jan), Festa major (weekend closest to 25 Sep).* 📷
www.besalu.cat

A magnificent medieval town, with a striking approach across a fortified bridge over the Riu Fluvià, Besalú has two fine Romanesque churches: **Sant Vicenç** and **Sant Pere** *(see p23).* The latter is the sole remnant of a Benedictine monastery founded in 977, but pulled down in 1835.

In 1964 a **mikvah**, a Jewish ritual bath, was discovered by chance. It was built in 1264 and is one of only three of that period to survive in Europe. The tourist office has the keys to all the town's attractions.

To the south, the sky-blue lake of **Banyoles**, where the 1992 Olympic rowing contests were held, is ideal for picnics.

Shop selling *llonganisses* in the mountain town of Camprodon

GIRONA TOWN CENTRE

Banys Arabs ②
Catedral ④
Centre Bonastruc Ça Porta ⑦
Església de Sant Feliu ③
Església de Sant Pere de
　Galligants ①
Museu d'Art ⑤
Museu d'Història
　de la Ciutat ⑥

0 metres　　　　250
0 yards　　　　250

Key to Symbols see back flap

Girona ⓭

Girona. 👥 96,000. 🚶 🚉 🚌 ℹ️
Rambla de la Llibertat 1 (972 22 65 75).
📅 Tue, Sat. 🎉 Sant Narcis (29 Oct
for a week). www.girona.cat/turisme

This handsome town puts on
its best face beside the Riu
Onyar, where tall, pastel-
coloured buildings rise above
the water. Behind them, in the
old town, the Rambla de la
Llibertat is lined with busy
shops and street cafés.

The houses were built in the
19th century to replace sections of the city wall damaged
during a seven-month siege
by French troops in 1809. Most
of the rest of the ramparts, first
raised by the Romans, are still

intact and have been turned
into the Passeig Arqueològic
(Archaeological Walk), which
runs right round the city.

The walk's starting point is
on the north side of the town,
near the **Església de Sant Pere
de Galligants** (St Peter of the
Cock Crows) *(see p23)*. The
church now houses the city's
archaeological collection.

From here, a narrow street
goes through the north gate,
where huge Roman foundation
stones are still visible. They
mark the route of the Via
Augusta, the road which once
ran from Tarragona to Rome.
The most popular place of
devotion in the town is the
Església de Sant Feliu. The
church, begun in the 14th

century, was built over the
tombs of St Felix and St
Narcissus, both patrons of the
city. Next to the high altar are
eight Roman sarcophagi.

Despite their name, the
nearby **Banys Àrabs** (Arab
Baths) were built in the late
12th century, about 300 years
after the Moors had left.

🏛 Centre Bonastruc Ça Porta
Carrer de la Força 8. **Tel** 972 21 67
61. ⬜ 10am–2pm Mon (to 8pm Jul–
Aug), 10am–6pm Tue–Sat (to 8pm
Jul–Aug), 10am–2pm Sun. ⬤ 1 & 6
Jan, 25 & 26 Dec. 🎫 ♿
This centre charts the history
of Jews in Girona. The
buildings it occupies in the
maze of alleyways and steps
in the old town were once
part of El Call, the Jewish
ghetto, which was inhabited
by the city's Jews from the
late 9th century until their
expulsion from Spain in 1492.

🔒 Catedral
⬜ Apr–Oct: 10am–8pm daily;
Nov–Mar: 10am–7pm daily. 🎫
Girona Cathedral's west face is
pure Catalan Baroque, but the
rest of the building is Gothic.
The single nave, built in 1416
by Guillem Bofill, possesses
the widest Gothic span in the
Christian world. Behind the
altar is a marble throne known
as "Charlemagne's Chair". It is

Painted houses packed tightly along the bank of the Riu Onyar in Girona

named after the Frankish king whose troops took Girona in 785. In the chancel is a 14th-century jewel-encrusted silver and enamel altarpiece, the best example in Catalonia. Among the fine Romanesque paintings and statues in the cathedral's museum are a 10th-century illuminated copy of St Beatus of Liébana's *Commentary on the Apocalypse*, and a 14th-century statue of the Catalan king, Pere the Ceremonious.

The collection's 11th- to 12th-century tapestry, *The Creation*, is decorated with lively figures. The rich colours of this large work are well preserved.

Tapestry of *The Creation*

🏛 Museu d'Art
Pujada de la Catedral 12. **Tel** *972 20 38 34.* ◯ *10am–7pm (to 6pm Oct–Feb) Tue–Sat, 10am–2pm Sun.* ◉ *1 & 6 Jan, 25 & 26 Dec.* 🎨 ♿
This gallery holds works from the Romanesque period to the 20th century. The many items from churches ruined by war or neglect tell of the richness of church interiors long ago.

🏛 Museu del Cinema
Carrer Sèquia 1. **Tel** *972 41 27 77.* ◯ *Tue–Sun.* ◉ *1 & 6 Jan, 25 &26 Dec.* 🎨 ♿
Next to Església de Mercadel, this collection includes film and artifacts from the mid-19th century to the present day.

🏛 Museu d'Història de la Ciutat
Carrer de la Força 27. **Tel** *972 22 22 29.* ◯ *Tue–Sun.* ◉ *1 & 6 Jan, 25 & 26 Dec.* 🎨 ♿
The city's history museum is in an 18th-century former convent. Recesses where the decomposing bodies of members of the Capuchin Order were placed can still be seen. Exhibits include old *sardana (see p129)* instruments.

Figueres ⑭

Girona. 🏠 *44,000.* 🚉 🚌 ℹ *Plaça del Sol (972 50 31 55).* 🛒 *Thu.* 🎉 *Santa Creu (3 May), Sant Pere (29 Jun).* **www**.figueresciutat.com

Figueres is the market town of the Empordà plain. Beside the plane-tree-shaded Rambla is the former Hotel de Paris, now home to the **Museu del Joguet** (Toy Museum). At the bottom of the Rambla is a statue of Narcís Monturiol i Estarriol (1819–95) who, it is said, invented the submarine.

Figueres was the birthplace of Salvador Dalí, who in 1974 turned the town theatre into the **Teatre-Museu Dalí**. Under its glass dome are works by Dalí and other painters. The museum is a monument to Catalonia's most eccentric artist.

Environs
The **Casa-Museu Castell Gala Dalí**, 55 km (35 miles) south of Figueres, is the medieval castle Dalí bought in the 1970s. It contains some of his paintings. East of Figueres is the Romanesque monastery, **Sant Pere de Rodes** *(see p23)*.

***Rainy Taxi*, a monument in the garden of the Teatre-Museu Dalí**

🏛 Museu del Joguet
C/ Sant Pere 1. **Tel** *972 50 45 85.* ◯ *Jun–Sep: daily; Oct–May: Tue–Sun.* 🎨 ♿ **www**.mjc.cat

🏛 Teatre-Museu Dalí
Pl Gala-Salvador Dalí 5. **Tel** *972 67 75 00.* ◯ *Jul–Sep: daily; Oct–Jun: Tue–Sun.* ◉ *1 Jan, 25 Dec.* 🎨 ♿ *by appt.* **www**.salvador-dali.org

🏛 Casa-Museu Castell Gala Dalí
C/ Gala Dalí, Púbol (La Pera). **Tel** *972 48 86 55.* ◯ *mid-Mar–Dec: Tue–Sun (mid-Jun–mid-Sep: daily).* 🎨 ♿

THE ART OF DALÍ

Salvador Dalí i Domènech was born in Figueres in 1904 and mounted his first exhibition at the age of 15. After studying at the Escuela de Bellas Artes in Madrid, and dabbling with Cubism, Futurism and Metaphysical painting, the young artist embraced Surrealism in 1929, becoming the movement's best-known painter. Never far from controversy, the self-publicist Dalí became famous for his hallucinatory images – such as *Woman-Animal Symbiosis* – which he described as "hand-painted dream photographs". Dalí's career also included writing and film-making, and established him as one of the 20th century's greatest artists. He died in his home town in 1989.

Ceiling fresco in the Wind Palace Room, Teatre-Museu Dalí

Cadaqués ⓯

Girona. 🏘 *3,000.* ⊞ ℹ *Carrer Cotxe 2 (972 25 83 15).* 🚍 *Mon.* 🎏 *Fiesta major de Verano (first week of Sep), Santa Esperança (18 Dec).*

This pretty resort is overlooked by the Baroque **Església de Santa Maria**. In the 1960s it was dubbed the "St Tropez of Spain", due to the young crowd that sought out Salvador Dalí in nearby Port Lligat. For six months of the year, from 1930 until his death in 1989, Dalí lived here.

Today the much modified house, which expanded far beyond the original fisherman's cabin, is known as the **Casa-Museu Salvador Dalí**. Managed by the Gala-Salvador Dalí Foundation, the museum provides a unique interpretation of the artist's life.

🏛 **Casa-Museu Salvador Dalí**
Port Lligat. **Tel** *972 25 10 15.*
⬤ *booking required.*
⬤ *1 Jan, 7 Jan–8 Feb, 25 Dec.*
📷 www.salvador-dali.org

Empúries ⓰

Girona. ⊞ *L'Escala.* **Tel** *972 77 02 08.*
◯ *Easter, Jun–Sep: 10am–8pm daily; Oct–May: 10am–6pm daily.* 📷 *ruins.* 📷 *by appointment.* www.mac.cat

The extensive ruins of this Greco-Roman town *(see p41)* occupy an imposing site beside the sea. Three separate settlements were built between the 7th and 3rd centuries BC: the old town (Palaiapolis); the new town (Neapolis); and the Roman town.

An excavated Roman pillar in the ruins of Empúries

Looking south along the Costa Brava from Tossa de Mar

The **old town** was founded by the Greeks in 600 BC as a trading port. It was built on what was a small island, and is now the site of the tiny hamlet of Sant Martí de Empúries. In 550 BC this was replaced by a larger new town on the shore which the Greeks named Emporion, meaning "trading place". In 218 BC, the Romans landed at Empúries and built a city next to the new town.

A nearby museum exhibits some of the site's finds, but the best are in Barcelona's Museu Arqueològic *(see p88).*

Peratallada ⓱

Girona. 🏘 *400.* ℹ *C/Unió 3, Ajuntament de Forallac, Vulpellac (972 64 55 22).* 🎏 *Herbs Fra Peratallada (last weekend in Apr), Festa Major (6 & 7 Aug), Medieval Market (first weekend in Oct).* www.forallac.com

This tiny village is the most spectacular of the many that lie a short inland trip from the Costa Brava. Together with Pals and Palau Sator it forms part of the 'Golden Triangle' of medieval villages. Its mountain-top position gives some dramatic views of the area. A labyrinth of cobbled streets wind up to the well-conserved castle and lookout tower, whose written records date from the 11th century. Peratallada's counts and kings made doubly sure of fending off any attackers by constructing a sturdy wall enclosing the entire village, which even today limits the nucleus from further expansion.

Tossa de Mar ⓲

Girona. 🏘 *6,000.* ⊞ ℹ *Avinguda Pelegri 25 (972 34 01 08).* 🚍 *Thu.* 🎏 *Festa Major d'Estin (22 Jan), Festa Major d'Hivern (29 Jun).* www.infotossa.com

At the end of a tortuous corniche, the Roman town of Turissa is one of the prettiest along the Costa Brava. Above the modern town is the **Vila Vella** (old town), a protected national monument. The medieval walls enclose fishermen's cottages, a 14th-century church and countless bars.

The **Museu Municipal** in the old town exhibits local archaeology and modern art.

🏛 **Museu Municipal**
Plaça Roig y Soler 1. **Tel** *972 34 07 09.* ◯ *Tue–Sun.* 📷

Blanes ⓳

Girona. 🏘 *40,000.* ⊞ ⊞ ℹ *Plaça Catalunya (972 33 00 45).* 🚍 *Mon.* 🎏 *Santa Ana (26 Jul); Festa Major Petita (21 Aug).* www.visitblanes.net

The working port of Blanes has one of the longest beaches on the Costa Brava. The highlight of the town is the **Jardí Botànic Mar i Murtra**. These gardens, designed by Karl Faust in 1928, are spectacularly sited above cliffs. Their 7,000 species of Mediterranean and tropical plants include African cacti.

🌺 **Jardí Botànic Mar i Murtra**
Pg Karl Faust 10. **Tel** *972 33 08 26.* ◯ *daily.* ⬤ *1 & 6 Jan, 25 & 26 Dec.* 📷 📷 ♿

The Costa Brava

The Costa Brava ("wild coast") runs for some 200 km (125 miles) from Blanes northwards to the region of Empordà, which borders France. It is a mix of rugged cliffs, pine-backed sandy coves, golden beaches and crowded, modern resorts. The busiest resorts – Lloret de Mar, Tossa de Mar and Platja d'Aro – are to the south. Sant Feliu de Guíxols and Palamós are still working towns behind the summer rush. Just inland there are medieval villages to explore, such as Peralada, Peratallada and Pals. Wine, olives and fishing were the mainstays of the area before the tourists came in the 1960s.

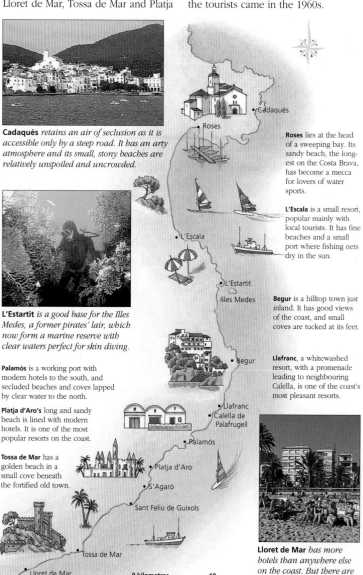

Cadaqués *retains an air of seclusion as it is accessible only by a steep road. It has an arty atmosphere and its small, stony beaches are relatively unspoiled and uncrowded.*

L'Estartit *is a good base for the Illes Medes, a former pirates' lair, which now form a marine reserve with clear waters perfect for skin diving.*

Palamós is a working port with modern hotels to the south, and secluded beaches and coves lapped by clear water to the north.

Platja d'Aro's long and sandy beach is lined with modern hotels. It is one of the most popular resorts on the coast.

Tossa de Mar has a golden beach in a small cove beneath the fortified old town.

Roses lies at the head of a sweeping bay. Its sandy beach, the longest on the Costa Brava, has become a mecca for lovers of water sports.

L'Escala is a small resort, popular mainly with local tourists. It has fine beaches and a small port where fishing nets dry in the sun.

Begur is a hilltop town just inland. It has good views of the coast, and small coves are tucked at its feet.

Llafranc, a whitewashed resort, with a promenade leading to neighbouring Calella, is one of the coast's most pleasant resorts.

Cadaqués
Roses
L'Escala
L'Estartit
Illes Medes
Begur
Llafranc
Calella de Palafrugell
Palamós
Platja d'Aro
S'Agaró
Sant Feliu de Guixols
Tossa de Mar
Lloret de Mar
Blanes

0 kilometres 10
0 miles 5

Lloret de Mar *has more hotels than anywhere else on the coast. But there are unspoiled beaches nearby, such as Santa Cristina.*

Monestir de Montserrat ⑳

The "serrated mountain" (*mont serrat*), its highest peak rising to 1,236 m (4,055 ft), is a superb setting for Catalonia's holiest place, the Monastery of Montserrat, which is surrounded by chapels and hermits' caves. A chapel was first mentioned in the 9th century, the monastery was founded in the 11th century, and in 1409 it became independent of Rome. In 1811, when the French attacked Catalonia in the War of Independence (*see p45*), the monastery was destroyed. Rebuilt and repopulated in 1844, it was a beacon of Catalan culture during the Franco years. Today Benedictine monks live here. Visitors can hear the Escolania singing the *Salve Regina i Virolai* (the Montserrat hymn) at various times throughout the day except on Saturdays, in July and August and during the Christmas period (*call ahead for details*).

A Benedictine monk

Plaça de Santa Maria
The focal points of the square are two wings of the Gothic cloister built in 1477. The modern monastery façade is by Francesc Folguera.

Gothic cloister

Funicular to the holy site of Santa Cova

The Museum has a collection of 19th- and 20th-century Catalan paintings and many Italian and French works. It also displays liturgical items from the Holy Land.

The Way of the Cross
This path passes 14 statues representing the Stations of the Cross. It begins near the Plaça de l'Abat Oliba.

STAR FEATURES

★ Basilica Façade

★ Black Virgin

View of Montserrat
The complex includes cafés and a hotel. A second funicular transports visitors to nature trails above the monastery.

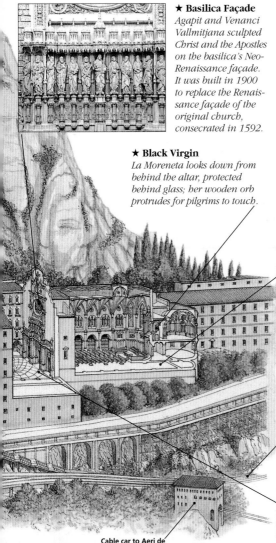

★ Basilica Façade
Agapit and Venanci Vallmitjana sculpted Christ and the Apostles on the basilica's Neo-Renaissance façade. It was built in 1900 to replace the Renaissance façade of the original church, consecrated in 1592.

★ Black Virgin
La Moreneta looks down from behind the altar, protected behind glass; her wooden orb protrudes for pilgrims to touch.

Cable car to Aeri de Montserrat station

VISITORS' CHECKLIST

Montserrat (Barcelona province). **Tel** 93 877 77 77. 🚡 Aeri de Montserrat, then cable car; Monistrol-Enllaç, then rack railway. 🚂 from Barcelona. **Basilica** ⏰ 7am–7:30pm Mon–Fri, 7am–8:30pm Sat–Sun (August: 7am–8:30pm daily). 🔔 11am & noon Mon–Fri; 11am, noon, & 7:30pm Sat; 9:30am, 11am, noon, 1pm & 7:30pm Sun. 🖼 **Museum** ⏰ 10am–5:45pm daily. 📷 ♿ 🌐 www.abadiamontserrat.cat

Basilica Interior
The sanctuary in the domed basilica is adorned by a richly enamelled altar and paintings by Catalan artists.

The rack railway from Monistrol de Montserrat follows the course of a rail line built in 1880.

THE VIRGIN OF MONTSERRAT

The small wooden statue of La Moreneta (the dark maiden) is the soul of Montserrat. It is said to have been made by St Luke and brought here by St Peter in AD 50. Centuries later, the statue is believed to have been hidden from the Moors in the nearby Santa Cova (Holy Cave). Carbon dating suggests, however, that the statue was carved around the 12th century. In 1881 Montserrat's Black Virgin became patroness of Catalonia.

The blackened Virgin of Montserrat

Inner Courtyard
On one side of the courtyard is the baptistry (1902), with sculptures by Carles Collet. A door on the right leads towards the Black Virgin.

Vic ㉑

Barcelona. 🚶 *40,000.* 🚇 🚌 🚍 C/
Ciutat 4 (93 886 20 91). 🚌 *Tue & Sat.*
🎭 *Mercat del Ram (Sat before Easter),*
Sant Miquel (5–15 Jul), Música Viva (3
days mid-Sep), Mercat medieval (6–10
Dec). **http://**victurisme.ajvic.net

Market days are the best time
to go to this small country
town. This is when the excellent local sausages *(embotits),*
for which the area is renowned, are piled high in the large
Gothic Plaça Major, along
with other produce from the
surrounding plains.

In the 3rd century BC Vic
was the capital of an ancient
Iberian tribe, the Ausetans. The
town was then colonized by
the Romans – the remains of
a Roman temple survive today.
Since the 6th century the town
has been a bishop's see. In the
11th century, Abbot Oliva commissioned El Cloquer tower,
around which the cathedral
was built in the 18th century.
The interior is covered with
vast murals by Josep-Maria
Sert (1876–1945, *see p29*).
Painted in reds and golds,
they represent Biblical scenes.

Adjacent to the cathedral is
the **Museu Episcopal de Vic**
(see p23), which has one of
the best Romanesque collections in Catalonia. The large
display of mainly religious art
and relics includes bright,
simple murals and wooden
carvings from rural churches.
Also on display are 11th- and
12th-century frescoes and
some superb altar frontals.

Cardona dominating the surrounding area from its hilltop site

🏛 **Museu Episcopal**
Plaça Bisbe Oliba, 3. **Tel** 93 886 93
60. ⏰ *Tue–Sun.* 🔴 *1, 6 Jan, 25,*
26 Dec. 🎟 ♿ 📷

Cardona ㉒

Barcelona. 🚶 *5,000.* 🚇 🚍
Avinguda Rastrillo (93 869 27 98).
🚌 *Sun.* 🎭 *Carnival (Feb), Festa*
major (second weekend of Sep).
www.cardona.cat

This 13th-century, ruddy-
stoned castle of the Dukes of
Cardona, constables to the
crown of Aragón, is set on the
top of a hill. The castle was
rebuilt in the 18th century and
is now a luxurious parador
(see p132). Beside the castle
is an early 11th-century church,
the **Església de Sant Vicenç**.

The castle gives views of the
town and of the Muntanya
de Sal (Salt Mountain), a huge
salt deposit beside the Riu
Cardener that has been mined
since Roman times.

12th-century altar frontal, Museu Episcopal de Vic

Solsona ㉓

Lleida. 🚶 *9,000.* 🚇 🚍 Carretera de
Bassella 1 (973 48 23 10). 🚌 *Tue &*
Fri. 🎭 *Carnival (Feb), Sant Isidro*
(closest weekend to 15 May), Corpus
Christi (May/Jun), Festa major (8–11
Sep). **www.**elsolsonesinvita.com

Nine towers and three gate-
ways remain of Solsona's
fortifications. Inside is an ancient town of noble mansions.
The cathedral houses a beautiful black stone Virgin. The
Museu Diocesà i Comarcal
contains Romanesque paintings and the **Museu del Ganivet**
has a fine knife collection.

🏛 **Museu Diocesà i Comarcal**
Plaça del Palau 1. **Tel** 973 48 21 01.
⏰ *Tue–Sun.* ♿ 🔴 *1 Jan, 25, 26 Dec.*

🏛 **Museu del Ganivet**
Trav. Sant Josep, 9. **Tel** 973 48 15
69. ⏰ *Tue–Sun.* 🔴 *6 Jan, 25, 26*
Dec. 🎟 ♿

Lleida ㉔

Lleida. 🚶 *136,000.* 🚇 🚍 🚍 C/ Major
31 (902 25 00 50). 🚌 *Thu & Sat.* 🎭
Sant Anastasi (11 May), Sant Miquel
(29 Sep). **http://**turisme.paeria.es

Dominating Lleida, the capital
of Catalonia's only inland province, is **La Suda**, a fort taken
from the Moors in 1149. The
cathedral, founded in 1203, lies
within the fort's walls, above
the town. It was transformed
into barracks by Felipe V in
1707. Today it is desolate, but
remains imposing, with magnificent Gothic windows.

A lift descends from La
Seu Vella to the Plaça de
Sant Joan in the busy,

pedestrianized shopping street that sweeps round the foot of the hill. The new cathedral is here, as is the reconstructed 13th-century town hall, the **Paeria**.

Poblet ㉕

See pp126–7.

Montblanc ㉖

Tarragona. 🏠 *7,000.* 🚌 🚉 ℹ️
Antigua Església de Sant Francesc (977 86 17 33). 🚌 *Tue & Fri.* 🎭
Festa major (8–11 Sep), Festa Medieval (two weeks in Apr).
www.montblancmedieval.org

The medieval grandeur of Montblanc lives on within its walls – possibly Catalonia's finest piece of military architecture. At the **Sant Jordi** gate St George allegedly slew the dragon. The **Museu Comarcal de la Conca de Barberà** has displays on local crafts.

🏛️ **Museu Comarcal de la Conca de Barberà**
Carrer de Josa 6. **Tel** *977 86 03 49.*
⭕ *Tue–Sun & public hols.* 🎫

Santes Creus ㉗

Tarragona. 🏠 *150.* 🚉 ℹ️ *Plaça de Sant Bernat 1 (977 63 81 41).* 🚌 *Sat & Sun.* 🎭 *Santa Llúcia (13 Dec).*

The tiny village of Santes Creus is home to the prettiest of the "Cistercian triangle"

monasteries. The other two, Vallbona de les Monges and Poblet, are nearby. The **Monestir de Santes Creus** was founded in 1150 by Ramon Berenguer IV *(see p42)* during his reconquest of Catalonia. The Gothic cloisters are decorated with figurative sculptures, a style first permitted by Jaume II, who ruled from 1291 to 1327. His tomb is in the 12th-century church, which features a rose window.

🏛️ **Monestir de Santes Creus**
Tel *977 63 83 29.* ⭕ *10am–3pm Tue–Sun & public hols.* 🚫 *1 Jan, 25 Dec.* 🎫 ♿ *by appointment.*

Vilafranca del Penedès ㉘

Barcelona. 🏠 *38,000.* 🚉 🚌
ℹ️ *Carrer Cort 14 (93 818 12 54).*
🚌 *Sat.* 🎭 *Fira de Mayo (2nd week of May), Festa major (end Aug).*
www.turismevilafranca.com

This market town is set in the heart of Penedès, the main wine-producing region of Catalonia. The **Vinseum** (Wine Museum) documents the history of the area's wine trade. Local *bodegues* can be visited for wine tasting.

Sant Sadurní d'Anoia, the capital of Spain's sparkling wine, *cava (see pp32–3),* is 8 km (5 miles) to the north.

🏛️ **Vinseum**
Plaça de Jaume I. **Tel** *93 890 05 82.*
⭕ *10am–2pm, 4–7pm Tue–Sat.*

Anxaneta climbing to the top of a tower of *castellers*

HUMAN TOWERS

The province of Tarragona is famous for its *casteller* festivals, in which teams of men stand on each other's shoulders in an effort to build the highest human tower *(castell)*. Configurations depend on the number of men who form the base. Teams wear similar colours, and often have names denoting their home town. The small child who has to undertake the perilous climb to the top, where he or she makes the sign of the cross, is called the *anxaneta. Castellers* assemble in competition for Tarragona province's major festivals throughout the year. In the wine town of Vilafranca del Penedès they turn out for Sant Fèlix (30 August), and in Tarragona city for Santa Tecla, its *festa major* on 23 September. Rival teams in Valls appear on St John's Day (24 June), but strive for their best achievement at the end of the tower-building season on St Ursula's Day (21 October), when teams from all over Catalonia converge on the town square.

Monestir de Santes Creus, surrounded by poplar and hazel trees

Monestir de Poblet ㉕

The monastery of Santa Maria de Poblet is a haven of tranquillity and a resting place of kings. It was the first and most important of three monasteries, known as the "Cistercian triangle" *(see p125)*, that helped to consolidate power in Catalonia after it had been re-captured from the Moors by Ramon Berenguer IV. In 1835, due to the Ecclesiastical Confiscation law, and during the Carlist upheavals, it was plundered and damaged by fire. Restoration of the impressive ruins began in 1930 and monks returned in 1940.

The dormitory is reached by stairs from the church. The vast 87-m (285-ft) gallery dates from the 13th century. Half of it is still in use by the monks.

The 12th-century refectory is a vaulted hall with an octagonal fountain and a pulpit.

View of Poblet
The abbey, its buildings enclosed by fortified walls that have hardly changed since the Middle Ages, is in an isolated valley near the Riu Francolí's source.

Museum

Wine cellar

Library
The Gothic scriptorium was converted into a library in the 17th century, when the Cardona family donated its book collection.

Former kitchen

Royal doorway

Museum

TIMELINE							
1150 Santes Creus founded – third abbey in Cistercian triangle		*Royal tombs*			**1812** Poblet desecrated by French troops	**1940** Monks return	
	1156 Founding of Cistercian monastery at Vallbona de les Monges	**14th century** Main cloister finished	**1479** Juan II, last king of Aragón, buried here				
1100	**1300**		**1500**	**1700**		**1900**	
	1196 Alfonso II is the first king to be buried here	**1336–87** Reign of Pere the Ceremonious, who designates Poblet a royal pantheon				**1952** Tombs reconstructed. Royal remains returned	
	1150 Poblet monastery founded by Ramon Berenguer IV		**1835** Disentailment *(p45)* of monasteries. Poblet ravaged				

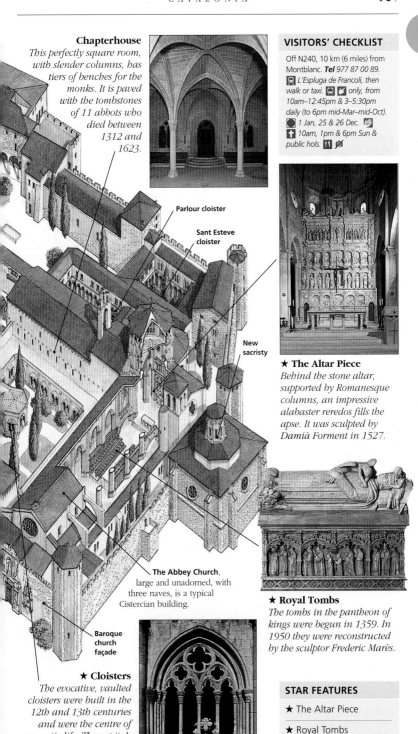

Chapterhouse
This perfectly square room, with slender columns, has tiers of benches for the monks. It is paved with the tombstones of 11 abbots who died between 1312 and 1623.

Parlour cloister

Sant Esteve cloister

New sacristy

The Abbey Church, large and unadorned, with three naves, is a typical Cistercian building.

Baroque church façade

★ Cloisters
The evocative, vaulted cloisters were built in the 12th and 13th centuries and were the centre of monastic life. The capitals are beautifully decorated with carved scrollwork.

VISITORS' CHECKLIST

Off N240, 10 km (6 miles) from Montblanc. **Tel** *977 87 00 89.*
🚉 *L'Espluga de Francolí, then walk or taxi.* ⬛ 🔲 *only, from 10am–12:45pm & 3–5:30pm daily (to 6pm mid-Mar–mid-Oct).* ⚫ *1 Jan, 25 & 26 Dec.* 📷 ✝ *10am, 1pm & 6pm Sun & public hols.* 🍴 📷

★ The Altar Piece
Behind the stone altar, supported by Romanesque columns, an impressive alabaster reredos fills the apse. It was sculpted by Damià Forment in 1527.

★ Royal Tombs
The tombs in the pantheon of kings were begun in 1359. In 1950 they were reconstructed by the sculptor Frederic Marès.

STAR FEATURES

★ The Altar Piece
★ Royal Tombs
★ Cloisters

Palm trees lining the waterfront at Sitges

Sitges ㉙

Barcelona. 🏠 28,000. 🚌 🚆
ℹ️ C/ Sinia Morera 1 (93 810 93 40).
🛥️ Thu (in summer). 🎉 Festa major
(22–27 Aug), Carnival (Feb/Mar).
www.sitgestour.com

Sitges has no less than nine
beaches. It has a reputation as
a gay resort but is just as
popular with Barceloneses.
Lively bars and restaurants
line its main boulevard, the
Passeig Marítim, and there are
many examples of
modernista architecture
scattered amongst the 1970s
apartment blocks. Modernista
artist Santiago Rusiñol *(see p29)*
spent much time here and bequeathed his quirky collection
of ceramics, sculptures, painting and ornate iron-work to
the **Museu Cau Ferrat**. It lies
next to Sitges's landmark, the
17th-century church of **Sant
Bartomeu i Santa Tecla**.

🏛️ **Museu Cau Ferrat**
Carrer Fonollar. **Tel** 93 894 03 64.
⭕ Tue–Sun. 🌑 public hols. 🈹🈺

Costa Daurada ㉚

Tarragona. 🚆 🚌 Calafell, Sant Vicenç
de Calders, Salou. ℹ️ Tarragona (977
23 34 15). **www**.costadaurada.org

The long sandy beaches of
the Costa Daurada (Golden
Coast) run along the shores of
Tarragona provine. **El Vendrell**
is one of the area's active ports.
The **Museu Pau Casals** in Sant
Salvador (El Vendrell) is dedi-
cated to the famous cellist.

Port Aventura, south of
Tarragona, is one of Europe's
largest theme parks and has
many exotically-themed
attractions, such as Polynesia
and Wild West. **Cambrils** and
Salou to the south are the liveliest resorts – the others are
low-key, family holiday spots.

🏛️ **Museu Pau Casals**
Avinguda Palfuriana 67.
Tel 977 68 42 76. ⭕ Tue–Sun.

🎢 **Port Aventura**
Autovia Salou–Vila-seca. **Tel** 902 20
22 20. ⭕ mid-Mar–6 Jan. 🈹🈺

Tarragona ㉛

Tarragona. 🏠 140,000. ✈️ 🚆 🚌
ℹ️ Carrer Major 39 (977 25 07 95).
🛥️ Tue, Thu & Sun. 🎉 Sant Magí
(19 Aug), Santa Tecla (23 Sep).
www.tarragonaturisme.cat

Tarragona is now a major
industrial port, but it has
preserved many remnants of
its Roman past. As the capital
of Tarraconensis, the Romans
used it as a base for the conquest of the peninsula in the
3rd century BC *(see p41)*.

The avenue of Rambla
Nova ends abruptly on the
clifftop Balcó de Europa, in
sight of the ruins of the
Amfiteatre Romà and the
ruined 12th-century church of
Santa Maria del Miracle.

Nearby is the Praetorium,
a Roman tower that was
converted into a palace in
medieval times. It now houses
the **Pretori i Circ Romans**. This
displays Roman and medieval
finds, and gives access to the
cavernous passageways of the
excavated Roman circus, built
in the 1st century AD. Next to
the Praetorium is the **Museu
Nacional Arqueològic**,
containing the most important
collection of Roman artifacts in
Catalonia. It has an extensive
collection of bronze tools and
beautiful mosaics, including a

The remains of the Roman amphitheatre, Tarragona

Head of Medusa. Among the most impressive remains are the huge Pre-Roman stones on which the Roman wall is built. An archaeological walk stretches 1-km (half a mile) along the wall.

Behind the wall lies the 12th-century **cathedral**, built on the site of a Roman temple. This evolved over many centuries, as seen from the blend of styles of the exterior. Inside is an alabaster altarpiece of St Tecla, carved by Pere Joan in 1434. The 13th-century cloister has Gothic vaulting, but the doorway is Romanesque *(see pp22–3)*.

In the west of town is a 3rd- to 6th-century Christian cemetery (ask about opening times in the archaeological museum). Some of the sarcophagi were originally used as pagan tombs.

Ruins of the Palaeo-Christian Necropolis

Environs
The **Aqüeducte de les Ferreres** lies just outside the city, next to the A7 motorway. This 2nd-century aqueduct was built to bring water to the city from the Riu Gaià, 30 km (19 miles) to the north. The **Arc de Berà**, a 1st-century triumphal arch on the Via Augusta, is 20 km (12 miles) northeast on the N340.

The bustling, provincial town of **Reus** lies inland from Tarragona. Although its airport serves the Costa Daurada, it is often overlooked by holiday-makers. However there is some fine *modernista* architecture to be seen here, notably some early work by Antoni Gaudí who was born in Reus. The Pere Mata Psychiatric Institute was designed by Domènech i Montaner before his master-piece, the Hospital de la Santa Creu i de Sant Pau *(see p79)*.

🏛 **Museu Nacional Arqueològic de Tarragona**
Plaça del Rei 5. **Tel** 977 23 62 09.
⏰ Tue–Sun. ▨ &
www.mnat.es

🏛 **Pretori i Circ Romans**
Plaça del Rei. **Tel** 977 23 01 71.
⏰ Tue–Sun. ▨

Tortosa 🌐

Tarragona. 🏘 35,000. 🚌 *Plaça Carrilet, 1 (977 44 96 48).* ⛵ *Mon.* 🎉 *Nostra Senyora de la Cinta (1st week Sep).* **www**.turismetortosa.com

A ruined castle and medieval walls are clues to Tortosa's historical importance. Sited at the lowest crossing point on the Riu Ebre, it has been strategically significant since Iberian times. The Moors held the city from the 8th century until 1148. The old Moorish castle, known as La Suda, is all that remains of their defences. It has now been renovated as a parador *(see p141)*. The Moors also built a mosque in Tortosa in 914. Its foundations were used for the present cathedral, on which work began in 1347. Although it was not completed for two centuries, the style is pure Gothic.

Tortosa was badly damaged in 1938–39 during one of the fiercest battles of the Civil War *(see p47)*, when the Ebre formed the front line between the opposing forces.

Delta de L'Ebre 🌐

Tarragona. 🚌 *Aldea.* 🚏 *Deltebre, Aldea.* 🛈 *Deltebre (977 48 96 79).* **www**.deltebre.net

The delta of the Riu Ebre is a prosperous rice-growing region and wildlife haven. Some 70 sq km (27 sq miles) have been turned into a nature reserve, the **Parc Natural del Delta de L'Ebre**. In Deltebre there is an information centre and an interesting **Eco-Museu**, with an aquarium containing species found in the delta.

The main towns in the area are **Amposta** and **Sant Carles de la Ràpita**, both of which serve as good bases for exploring the reserve.

The best places to see the variety of wildlife are along the shore, from the Punta del Fangar in the north to the Punta de la Banya in the south. Everywhere is accessible by car except the Illa de Buda. Flamingoes breed on this island and, together with other water birds such as herons and avocets, can be seen from tourist boats that leave from Riumar and Deltebre.

🏛 **Eco-Museu**
Carrer Martí Buera 22. **Tel** 977 48 96 79. ⏰ *daily.* ▨ & ✓

THE SARDANA
Catalonia's national dance is more complicated than it appears. The dancers must form a circle and accurately count the complicated short- and long-step skips and jumps. Music is provided by a *cobla*, an 11-person band consisting of a leader playing a three-holed flute *(flabiol)* and a little drum *(tamborí)*, five woodwind players and five brass players. The *sardana* is performed during most *festes* and at special day-long gatherings called *aplecs*. In Barcelona it is danced on Saturday evenings at 6 in front of the cathedral and usually every Sunday evening at 6 in the Plaça de Sant Jaume.

A group of *sardana* dancers captured in stone

TRAVELLERS' NEEDS

WHERE TO STAY

Sign for a luxury
five-star hotel

Catalonia has an unrivalled variety of accommodation. The Barcelona and Catalonia tourist authorities have complete listings of hotels, country houses and camp sites as well as information on a range of other options. In Barcelona you can stay in the modern luxury of one of Spain's highest skyscrapers, while on the coast you can try a self-catering holiday village (efficiencies) with all sorts of sports and entertainments provided. Family-run *cases de pagès,* which are stone-built farm or village houses or country manors, are Catalonia's most distinctive alternative. Some of the best hotels in every price range are listed on pages 134–41.

Façade of the Hotel Lloret in Barcelona's Rambla de Canaletes

HOTEL GRADING AND FACILITIES

The different types of hotel in Catalonia are denoted by the blue plaques near their doors. These show a star-rating which reflects the number and range of facilities available rather than quality of service. *Hotels* (H) and *hotel-residències* (HR) are graded from one to five stars; *motels* (M), *hostals* (H) and *hostal-residències* HR) from one to three stars; and *pensions* (P), with the simplest accommodation, have one or two stars. Hotels, *hostals, pensions* and motels may not have restaurants. *Hotel-residències* and *hostal-residències* do not have full dining rooms, but some serve breakfast.

PRICES AND PAYING

Spanish law requires all hotels to display their prices at reception and in every room. As a rule, the higher the star-rating, the greater the price. Rates are almost invariably quoted per room (but meal prices per person). A double room in a one-star *hostal* can be as little as €30 a night; one in a five-star hotel will cost more than €150 a night. Prices vary according to region, season, day of the week or special feature such as a view or balcony. The prices given on pages 134–41 are based on mid-season or high (tourist)-season rates. Prices for rooms and meals are usually quoted without including VAT *(IVA),* currently eight per cent.

BOOKING AND CHECK-IN

Hotels in Barcelona can be very busy during the many trade fairs held all year round, so booking in advance is advisable. Off-season in rural Catalonia there is rarely any need to book ahead, but if you want a room in a busy season or in a particular hotel it is a good idea to do so. Resort hotels on the Costa Brava often close from autumn to spring. On the warmer Costa Daurada, hotels may have a shorter winter closing period. You will not normally be asked for a deposit when you book a room. However, a deposit of 20–25 per cent may be levied for bookings during peak periods or for a stay of more than a few nights. You may lose all or some of it if you cancel at less than a week's notice. Most hotels will honour a booking only until 8pm. If you are delayed, telephone to tell them when to expect you.

When checking in you will be asked for your passport or identity card to comply with police regulations. It will normally be returned as soon as your details have been copied.

PARADORS

There are seven paradors in Catalonia – at Aiguablava, Artíes, Cardona, Seu de Urgell, Vic, Vielha and Tortosa. They form part of Spain's chain of high-quality, government-run hotels in historic buildings, or in purpose-built, new buildings in spectacular settings. Reservations for paradors can be made through the **Central de Reservas** (Madrid), **Keytel International** (London) and **Marketing Ahead** (New York).

The spacious and comfortable interior of the parador at Vic

◁ Christmas market in front of the cathedral, Barcelona

Solid, stone-built architecture typical of traditional Catalan farmhouses

RURAL ACCOMMODATION

Cases de Pagès (also called *cases rurales*) are Catalan farmhouses *(masies)* that accept visitors. Some do B&B, some an evening meal or full board and many are self-catering. Tourist offices have the *Guia residències-casa de pagès*, published by the Generalitat de Catalunya. You can book directly or through websites such as www.toprural.com.

The **Associació Fondes de Catalunya** is a group of *cases fonda* (simple country hotels, offering wholesome regional cuisine). Keep in mind that the facility closes for two weeks during August.

The **Xarxa d'Albergs de Catalunya** runs youth hostels, which also cater for adults and families, and the **Federació d'Entitats Excursionistes de Catalunya** runs mountain refuges for hikers.

SELF-CATERING

Villas and apartments let by the week are plentiful on the Costa Daurada and Costa Brava. *Aparthotels (*or *hotels-apartament)* and *residències-apartament* are a type of self-catering accommodation. Ranked from one to four stars, each apartment has a kitchen, but each complex also has a restaurant and often a swimming pool and other facilities. Generalitat de Catalunya tourist offices *(see p174)* and most travel agents have details of all types of villas and apartments.

Holiday (vacation) villages *(ciutats de vacances),* such as Cala Montjoi and Club-Hotel Giverola on the Costa Brava, are similar, but accommodation is in bungalows and includes

Sign for a camp site

sports and entertainments. *Gites de Catalunya* are superior country houses rented out on a week-by-week basis by Turisverd or **Villas 4 You**. Many *cases de pagès* are also self-catering.

CAMP SITES

Catalonia has over 300 camp sites, classified as deluxe (L), 1-star, 2-star, 3-star, or farm (M, *càmpings-masia*). All have basic amenities, guards and a safe. *Catalunya Càmpings,* published by the Generalitat *(see p174),* is available from tourist offices. Many sites in Barcelona are grouped under the **Associació de Càmpings de Barcelona** (which closes for three weeks in August, so ring in advance). A camping carnet from your home camping association can be used instead of a passport at sites and also covers you for third-party insurance. Camping is permitted only at official sites.

DISABLED TRAVELLERS

Few hotels are well equipped for disabled guests, although some youth hostels are. The **Federació ECOM** and Viajes 2000 *(see p175)* will advise on hotels throughout Catalonia for visitors with special needs.

DIRECTORY

PARADORS

Central de Reservas
Calle Requena 3, 28013 Madrid. **Tel** 902 547 979.
Fax 902 525 432.
www.parador.es

Keytel International
402 Edgware Road, London W2 1ED.
Tel 027 953 3020 *in UK.*
www.keytel.co.uk

Marketing Ahead
381 Park Av. Sth., Suite 718, New York, NY 10016. **Tel** 800 223 1356 *(toll free).* **Fax** (212) 686 0271 *in NY.*
www.marketing ahead.com

RURAL ACCOMMODATION

Associació Fondes de Catalunya
Ramón Turró 63–65, 2 08005 Barcelona.
Tel 93 300 16 26.
Fax 93 300 16 58.
www.casafonda.com

Federació d'Entitats Excursionistes de Catalunya
La Rambla 41, Ppal., 08002 Barcelona.
Tel 93 412 07 77.
Fax 93 412 63 53.
www.feec.cat

Xarxa d'Albergs de Catalunya
Carrer Calàbria 147, 08015 Barcelona.
Tel 93 483 83 41.

Fax 93 483 83 62.
www.tujuca.com

SELF-CATERING

Villas 4 You
Spring Mill, Earby, Barnoldswick, Lancs BB94 0AA.
Tel 0845 268 0770.
www.villas4you.co.uk

CAMPING

Associació de Càmpings de Barcelona
Gran Via Corts Catalanes 608, 3ª, 08007 Barcelona.
Tel 93 412 59 55.
Fax 93 302 13 36.
www.campings barcelona.com

DISABLED TRAVELLERS

Federació ECOM
Gran Via de les Corts Catalanes 562, principal, 2a, 08011 Barcelona.
Tel 93 451 55 50.
Tel 93 451 69 04.
www.ecom.cat

SPANISH TOURIST OFFICES

UK
22–23 Manchester Sq., London W1U 3PX.
Tel 020 7486 8077.
www.spain.info

US
666 Fifth Ave, Floor 35, New York, NY 10103.
Tel (212) 265 8822.
www.spain.info

Choosing a Hotel

The hotels in the following pages have been selected across a wide price range for the excellence of their facilities, location or character. The chart below first lists hotels in Barcelona by area, followed by a selection in the rest of Catalonia. Hotels within the same price category are listed alphabetically.

PRICE CATEGORIES
For a standard double room per night, with tax, breakfast and service included.

€ under €75
€€ €75–€125
€€€ €125–€200
€€€€ €200–€275
€€€€€ over €275.

OLD TOWN

Downtown Paraiso　€
C/Junta de Comerç 13, 08001　**Tel** 93 302 61 34　**Fax** 93 302 61 34　**Rooms** 8　　**Map** 2 F3

Established by four former travellers, this friendly *hostal* is located in a renovated townhouse on a quiet street in the lively Raval area. A hit with young backpackers, there is no curfew, a range of rooms, with or without bathrooms, Wi-Fi access and a kitchen for guests' use. **www.downtownparaisohostel.com**

Pensió 2000　€
Carrer de Sant Pere més Alt 6, 1st floor, 08003　**Tel** 93 310 7466　**Fax** 93 319 42 52　**Rooms** 6　　**Map** 5 B1

This welcoming little *hostal* has a perfect location overlooking the flamboyant Modernista Palau de la Música. The cosy bedrooms, some with shared bathroooms, lead off a large, comfortable sitting room with a big TV. Triple and quadruple rooms are also available. **www.pensio2000.com**

Pension Mari-Luz　€
Carrer Palau 4, 08002　**Tel & Fax** 93 317 34 63　**Rooms** 14　　**Map** 5 A3

A welcoming, family-run pension on the upper floors of a grand 18th-century mansion. There are sparsely furnished but spotless doubles, singles and dorms, along with self-contained apartments to rent in the nearby Raval neighbourhood. Guests have use of a kitchen and access to Wi-Fi. **www.pensionmariluz.com**

Quartier Gothic　€
Carrer d'Avinyó 42, 08002　**Tel** 93 318 79 45　**Rooms** 28　　**Map** 5 A3

This very simple hotel has a central position, near Port Vell, La Rambla and the Picasso Museum. Best of all, it's on one of the Old Town's best shopping streets, with trendy fashion boutiques and hip bars and restaurants. The rooms are basic but clean. They are better value in the low season. **www.hostalquartiergothic.com**

Banys Orientals　€€
Carrer Argenteria 37, 08003　**Tel** 93 268 84 60　**Fax** 93 268 84 61　**Rooms** 56　　**Map** 5 B3

Situated on a lively and mostly traffic-free street in the chic Born neighbourhood, this is an affordable boutique hotel with a sleek, less-is-more approach to design and small but comfortable rooms. Slightly more spacious suites are available in two other buildings a short walk away. Free Wi-Fi. **www.hotelbanysorientals.com**

Gat Raval　€€
Carrer de Joaquin Costa 44, 08001　**Tel** 93 481 66 70　**Fax** 93 342 66 97　**Rooms** 24　　**Map** 2 F1

A hip, newish *hostal*, painted in an eye-catching lime green and brilliant white, this is an excellent budget choice in the heart of the trendy Raval district. Huge blown-up photographs of Barcelona give it a stylish edge. Rooms are plain, but crisp and modern, and there is Internet access for guests. **www.gatrooms.es**

Gat Xino　€€
C/Hospital 149-155, 08001　**Tel** 93 324 88 33　**Fax** 93 324 88 34　**Rooms** 34　　**Map** 2 E2

This is the second *hostal* from the Gat Accommodation group, and it repeats the formula that has worked so well: simple, modern design and great prices. It is worth splashing out on the suite, which has its own private terrace. All rooms have free Wi-Fi. Family rooms are also available. **www.gatrooms.es**

Hosteria Grau　€€
Carrer de Ramalleres 27, 08001　**Tel** 93 301 81 35　**Fax** 93 317 68 25　**Rooms** 27

Close to the Museum of Contemporary Art (MACBA) and the nightlife of El Raval, this is a delightful little *hostal*. Rooms are simply decorated with floral prints and come with or without en suite facilities. They also rent apartments, a good choice for families or for longer stays. **www.hostalgrau.com**

Market　€€
Passatge Sant Antoni Abad 10, 08015　**Tel** 93 325 12 05　**Fax** 93 424 29 65　**Rooms** 52　　**Map** 2 E1

Close to the Modernista market of Sant Antoni, this stylish hotel has oriental-themed rooms, with glossy, lacquered wood and a red, white and black colour theme. The hotel has a popular restaurant, where breakfast is served. Free Wi-Fi. Book well in advance. **www.markethotel.com.es**

Key to Symbols *see back cover flap*

Metropol

Carrer Ample 31, 08002 **Tel** *93 310 51 00* **Fax** *93 319 12 76* **Rooms** *71* €€

Map *5 A3*

This handsome 19th-century hotel has been thoroughly modernized but retains some old-fashioned charm. It is tucked away down a quiet street in the Barri Gòtic, and the streetside rooms, many with balconies, are bright and modern. Interior rooms can be a little gloomy. **www.hesperia-metropol.com**

Barceló Raval

Rambla del Raval 17–21, 08001 **Tel** *93 320 14 90* **Fax** *93 320 14 94* **Rooms** *188* €€€

Map *2 F3*

This striking hotel dominates the otherwise down-at-heel Rambla del Raval. The rooftop terrace with its stunning views is a huge draw, and the open-plan rooms are stylish, with retro fittings and soft neon glows. Gadget fans are catered for with Nespresso machines and iPod docks. Free Wi-Fi. **www.barcelo.com**

Barcelona Catedral

Carrer Capellans 4, 08002 **Tel** *93 304 22 55* **Fax** *93 304 23 66* **Rooms** *80* €€€

Map *5 A3*

In the very heart of the medieval quarter, the Barcelona Catedral is named for its proximity to the Gothic cathedral, but that's where the nod to the past ends. Rooms are sharply modern, with flat-screen TVs and mood lighting. The lobby café is a good meeting place and serves a decent breakfast. Free Wi-Fi. **www.barcelonacatedral.com**

Chic and Basic

Carrer de la Princesa 50, 08003 **Tel** *93 295 46 52* **Fax** *93 295 46 53* **Rooms** *31* €€€

Map *5 C2*

This converted 19th-century townhouse is popular with visiting fashionistas. The rooms are decorated completely in white, with contemporary glass and steel bathrooms, but they are given a touch of kitsch glamour with a colourful LED light system. The White Bar is very hip. Free Wi-Fi. **www.chicandbasic.com**

Jazz Hotel

Carrer Pelai 3, 08001 **Tel** *93 552 96 96* **Fax** *93 552 96 97* **Rooms** *108* €€€

Map *5 A1*

A glassy ultra-modern hotel near the Plaça de Catalunya, this offers better facilities than its three-star rating would suggest. There's a small rooftop pool with sun-deck, and the rooms (all soundproofed) are stylishly decorated with contemporary furniture and fabrics. Free Wi-Fi. **www.hoteljazzbarcelona.com**

Montecarlo

La Rambla 124, 08002 **Tel** *93 412 04 04* **Fax** *93 318 73 23* **Rooms** *55* €€€

Map *5 A2*

This beautiful hotel right on La Rambla in the centre of Barcelona occupies a former 19th-century palace. The lobby is a gorgeous whirl of gilt and marble, but rooms are smart and modern. Staff are particularly helpful here, and there are fantastic deals available on the website. Free Wi-Fi. **www.montecarlobcn.com**

Nouvel

Carrer de Santa Anna 18–20, 08002 **Tel** *93 301 82 74* **Fax** *93 301 83 70* **Rooms** *78* €€€

Map *5 A1*

In a pretty little shopping street off La Rambla, near the Plaça de Catalunya, this well-managed old-style hotel is tastefully decorated and furnished. The best rooms have curving Modernista-style balconies, and there's a charming lobby and lounge area with 1920s-style chandeliers. Free Wi-Fi. **www.hotelnouvel.com**

Park Hotel

Carrer de Marquès de l'Argentera 11, 08003 **Tel** *93 319 60 00* **Fax** *93 319 45 19* **Rooms** *91* €€€

Map *5 C3*

A rare gem of 1950s architecture, designed by Antonio Moragas in 1951 and well preserved during his son's award-winning renovations in 1990. The slim wraparound staircase is a highlight. Rooms are small but smartly furnished and the best have balconies. Free Wi-Fi. **www.parkhotelbarcelona.com**

Petit Palace Opera Garden

Carrer de la Boqueria 10, 08002 **Tel** *93 302 00 92* **Fax** *93 302 15 66* **Rooms** *61* €€€

Map *5 A2*

A handsomely converted townhouse just off La Rambla houses this smart, boutique hotel. Modern, colourful rooms have a musical theme (the city's Opera House is around the corner). The large and shady interior garden with its ancient trees and candle-lit corners is deeply romantic. Free Wi-Fi. **www.hthoteles.com**.

1898

La Rambla 109, 08002 **Tel** *93 552 95 52* **Fax** *93 552 95 50* **Rooms** *169* €€€€

Map *5 A2*

This chic hotel is located in a 19th-century tobacco factory at the top of Las Ramblas. The decor has retained some of the original fittings and combined them with 21st-century amenities, such as indoor and outdoor swimming pools, a state-of-the art spa, a fitness centre and a good restaurant and bar. Free Wi-Fi. **www.hotel1898.es**

Grand Hotel Central

Via Laietana 30, 08003 **Tel** *93 295 79 00* **Fax** *93 268 12 15* **Rooms** *147* €€€€

Map *5 B2*

A rooftop infinity pool, with a great view across the Born neighbourhood to the sea, is perhaps the Grand Central's finest feature. Rooms are large and airy, if dimly lit, with wide comfortable beds, and even the standard rooms come with CD, DVD and MP3 players. Special two-night packages are available. Free Wi-Fi. **www.grandhotelcentral.com**

Arts

Carrer de Marina 19–21, 08005 **Tel** *93 221 10 00* **Fax** *93 221 10 70* **Rooms** *483* €€€€€

Map *6 E4*

Set in a soaring tower overlooking the Port Olímpic, this is one of Europe's most luxurious and glamorous hotels. Huge rooms boast spectacular views along with every imaginable modern convenience, and there are stunning suites on the upper floors for those with very deep pockets. The best spa in town. Free Wi-Fi. **www.hotelartsbarcelona.com**

Hotel W   €€€€€

Moll de Levant, Passeig Joan de Borbó, 08039 **Tel** *93 221 08 30* **Fax** *91 360 72 14* **Rooms** *473*   **Map** *5 B4*

Designed by Ricardo Bofill to resemble a giant silvery sail, the enormous W Hotel dominates the port. Each sleek room boasts extraordinary views through floor-to-ceiling windows, and comes equipped with Munchie boxes and an iPod docking station. Several restaurants for fine dining, a spa and a stunning rooftop bar. Free Wi-Fi. **www.starwoodhotels.com**

Le Méridien   €€€€€

La Rambla 111, 08002 **Tel** *93 318 62 00* **Fax** *93 301 77 76* **Rooms** *233*   **Map** *5 A1*

A very elegant hotel on La Rambla, this is popular with visiting film stars and opera singers from the nearby Liceu opera house. Rooms are handsomely furnished and the hotel is well equipped for business travellers. For a treat, book the extravagant Presidential Suite. Free Wi-Fi. **www.lemeridienbarcelona.com**

Neri   €€€€€

Carrer de Sant Sever 5, 08002 **Tel** *93 304 06 55* **Fax** *93 304 03 37* **Rooms** *22*   **Map** *5 A2*

An enchanting hotel which combines the architectural features of the original 18th-century palace with sleek contemporary fittings. Airy, stylish rooms are draped in sensuous fabrics, and there's a magnificent rooftop terrace with views of the Gothic cathedral. Fabulous restaurant too serving Mediterranean cuisine. Free Wi-Fi. **www.hotelneri.com**

EIXAMPLE

Hostal Eden   €

Carrer Balmes 55, principal 1a, 08007 **Tel** *93 452 66 20* **Fax** *93 452 66 21* **Rooms** *30*   **Map** *3 A4*

An excellent-value pensión where guests can use a lounge with DVD player and a free internet connection along with a sunny terrace. The rooms themselves are plain but clean and adequate, making this a good deal for those who wish to be near some of Gaudí's best-known buildings without spending a fortune. **www.hostaleden.net**

Hostal San Remo   €

Carrer Ausias Marc 19, 08026 **Tel** *93 302 19 89* **Rooms** *7*   **Map** *5 C1*

Run by the owner, the San Remo is a very friendly option for those on a budget, but be warned that it can get noisy. The rooms are basic but comfortable enough; all have TVs and most have small, clean en suite bathrooms and balconies. Free Wi-Fi. **www.hostalsanremo.com**

Hostal Ciudad Condal   €€

Carrer de Mallorca 255, 08008 **Tel** *93 215 10 40* **Fax** *93 487 04 59* **Rooms** *15*   **Map** *3 A4*

A modest *hostal* located in a handsome Modernista building on one of the Eixample's most elegant streets. All rooms have free Wi-Fi, mini-bars and air conditioning. Rear rooms on the second floor are quieter than those closer to street level. No breakfasts, but there are dozens of cafés close by. **www.hostalciudadcondal.com**

Hostal Girona   €€

Carrer Girona 24, 08010 **Tel** *93 265 02 59* **Fax** *93 265 85 32* **Rooms** *26*   **Map** *5 C1*

After the terracotta walls, antique furnishings, oil paintings and velvet sofas of the entrance and hallway, the rooms here can seem something of a disappointment. In fact they are exactly as you would expect from a pensión – simple, modestly-sized and clean – and most are en suite. Free Wi-Fi. **www.hostalgirona.com**

Hotel Paseo de Gràcia   €€

Passeig de Gràcia 102, 08008 **Tel** *93 215 06 03* **Fax** *93 215 37 24* **Rooms** *33*   **Map** *3 B3*

There are few budget choices in the chi-chi Eixample district, but this modest little hotel is a good option. It has a fabulous location on the city's most desirable boulevard, close to the finest Gaudí buildings, and some of the simple rooms offer views of the Plaça de Catalunya. **www.hotelpaseodegracia.es**

Actual   €€€

Carrer Rosselló 238, 08008 **Tel** *93 552 05 50* **Fax** *93 552 05 55* **Rooms** *29*   **Map** *3 B3*

This modern, stylish hotel is fashionably decorated in sleek minimalist style. It has a superb location on the same block as Gaudí's La Pedrera, and the upmarket boutiques of the Passeig de Gràcia are on the doorstep. Like many hotels in this area, it is geared towards business travellers, which means good weekend deals. Free Wi-Fi. **www.hotelactual.com**

Axel   €€€

Carrer Aribau 33, 08011 **Tel** *93 323 93 93* **Fax** *93 323 93 94* **Rooms** *66*

This is Barcelona's best gay hotel, a stylish four-star establishment with a wealth of excellent facilities. The rooms are sleek and modern, there's a fabulous rooftop bar, and business facilities are available in the small library. There's also a dipping pool, and a good restaurant with drag shows. Free Wi-Fi. **www.axelhotels.com**

Catalunya Plaza   €€€

Plaça de Catalunya 7, 08002 **Tel** *93 317 71 71* **Fax** *93 317 78 55* **Rooms** *46*   **Map** *5 A1*

A reliable chain hotel in the city centre which is popular with business people. The 19th-century building has large sitting rooms decorated with some intricate frescoes. Rooms are attractively if generically decorated, but vary in size; request a larger room when booking. Free Wi-Fi. **www.hotelcatalunyaplaza.com**

Key to Price Guide *see p134* **Key to Symbols** *see back cover flap*

Granados 83

🔵🔲👤🎒📶📶👤📶 €€€

Carrer d'Enric Granados 83, 08008 **Tel** *93 492 96 70* **Fax** *93 492 96 90* **Rooms** *77*   **Map** *3 A3*

The rooms at this designer hotel are stylishly decorated with African zebrawood, chocolate brown leather and original pieces of Buddhist and Hindu art. Suites have private terraces overlooking a small plunge pool. There is an excellent restaurant and a small rooftop with a very fashionable bar. Free Wi-Fi. **www.derbyhotels.es**

Hotel Murmuri

🔵🔲📶 €€€

Rambla Catalunya 104, 08008 **Tel** *93 550 06 00* **Fax** *93 550 06 01* **Rooms** *53*   **Map** *3 A3*

One of the fanciest establishments on the Barcelona hotel scene, the Murmuri is part of a small luxury chain that includes the nearby Hotel Majestic. Rooms are suitably plush, and there is a fabulously trendy cocktail bar as well as an acclaimed Asian restaurant. Tapas are served on a quiet terrace. Free Wi-Fi. **www.murmuri.com**

Hotel Soho

🔵🔲👤📶📶 €€€

Gran Via de les Corts Catalanes 543, 08011 **Tel** *93 552 96 10* **Fax** *93 552 96 11* **Rooms** *51*   **Map** *2 E1*

The Hotel Soho is chic without being intimidating, and staff are helpful and friendly. The decked rooftop terrace with plunge pool and bar is a popular place to hang out, while the rooms are a good size, with glassed-in bathrooms. The hotel can get busy so book well in advance. Free Wi-Fi. **www.hotelsohobarcelona.com**

SixtyTwo

🔲👤📶📶 €€€

Passeig de Gràcia 62, 08007 **Tel** *93 272 41 80* **Fax** *93 272 41 81* **Rooms** *45*   **Map** *3 A4*

Zen meets Modernism in this tasteful, luxury hotel near Gaudí's most important buildings. Rooms are light-filled and stylish, with up-to-the-minute amenities including Bang and Olufsen TVs and music systems. In the chilled-out Zeroom, you can browse through art and design books. **www.sixtytwohotel.com**

Claris

🔵🔲📶👤📶📶📶 €€€€

Carrer Pau Claris 150, 08009 **Tel** *93 487 62 62* **Fax** *93 215 79 70* **Rooms** *124*   **Map** *3 B4*

Antique kilims and elegant English and French furniture ornament this hotel off the Passeig de Gràcia. It occupies the converted Vedruna Palace, and is scattered with fabulous artworks from around the world. There's a panoramic rooftop pool and sun-deck, and guests may use the hotel Smart cars. Free Wi-Fi. **www.derbyhotels.es**

Condes de Barcelona

🔲📶👤📶📶📶 €€€€

Passeig de Gràcia 73–75, 08008 **Tel** *93 445 00 00* **Fax** *93 445 32 32* **Rooms** *235*   **Map** *3 A4*

This hotel is located in two handsomely renovated Modernista palaces, with marble lobbies and creamy façades. The rooms in both locations are coolly contemporary and some have Jacuzzis. Choose a room with terrace to admire Gaudí's La Pedrera directly across the street. Free Wi-Fi. **www.condesdebarcelona.com**

Hispanos Siete Suiza

🔲📶👤📶📶📶 €€€€

Carrer Sicilia 255, 08025 **Tel** *93 208 20 51* **Fax** *93 208 20 52* **Rooms** *19*   **Map** *4 D3*

This *aparthotel* has a stunning location next to Gaudí's Sagrada Família cathedral. The 18 two-bedroom apartments and one suite are traditionally decorated. Proceeds from the *aparthotel* go to the Dr Melchor Colet foundation for cancer research. Colet's collection of vintage cars is on permanent show. Free Wi-Fi. **www.hispanos7suiza.com**

Majèstic

🔲📶👤📶📶👤📶📶 €€€€

Passeig de Gràcia 68, 08007 **Tel** *93 488 17 17* **Fax** *93 488 18 80* **Rooms** *303*   **Map** *3 A4*

A grand, traditional hotel in Neo-Classical style in a chic street (adjoining the Carrer de València). The stylish bedrooms are decorated with plush drapes and elegant prints, and are all equipped with five-star amenities. There is a beautiful spa and a small rooftop pool with spectacular views. Free Wi-Fi. **www.hotelmajestic.es**

Omm

🔲📶👤📶📶📶 €€€€€

Carrer Rosselló 265, 08008 **Tel** *93 445 40 00* **Fax** *93 445 40 04* **Rooms** *91*   **Map** *3 B3*

From the glistening ultra-modern façade with its peeled-back balconies, to the fluid, glassy public spaces, this hotel is the epitome of sleek Barcelona design. The fashionably minimalist rooms are very comfortable, and the slick bar and club make it popular with fashionistas. Free Wi-Fi. **www.hotelomm.es**

FURTHER AFIELD

GRÀCIA Casa Fuster

🔲📶👤📶👤📶📶 €€€€€

Passeig de Gracia 132, 08008 **Tel** *93 255 30 00* **Fax** *93 553 30 02* **Rooms** *96*

Lluís Domènech i Montaner, the architect responsible for the dazzling Palau de la Musica, designed the lavish Casa Fuster, a Modernista building dating back to 1908. After a long restoration project, the house has opened as one of the city's most prestigious and luxurious hotels. Do not miss the stunning rooftop views. Free Wi-Fi. **www.hotelcasafuster.com**

POBLENOU Hostal Poble Nou

📶 €€

Carrer Taulat 30, 08005 **Tel** *93 221 26 01* **Fax** *93 221 26 01* **Rooms** *10*

This charming, little *hostal* is located in a colourful 1930s townhouse in the traditional neighbourhood of Poblenou. It's close to the best city beaches and well connected by metro and tram to the city centre. The en suite rooms are simple, but there's a pretty breakfast terrace. Breakfast included in price. **www.hostalpoblenou.com**

SARRIA-SANT GERVASI Petit Hotel

Carrer Laforja 67, 08021 **Tel** *93 202 36 63* **Fax** *93 202 34 95* **Rooms** *4*

As the name suggests, the Petit Hotel is not huge and has just four bedrooms set around a comfortable seating area. Two are en-suite and two have separate private bathrooms, which are bigger. The area is not particularly central, but is upmarket and home to some of the city's finest restaurants. Free Wi-Fi. **www.petit-hotel.net**

SARRIA-SANT GERVASI Rekord

Carrer de Muntaner 352, 08021 **Tel** *93 200 19 53* **Fax** *93 414 50 84* **Rooms** *15*

A small, modern hotel oriented towards business travellers in the uptown shopping area. The large rooms are sleekly furnished with contemporary fabrics and fittings, and all come equipped with exercise bikes and office space. The facilites for business travellers are excellent. Free Wi-Fi. **www.hotelrekord.com**

CATALONIA

ARTIES Parador Don Gaspar de Portolà

Ctra Bequeira-Beret, 25599 (Lleida) **Tel** *973 64 08 01* **Fax** *973 64 10 01* **Rooms** *58*

A modern, warm, comfortable parador built in the local traditional stone and slate. It's in one of the prettiest villages of the Vall d'Aran, with attractive narrow streets dotted with medieval chapels. It's handy for local ski resorts, and makes a good base for mountain walkers. Free Wi-Fi. **www.parador.es**

AVINYONET DE PUIGVENTÓS Mas Pau

Carretera de Figueres a Olot, 17742 (Girona) **Tel** *972 54 61 54* **Rooms** *20*

A beautiful hotel in a 16th-century house, surrounded by gardens and wooded farmland. Many of the luxurious bedrooms and suites are located in the 25-metre-high tower, and have splendid views. There's a spectacular restaurant too. Free Wi-Fi. Closed Jan, Feb, early Mar. **www.maspau.com**

BANYOLES Mirallac

Passeig Darder 50, 17820 (Girona) **Tel** *972 57 10 45* **Fax** *972 57 10 39* **Rooms** *27*

A cheerful, old-style hotel overlooking the vast lake at Banyoles, they offer traditionally decorated rooms, a huge swimming pool and lots of lakeside activities. There's a good restaurant serving tasty local specialities. Mirallac is also an ideal place for adventure sports lovers. Free Wi-Fi. **www.hotelmirallac.com**

BEGUR Aigua Blava

Platja de Fornells, 17255 (Girona) **Tel** *972 62 45 62* **Fax** *972 62 21 12* **Rooms** *86*

This charming, whitewashed Mediterranean-style hotel overlooks Fornells Bay, one of the prettiest spots on the Costa Brava. Arches frame beautiful sea views, and it is surrounded by pine trees and gardens. The rooms are light and airy, and it also offers ten fully-equipped apartments. Minimum two-night stay. Closed Nov–mid-Mar. **www.aiguablava.com**

BEGUR El Convent

Carrer del Racó (Sa Riera) 2, 17255 **Tel** *972 62 30 91* **Fax** *972 62 31 04* **Rooms** *25*

A tranquil retreat amid a forest of pine and Mediterranean oak, this serene hotel is perfectly located mid-way between medieval Begur and the charming cove of Sa Riera. It occupies a handsomely restored 18th-century convent, which combines original details with elegant, contemporary design. Free Wi-Fi. Excellent restaurant. **www.hotelconventbegur.com**

BEQUEIRA-BERET Royal Tanau

Ctra de Beret, 25598 (Lleida) **Tel** *902 10 65 52* **Fax** *973 64 43 44* **Rooms** *30*

This luxurious boutique hotel in the Tanau skiing area has several amenities, including indoor and outdoor Jacuzzis and a spa. In winter, a private ski lift whisks guests directly to the pistes. There are full après-ski facilities and it offers elegant, fully-equipped suites as well as rooms. Free Wi-Fi. Open only Jan–mid-Apr. **www.solmelia.com**

BEUDA Can Felicià

Segueró, 17850 (Girona) **Tel** *972 59 05 23* **Fax** *972 59 05 23* **Rooms** *8*

Beautiful views make this charming, rural hotel in a former school a good place to stay. The rooms are painted in fresh, light colours and overlook a lovely garden, perfect for children and complete with a small swimming pool. The price includes delicious home-cooked dinners for hotel guests only. **www.canfelicia.com**

BEUDA Mas Salvanera

Mas Salvanera s/n, 17850 (Girona) **Tel** *972 59 09 75* **Fax** *972 59 08 63* **Rooms** *10*

This handsome 17th-century Catalan farmhouse has been attractively converted into a small, family-run rural hotel. It is beautifully set in gardens, and offers delicious home-cooked food to its guests. Lots of opportunities for hiking, fishing and horseback riding in the local area. **www.salvanera.com**

BOLVIR DE CERDANYA Torre del Remei

Camí Reial s/n, 17539 (Girona) **Tel** *972 14 01 82* **Fax** *972 14 04 49* **Rooms** *20*

One of the most luxurious hotels in the region, this opulent Modernista mansion is set in magnificent gardens with a stunning mountain backdrop. The classically decorated rooms are perfectly equipped with up-to-the-minute gadgetry, and the extensive facilities include a new spa and gym. Free Wi-Fi. **www.torredelremei.com**

Key to Price Guide *see p134* **Key to Symbols** *see back cover flap*

CADAQUÈS Misty

P 🏊 🖥 €

Carretera Nova Port Lligat, 17488 (Girona) **Tel** *972 25 89 62* **Fax** *972 15 90 90* **Rooms** *12*

Three houses and a swimming pool surrounded by shady gardens comprise this appealing hotel, one of the most unusual on the Costa Brava. It's a good spot for families, with a barbecue area, billiard room and a swimming pool. There's a snack bar in high season, but no restaurant. Closed Jan–Mar. **www.hotel-misty.com**

CARDONA Parador de Cardona

🖥 P 🛏 📺 🖥 €€€

Carrer de Castell s/n, 08261 (Barcelona) **Tel** *93 869 12 75* **Fax** *93 869 16 36* **Rooms** *54*

One of the most striking paradors in Spain, this luxuriously converted medieval castle dominates Cardona and offers spectacular views of the countryside. Many of the elegant rooms boast four-poster beds, and it has a fine Catalan restaurant. Free Wi-Fi. **www.parador.es**

CASTELLDELFELS Gran Hotel Rey Don Jaime

🖥 🖥 P 🛏 🏊 🖥 📺 🖥 €€

Avinguda del Hotel 22, 08860 (Barcelona) **Tel** *93 665 13 00* **Fax** *93 664 51 51* **Rooms** *220*

This huge Mediterranean-style hotel has arches and whitewashed walls. Choose between modern rooms or more traditional decor in the rustic zone. There are excellent sports facilities, with everything from squash courts to a swimming pool. The hilltop setting offers wonderful views of the coast. Free Wi-Fi. **www.hotelreydonjaime.es**

CÓLL Casa Peiró

€

Carrer La Plaça 7, 25527 (Lleida) **Tel** *973 29 70 02* **Rooms** *8*

A delightful, family-run little hostelry hidden away in a pretty mountain village. All the traditionally decorated rooms are en suite, and there's a sauna and facilities for massage. The rustically decorated restaurant offers tasty regional dishes including *butifarra negra i ceps* (local sausage with wild mushrooms). **www.hotelcasapeiro.com**

FIGUERES Hotel Durán

🖥 🖥 P 🛏 🖥 €€

Carrer de Lasauca 5, 17600 (Girona) **Tel** *972 50 12 50* **Fax** *972 50 26 09* **Rooms** *65*

This ochre-and-pink hotel is set above one of the finest restaurants in the region, established in 1855. It is still owned by the same family, who provide a friendly welcome. Rooms are attractively, if simply, furnished, and many have pretty wrought-iron balconies overlooking the street below. Free Wi-Fi. **www.hotelduran.com**

GIRONA Hotel Aatu

P 🛏 🏊 €€€

Afueras s/n, Peratallada (Girona), 17113 **Tel** *617 46 49 14* **Fax** *972 63 42 00* **Rooms** *13*

Set in exquisite gardens on the outskirts of the magical medieval village of Peratallada, this is a peaceful and very stylish rural hotel. There are two swimming pools in the grounds and various activities, including golf, cycling, horse-riding and even hot-air balloon rides, can be arranged via the hotel. The restaurant has an open fire. **www.hotelaatu.net**

GIRONA Hotel Llegendes de Girona Catedral

🖥 🖥 🛏 🖥 🖥 €€€

Portal de la Barça 4, 17004 (Girona) **Tel** *972 22 09 05* **Rooms** *15*

A charming hotel located in the historic centre of Girona, it is housed in an emblematic medieval stone building with an 18th-century staircase. The hotel has the latest modern facilities and is elegantly decorated. The hotel publishes a book of legends of Girona for its guests. Free Wi-Fi. **www.llegendeshotel.com**

GOMBRÈN Fonda Xesc

🖥 P 🛏 🖥 €

Plaça Roser 1, 17531 (Girona) **Tel** *972 73 04 04* **Rooms** *14*

Perfectly located in the heart of a traditional mountain village, this old-fashioned hotel offers modest, but immaculate rooms. The renowned restaurant serves fine Catalan specialities, including home-made *embutits*, which you can also pick up at their shop. Free Wi-Fi. **www.fondaxesc.com**

GRANOLLERS Fonda Europa

🖥 🖥 🛏 🖥 €€

Carrer Anselm Clavé 1, 08400 (Barcelona) **Tel** *93 870 03 12* **Fax** *93 870 79 01* **Rooms** *7*

This small hotel has been an inn for travellers since 1714, and is still owned by the same family. The bedrooms, on the second floor, have been completely modernized, and are simply decorated. The restaurant is the big draw here, with its hearty Catalan specialities prepared to traditional recipes. Free Wi-Fi. **www.casafondaeuropa.com**

LA GARRIGA Gran Hotel Balneario Blancafort

🖥 🖥 P 🛏 🏊 📺 🖥 €€€€

Carrer Mina, 7, 08530 (Barcelona) **Tel** *93 860 56 00* **Fax** *93 871 94 22* **Rooms** *312*

This handsome 19th-century hotel and thermal centre has been converted to include modern five-star luxuries, and is located in a relaxing spa town near Barcelona. The rooms are classically decorated with prints and drapes, and excellent facilities include a beauty spa and gardens. Free Wi-Fi. **www.spablancafort.com**

LA SEU D'URGELL Parador de La Seu d'Urgell

🖥 🖥 P 🛏 🏊 🖥 €€€

Carrer Sant Domènec 6, 25700 (Lleida) **Tel** *973 35 20 00* **Fax** *973 35 23 09* **Rooms** *80*

Only the Renaissance cloister, now used as the lounge, remains of a convent that occupied this site close to the 12th-century cathedral of La Seu. The modern parador has good facilities, including a covered pool, and there are excellent opportunities on the doorstep for hiking and skiing. Free Wi-Fi. **www.parador.es**

L'ESCALA El Roser

🖥 P 🛏 🖥 €

Carrer L'Església 7, 17130 (Girona) **Tel** *972 77 02 19* **Fax** *972 77 45 29* **Rooms** *22*

This family-run, old-fashioned seaside hotel is right on the beach in the heart of the historic centre of L'Escala. The restaurant is one of the best in the area. Rooms are immaculate and brightly furnished and each has a full bathroom, telephone and television. Free Wi-Fi. Closed Nov. **www.elroserhostal.com**

L'ESPLUGA DEL FRANCOLÍ Hostal del Senglar   €€

Plaça de Montserrat Canals 1, 43440 (Tarragona) **Tel** *977 87 04 11* **Fax** *977 87 01 27* **Rooms** *38*

A three-storey, whitewashed hotel with simply furnished, traditional rooms including family rooms. There's a delightful shady garden where barbecues are held in summer. A menu of delicious dishes traditional to the area is served in the restaurant. **www.hostaldelsenglar.com**

LLORET DE MAR Hotel Santa Marta   €€€€€

Platja Santa Cristina, 17310 (Girona) **Tel** *972 36 49 04* **Fax** *972 36 92 80* **Rooms** *76*

The modern Hotel Santa Marta overlooks a beautiful cove on the fringes of the frenetic resort of Lloret de Mar. Tranquil pine woods and gardens extend to the shore, and there are tennis courts and other sporting facilities. Free Wi-Fi. Closed mid-Nov–mid-Feb. **www.hstamarta.com**

MONTSENY Can Barrina   €€

Ctra Palautorder al Montseny, 08460 (Barcelona) **Tel** *938 47 30 65* **Fax** *938 47 31 84* **Rooms** *14*

A traditional country house lost in a verdant fold of the glorious Montseny hills, Can Barrina is famous for its excellent Catalan restaurant. Few people realise, however, that it also has a handful of antique-filled guestrooms, each with original beams and rustic decoration. The gardens boast sublime views and there is a small pool. **www.canbarrina.com**

MONTSENY Sant Bernat   €€

Finca El Clot, Ctra Sta Ma de Palautordera a Seva, km 20.8, 08460 (Barcelona) **Tel** *93 847 30 11* **Rooms** *23*

A gorgeous country house with beautiful views over the Serra de Montseny, the old stone walls are cloaked in greenery. The rooms and suites are stylishly decorated with traditional prints and rustic furniture. It's surrounded by extensive gardens with lawns and a pond, and all kinds of outdoor activities can be arranged. **www.hotelhusasantbernat.com**

PERAMOLA Can Boix de Peramola   €€€

Carrer Afores s/n, 25790 (Lleida) **Tel** *973 47 02 66* **Fax** *973 47 02 81* **Rooms** *41*

This good-value, traditional mountain hotel has been in the same family for ten generations. It has charming rooms and apartments with breathtaking views, and is very convenient for walking in the Pyrenean foothills. The service is outstanding. Closed Jan–mid-Feb. **www.canboix.cat**

REGENCÓS Hotel del Teatre   €€€€

Plaça Major s/n, 17214 (Girona) **Tel** *972 30 62 70* **Fax** *972 30 62 73* **Rooms** *7*

In the heart of a rambling, medieval village, this boutique-style hotel is located in a pair of handsomely restored 18th-century mansions. Sleek minimalism and charming original features are stylishly combined in the bedrooms. There's a lovely semi-shaded pool in the garden. Free Wi-Fi. **www.hoteldelteatre.com**

SA TUNA (BEGUR) Hotel Sa Tuna   €€€

Platja Sa Tuna, 17255 (Girona) **Tel** *972 62 21 98* **Fax** *972 62 41 82* **Rooms** *5*

A simple, whitewashed small hotel on one of the Costa Brava's prettiest coves. Improvements by the grandson of the original owner have added to its charms. Rooms with own terrace overlooking the bay. The restaurant is well known in the area. Free Wi-Fi. Open Apr–Sep only. **www.hostalsatuna.com**

SADURNI D'ANOIA Sol I Vi   €€

Ctra San Sadurni–Vilafranca km 4, Lavern, 08739 (Barcelona) **Tel** *938 99 32 04* **Fax** *938 99 34 35* **Rooms** *25*

A cheerful, traditional hotel set in a sea of vines, this is a good base for exploring the wine- and *cava*-producing region southwest of Barcelona. It offers comfortable, simple rooms and boasts a superb restaurant which specialises in traditional Catalan dishes. Free Wi-Fi. **www.solivi.com**

S'AGARÓ Hostal de la Gavina   €€€€€

Plaça de la Rosaleda, 17248 (Girona) **Tel** *972 32 11 00* **Fax** *972 32 15 73* **Rooms** *74*

This elegant Mediterranean-style beach mansion is set in its own exclusive estate with beautiful gardens and a sea water pool. Bedrooms are impressively decorated with silk-lined walls and burnished antiques, and the many facilities include a luxurious spa and a fine restaurant. Free Wi-Fi. **www.lagavina.com**

SANT PERE DE RIBES Els Sumidors   €€

Carretera de Vilafranca km 2.4, 18810 (Barcelona) **Tel** *93 896 20 61* **Fax** *93 896 20 61* **Rooms** *9*

On the slope of a hill, with views of the Penèdes wine region, this rustic 18th-century house has plenty of atmosphere and charm but few luxuries. Half lost in greenery, it's a tranquil world away from the frenzied nightlife of nearby Sitges. No restaurant but home-cooked meals are available. **www.sumidors.com**

SANTA CRISTINA D'ARO Mas Torrellas   €€

Carretera Santa Cristina-Platja d'Aro, 17246 (Girona) **Tel** *972 83 75 26* **Fax** *972 83 75 27* **Rooms** *18*

An attractive 18th-century country house hotel, with ancient stone walls and flower-filled gardens. Its most comfortable bedroom is in the distinctive yellow tower, built at a later date. There's a pool and tennis courts and horseback riding can be arranged. The restaurant is excellent. Closed Oct–Mar. **www.mastorrellas.com**

SANTA PAU Cal Sastre   €€€

Carrer de les Cases Noves, 1, 17811 (Girona) **Tel** *902 99 84 79* **Rooms** *11*

A modernized 18th-century rural house has been converted into this elegant, comfortable hotel. It is tucked into the ancient walls which circle medieval Santa Pau, and is surrounded by a shady garden. Rooms and self-catering bungalows available. The area has excellent opportunities for hiking and volcano spotting. **www.calsastre.com**

Key to Price Guide *see p134* **Key to Symbols** *see back cover flap*

SITGES Romàntic

Carrer Sant Isidre 33, 08870 (Barcelona) **Tel** *93 894 83 75* **Fax** *93 894 41 29* **Rooms** *60*

Well known in Sitges, this memorable hotel lives up to its name. Bedrooms are simple, but attractively decorated with antiques and paintings. A gloriously shady garden, with tinkling fountains, is perfect for breakfast and evening cocktails. Closed Nov–Mar. **www.hotelromantic.com**

TARRAGONA Imperial Tarraco

Passeig Les Palmeres s/n, 43003 (Tarragona) **Tel** *977 23 30 40* **Fax** *977 21 65 66* **Rooms** *170*

The plushest option in Tarragona, this large, modern hotel has a panoramic location right on the Balconi del Mediterrani. Many of the spacious, elegant rooms and suites have large terraces and the hotel is conveniently close to the historic centre of the city. Free Wi-Fi. **www.hotelhusaimperialtarraco.com**

TARRAGONA Lauria

Rambla Nova 20, 43004 (Tarragona) **Tel** *977 23 67 12* **Fax** *977 23 67 00* **Rooms** *72*

A modern, functional hotel in the town centre and close to the sea, with an elegant entrance under balustraded stone stairs. Rooms are large, although the decor is dated, but the hotel offers good amenities for the price, including a pool and facilities for business travellers. Self-catering apartments also available. **www.hlauria.es**

TAVERTET El Jufré

Tavertet, 08511 (Barcelona) **Tel** *93 856 51 67* **Fax** *93 856 51 67* **Rooms** *8*

This converted farmhouse is now a delightful *casa rural* with stunning mountain views, which has been in the same family for over 800 years. Warm, comfortable rooms have replaced the animal quarters. A perfect base for walking and exploring Osona. Price includes bed, breakfast and dinner. **www.mundo-rural.com**

TORRENT Mas de Torrent

Afueras, 17123 (Girona) **Tel** *902 55 03 21* **Fax** *972 30 32 93* **Rooms** *39*

A superbly converted 18th-century country house, this offers luxurious accommodation in one of ten beautiful rooms in the main house, or in elegant bungalows scattered around the extensive gardens. There are also deluxe suites with private pools available. Free Wi-Fi. **www.mastorrent.com**

TORTOSA Parador Castillo de la Zuda

Castillo de la Zuda, 43500 (Tarragona) **Tel** *977 44 44 50* **Fax** *977 44 44 58* **Rooms** *72*

A medieval Moorish castle makes a superb hilltop parador with views of the town and valley of the Riu Ebre. The fine restaurant offers al fresco dining on the terrace, and there are plenty of luxurious extras including a swimming pool, in summer only. Free Wi-Fi. **www.parador.es**

TOSSA DE MAR Diana

Plaça d'Espanya 6, 17320 (Girona) **Tel** *972 34 18 86* **Fax** *972 34 11 03* **Rooms** *21*

A fine, Modernista mansion is the gorgeous setting for this delightful hotel. There are great views of the castle from the terrace and the best of the modest rooms have private balconies. The elegant lobby is full of original details and has been converted into a comfortable lounge area. Closed mid-Nov–Mar. **www.diana-hotel.com**

TREDÒS Hotel de Tredòs

Carretera a Baqueira-Beret km 177.5, 25598 (Lleida) **Tel** *973 64 40 14* **Fax** *973 64 43 00* **Rooms** *45*

Skiers and mountain-walkers find this hotel in the Val d'Aran good value. It is built of stone and slate in the local style, and offers attractive rooms with wooden beams. There's a cosy lounge with fireplace in winter, and a heart-shaped outdoor pool to cool off in summer. Free Wi-Fi. Closed Oct, Nov, May and Jun. **www.hoteldetredos.com**

VIC Parador de Turismo de Vic

Paratge Bac de Sau, 08500 (Barcelona) **Tel** *93 812 23 23* **Fax** *93 812 23 68* **Rooms** *36*

This comfortable stone-built parador, 14 km (9 miles) from Vic, has magnificent views of the Sau reservoir. It's a peaceful retreat amid pine forests and dramatic rock formations. Facilities include a tennis court and an outdoor pool in summers. Free Wi-Fi. **www.parador.es**

VIELHA (VIELLA) Parador Valle de Arán

Carretera de túnel, 25530 (Lleida) **Tel** *973 64 01 00* **Fax** *973 64 11 00* **Rooms** *118*

This modern parador has a panoramic circular lounge dominated by a large window from which there are magnificent mountain views. There's a wonderful spa and a fine restaurant, and the rooms are spacious and well appointed. Free Wi-Fi. **www.parador.es**

VILADRAU Hostal de la Glòria

Carrer Torreventosa 12, 17406 (Girona) **Tel** *938 84 90 34* **Fax** *938 84 94 65* **Rooms** *26*

A traditional hotel with a family atmosphere in a conventional Catalan house above the Serra de Montseny. The fine restaurant serves creative Catalan specialities and the outdoor pool is surrounded by gardens. You can rent bikes and horseback-riding can be arranged. **www.hoteldelagloria.com**

VILANOVA I LA GELTRÚ César

Carrer Isaac Peral 4, 08800 (Barcelona) **Tel** *93 815 11 25* **Fax** *93 815 67 19* **Rooms** *30*

This hotel, near the Ribes Roges beach, is located in a marvellous turn-of-the-19th-century mansion. It is owned by two sisters who pay great attention to detail, from the furniture and the fabrics in the bedrooms to the well-known restaurant. There are delightful gardens with a pool, which is covered in winter. Free Wi-Fi. **www.hotelcesar.net**

RESTAURANTS, CAFES AND BARS

Wall tile advertising a
Barcelona restaurant

Eating out remains both a common practice and one of the convivial joys of life in Catalonia. Catalans are proud of their regional cuisine and expect to eat well in restaurants, not only at celebratory dinners, but also at work-day meal breaks or at family Sunday lunches out. Country restaurants in particular are packed on Sundays. Barcelona has an unusually large number of restaurants. From the sophisticated feast to the simple tapa, fresh ingredients are usually in evidence as Catalans tend to despise convenience food. The restaurants and cafés listed on pages 146–53 have been selected for their food and atmosphere. Pages 30–1 and 144–5 illustrate some of Catalonia's best dishes.

Comerç 24, one of Barcelona's most innovative restaurants *(see p148)*

RESTAURANTS AND BARS

Barcelona and Catalonia possess some of Spain's best restaurants, testifying to the quality of Catalan cooking, but the cheapest and quickest places to eat are the bars and cafés that serve *tapes* (tapas). Some bars, however, especially *pubs* (late-opening bars for socializing) do not serve food.

Family-run *bars i restaurants, hostals* and *fondes* – old Catalan words for the various types of inn – serve inexpensive, sit-down meals. *Xiringuitos* are beachside bars that are open only during the busy summer season.

Most restaurants close one day a week, some for lunch or dinner only, and most for an annual holiday. They also close on some public holidays. The main closing times of the restaurants on pages 146–53 are listed at the end of each entry. Always check the opening times, however, when phoning to book a table.

EATING HOURS

Catalans, in common with other Spaniards, often eat a light breakfast (*l'esmorzar*) of biscuits or toast with butter and jam and *cafè amb llet* (milky coffee), then follow with a second breakfast or snack between 10 and 11am, perhaps in a café. This may consist of a croissant, or an *entrepà* (sandwich) with sausage, ham or cheese, or a slice of the ubiquitous *truita de patates* (potato omelette). Fruit juice, coffee or beer are the usual accompaniments.

From about 1pm onwards, people will stop in the bars for a beer or an *aperitivo* with tapas. By 2pm those who can will have arrived home from work for *dinar* (lunch), which is the main meal of the day. Others will choose to have lunch in a restaurant.

The cafés, *salons de te* (tea rooms) and *pastisseries* (pastry shops) fill up by about 6 or 7pm for *el berenar* (tea)

Tèxtil Cafè logo
(see p153)

of sandwiches, pastries or cakes, with coffee, tea or fruit juice. Snacks such as *xurros* (fried, sugar-coated batter sticks) can also be bought from stalls.

By 7pm, bars are crowded with people having tapas with sherry, wine or beer. In Catalonia *el sopar* (dinner or supper), begins at about 9pm. However, restaurants sometimes begin serving earlier for tourists. In summer, however, families and groups of friends often do not sit down to dinner until as late as 11pm. At weekend lunch times, especially in the summer, you will often find that restaurants are filled by large and noisy family gatherings.

HOW TO DRESS

A jacket and tie are rarely required, but Catalans dress smartly, especially for city restaurants. Day dress is casual in beach resorts, but shorts are frowned on in the evenings.

Eating out at Barcelona's Port Olímpic, a busy venue all year round

Outdoor tables at a *cafeteria* in Cadaqués on the Costa Brava

READING THE MENU

Aside from tapas, perhaps the cheapest eating options in Catalan restaurants are the fixed-price *plats combinats* and the *menú del dia*. A *plat combinat* (meat or fish with vegetables and, usually, fried potatoes) is offered only by cheaper establishments. Most restaurants – but not all – offer an inexpensive, fixed-price *menú del dia*, normally of three courses. This menu is generally offered at lunchtime (on weekdays), and it can be a good opportunity to try out an expensive restaurant at a more reasonable price.

The Catalan word for menu is *la carta*. It starts with *sopes* (soups), *amanides* (salads), *entremesos* (hors d'oeuvres), *ous i truites* (eggs and omelettes) and *verdures i llegums* (vegetable dishes).

Main courses are *peix i marisc* (fish and shellfish) and *carns i aus* (meat and poultry). Daily specials are chalked on a board or clipped to menus. *Paella* and other rice dishes may be served as the first course. A useful rule is to follow rice with meat, or start with *fuet or llonganissa* (two popular types of sausage) or salad and follow with *paella*. Desserts are called *postres*. All restaurants offer fresh fruit, but otherwise the range of *postres* is often limited – perhaps the famous *crema catalana (crème brûlée)*, or *flam* (crème caramel) and *natillas* (custard). Gourmet restaurants have more creative choices.

Vegetarians are rather poorly catered for. Some vegetable, salad and egg dishes will be vegetarian, but may contain pieces of ham or fish, so ask before you order.

All eating places welcome children and will serve small portions if requested.

Las Torres de Àvila *(see p163)*, a distinctive Barcelona bar

WINE CHOICES

Dry fino wines are perfect with shellfish, sausage, olives and soups. Main dishes are often accompanied by wines from Penedès or Terra Alta *(see p32)* in Catalonia, or from Rioja, Ribera del Duero and Navarra. Oloroso wines are often drunk as a *digestif*. *Cava (see pp32–3)* is popular for Sunday lunch.

SMOKING

All restaurants, bars and cafés larger than 100 sq m (1100 sq ft) must have a non-smoking area. Smaller venues have a sign at the door stating whether smoking is permitted. A new law is proposed to ban smoking in public places competely.

PRICES AND PAYING

If you order from *la carta* in a restaurant, your bill can soar way above the price of the *menú del dia*, especially if you order pricey items, such as fresh seafood, fish or *ibèric* ham. If there is an expensive fish such as sole or swordfish on the menu at a bargain price, it may be frozen. Sea bass and other popular fish and shellfish, such as large prawns, lobster and crab, are generally priced by weight.

El compte (the bill) does not usually include service charges, but may include a small cover charge. Menu prices do not include eight per cent VAT *(IVA)*, which is usually added when the bill is calculated. Clients rarely tip waiters more than five per cent, often just rounding up the bill.

Cheques are never used in restaurants. Traveller's cheques are rarely accepted. Major credit cards and international debit cards are now accepted in most restaurants. However, do not expect to pay by credit card in smaller eating or drinking places like tapas bars, cafés, village *hostals* roadside *pubs* or *cellers*.

WHEELCHAIR ACCESS

All new restaurants have disabled access, but since older restaurants were rarely designed for wheelchairs, phone in advance (or ask the hotel staff to call) to check on access to tables and toilets.

Interior of Set Portes restaurant *(see p147)*, Port Vell, Barcelona

A Glossary of Typical Dishes

Catalan cuisine at its best, using fresh food, is known as *cuina de mercat* (market cuisine) and there is nowhere better to see produce laid out than at Barcelona's Boqueria market *(see p155)*. Peppers glisten, fish sparkle and no meat is wasted – even cocks' combs are sold for the pot. Olives come in all sorts of varieties.

Olives

Spring brings *calçot* onions and broad (fava) beans, while strawberries, from Easter onwards, are eaten with *cava*. In autumn 30 varieties of mushroom spill across the stalls.

TAPES (TAPAS – SNACKS)

Bar-hopping around Barcelona is a delightful way to spend an evening, and a good way to try the many local dishes laid out on the counters.

Anxoves: anchovies.
Escopinyes: cockles.
Bunyols de bacallà: salt cod fritters.
Calamars a la romana: fried squid rings.
Pa amb tomàquet: bread rubbed with tomato, garlic and olive oil – a good filler.
Panadons d'espinacs: small spinach pasties or pies.
Patates braves: potato chunks in spicy tomato sauce.
Pernil: ham – leg of pork seasoned and hung to dry.
Peixet fregit: small fried fish.
Popets: baby octopus.
Truita: omelette.
Truita de patates: traditional potato and onion omelette.

Pa amb tomàquet (bread with tomato), often served with ham

ENTRANTS (STARTERS)

These are often unusual dishes and two may be enough for a meal. Some may appear as main courses.
Amanida catalana: Catalan mixed salad.
Arròs negre: squid-ink rice. Can be a main course.

Produce at La Boqueria, Barcelona's huge covered market on La Rambla

Cargols a la llauna: snails in a spicy sauce.
Empedrat: salad of salt cod and white beans.
Escalivada: char-grilled or roasted aubergines (eggplant) and peppers, all drizzled with olive oil.
Espinacs a la catalana: spinach with pine nuts, raisins and ham; sometimes made with chard *(bledes)*.
Esqueixada: raw salt cod salad.
Faves a la catalana: a broad (fava) bean stew of black pudding, bacon, onion and garlic.
Fideus: noodles, usually served with fish and meat.
Garotes: raw sea urchins, from the Costa Brava, eaten with bread, garlic or spring onions.
Musclos: mussels.
Ous remenats amb camasecs: scrambled eggs with wild mushrooms.
Pa de fetge: liver pâté.
Sardines escabetxades: pickled sardines.
Xató: salt cod and tuna salad with *romesco* sauce.

SOPES (SOUPS)

Caldereta de llagosta: spiny lobster soup.
Escudella i carn d'olla: the liquid from Catalonia's traditional hotpot; the meat and vegetables *(carn i olla)* are served as a main course.
Gaspatxo: a clear, cold tomato soup with raw vegetables.
Sopa de farigola: thyme soup.
Sopa de bolets: mushroom soup.

MAIN DISHES

Methods of cooking are: *a la brasa* (over open flames); *bullit* (boiled); *cremat* (crisp fried or caramelized); *estofat* (stewed); *farcit* (stuffed); *al forn* (in the oven); *a la graella/ planxa* (cooked on a griddle, pan-fried or barbecued); *a la pedra* (on a hot stone).

PEIX I MARISCOS (FISH AND SHELLFISH)

Allipebre d'anguiles: spicy eel stew.
Anfós al forn: baked stuffed grouper.
Calamars farcits: squid stuffed with pork, tomatoes and onions.
Cassola de peix: fish casserole.
Congre amb pèsols: conger eel with peas.
Escamarlans bullits: boiled crayfish.
Gambes a la planxa: prawns cooked on a griddle.
Graellada de peix: mixed seafood grill.
Llagosta a la brasa: lobster cooked over open flames.
Llagostins amb maionesa: king prawns and mayonnaise.
Llobarro al forn: baked, sea bass.
Lluç a la planxa: hake cooked on a griddle.
Molls a la brasa: red mullet cooked over open flames.
Orada a la sal: gilthead bream baked in salt, which is removed on serving.
Paella valenciana: paella with chicken and seafood.
Peix amb romesco: seafood with the famous *romesco* sauce. Tarragona's master *romesco* makers compete each summer.
Rap a l'all cremat: angler fish with crisped garlic.
Sarsuela: fish, shellfish and spices, everything goes into

the pot that gives its name to a light Spanish opera.

Sèpia amb pèsols: cuttlefish with peas.

Suquet de peix: Catalonia's principal fish stew, made with various fish, tomatoes, peppers, potatoes and almonds.

Verats a la brasa: mackerel cooked over open flames.

CARN (MEAT)

Ànec amb naps: duck with turnips, ideally the "black" turnips of the Empordà region; also sometimes served with pears (*ànec amb peres*).

Boles de picolat: meatballs in tomato sauce. Meatballs with cuttlefish (*sèpia*) is classic *mar i muntanya* food.

Botifarra amb mongetes: sausage and beans.

Bou a l'adoba: beef casserole.

Costelles a la brasa amb allioli: flame-roast lamb cutlets with garlic mayonnaise.

Costelles de cabrit rostides: roast goat kid cutlets.

Cuixa de xai al forn: roast leg of lamb.

Estofat de bou: beef stew with sausages, potatoes, herbs and sometimes a little chocolate.

Barcelona's cheese and honey market *(see p155)* in the Plaça del Pi

Estofat de quaresma: a filling Lenten vegetable stew.

Freginat: calf's liver with onions.

Fricandó: braised veal with wild mushrooms.

Llom de porc: pork chops.

Oca amb peres: goose with pears – traditional village festival fare.

Niu: a huge fish and meat stew from Palafrugell, Costa Brava, with pigeon, cuttlefish, cod tripe, pig's trotters, egg and garlic mayonnaise.

Peus de porc a la llauna: pig's trotters in a spicy sauce.

Pollastre amb samfaina: chicken with *samfaina*.

Pota i tripa: lamb's trotters and tripe.

Tripa a la catalana: tripe in *sofregit* and wine with pine nuts and almonds.

Xai amb pèsols: lamb with peas.

Aubergines (eggplant) and peppers, used in abundance

CAÇA (GAME)

Although the hunting season is from October to February, some game is available all year round, especially rabbit.

Becada amb coc: woodcock in a bread roll.

Civet de llebre: jugged hare.

Conill a la brasa amb allioli: rabbit with garlic mayonnaise.

Conill amb cargols: rabbit with snails.

Conill amb xocolata: rabbit with garlic, liver, almonds, fried bread, chocolate and old wine.

Estofat de porc senglar amb bolets: wild boar casserole with wild mushrooms.

Guatlles amb salsa de magrana: quail in pomegranate sauce.

Perdiu: partridge.

Perdius amb farcellets de col: partridge with cabbage dumplings.

VERDURES (VEGETABLES)

Albergínies: aubergines (eggplant).

Bledes: chard.

Bolets: mushrooms.

Calçots: leek-sized green onions, roasted on an open fire and dipped in a spicy tomato sauce. A spring-time speciality of the Tarragona region.

Carbassó arrebossat: battered courgettes (zucchini).

Carxofes: artichokes.

Julivert: parsley.

Mongetes tendres i patates: French beans and potatoes.

Pastanagues: carrots.

Pebrots: red peppers.

POSTRES (DESSERTS)

Although *pastisseria* (pastries) and *dolços* (sweets) are very popular in Catalonia, desserts in restaurants are generally uneventful. The choice may be simply ice cream or fruit: apple *(poma)*, peach *(préssec)*, banana *(plàtan)*, orange *(taronja)*, grapes *(raïm)*.

Crema catalana: rich egg custard.

Figues amb aniset: figs in anise.

Flam: crème caramel.

Formatge: cheese. There is little local cheese.

Gelat: ice cream.

Mel i Mató: fresh goat's cheese, eaten with honey.

Menjar blanc: an almond blancmange.

Peres amb vi negre: pears in red wine.

Postre de músic: a bowl of mixed nuts and dried fruit, once given as a reward to itinerant musicians.

Recuit: curdled sheep's (or cow's) milk in a small pot.

Mel i mató – a traditional dessert of soft cheese served with honey

Choosing a Restaurant

The restaurants in this guide have been selected for their good value, food and location. The chart below lists restaurants in Barcelona by area, and the entries are alphabetical within each price category. Restaurants in the Further Afield section are listed by district and those in the rest of Catalonia are arranged by town.

PRICE CATEGORIES
For a three-course evening meal for one, including a half-bottle of house wine, tax and service.

€ under €20
€€ €20–€35
€€€ €35–€50
€€€€ over €50.

OLD TOWN

Bar Pinotxo
€

Mercat de la Boqueria (La Rambla 89), 08002 **Tel** *93 317 17 31*   **Map** *5 A1*

The most famous of all the bars in the Boquería. Steel buckets hold chilled bottles of *cava*, and fresh ingredients from neighbouring market stalls are cooked and served hot on the spot. The bar is open from early in the morning. Closed Sun, evenings after 6pm.

Elisabets
€

C/Elisabets 2, 08001 **Tel** *93 317 58 26*   **Map** *2 F2*

A local institution, this homely bustling restaurant specialises in traditional Catalan cuisine. It is a favourite for diners in search of hearty, home-cooked midday meals, and Friday night tapas. Elisabets also has a lively bar where you can have a sandwich or drink at any time of the day. Closed 3 wks Aug (bar); Sun; dinner, except Fri (restaurant only).

Organic
€

C/Junta de Comerç 11, 08001 **Tel** *93 301 09 02*   **Map** *2 F3*

Spacious, clean and softly lit, this good-value vegetarian restaurant offers an imaginative menu of Asian dishes, lasagnes, stews and an all-you-can-eat salad buffet. The home-made bread with nuts is a must. They have a very reasonably priced set menu. They also have a small shop selling organic products.

Can Culleretes
€€

C/Quintana 5, 08002 **Tel** *93 317 30 22*   **Map** *5 A2*

The oldest restaurant in Barcelona dates from 1786 and oozes history from its many dining rooms, nooks and crannies. Original frescoes and tiles decorate the walls. Staff are brusque but efficient. Food is cheap, plentiful and satisfying. Try the goose with apples or duck with prunes. Closed Sun dinner, Mon; 2 wks Aug; 25 Dec.

Inopia
€€

Carrer de Tamarit 104, 08015 **Tel** *93 424 52 31*   **Map** *5 D5*

It may be off the beaten track, but dedicated foodies should seek out this restaurant. Owner Albert Adrià (brother of Ferran who runs the famous El Bulli) has gone back to basics, and the bar serves classic tapas prepared with the finest of local ingredients. Albert also has a sweet shop, Cacao Sampaka *(see p156)*. Closed Sun, Mon.

Kaiku
€€

Plaça del Mar 1, 08003 **Tel** *93 221 90 82*   **Map** *5 B5*

You would not know it from the exterior, but this unassuming, beachfront restaurant makes what is probably the best paella in the city. It is on the menu as *arròs del xef*, and it is prepared with smoked rice and succulent shellfish. Book the terrace in summer for sea views and a breeze. Great desserts too. Tue–Sun lunch only. Closed 2 wks Aug.

Mam i Teca
€€

C/Lluna 4, 08001 **Tel** *93 441 33 35*   **Map** *2 F2*

Tiny, sunflower-yellow bar that plays well-known jazz, blues and rock tunes. The tapas are superb, and include locally sourced cheeses, organic sausages, and country dishes such as ham and broad beans. They also have an excellent wine list, and a good range of Scottish single malts. Closed Tue, Sat lunch; 3 wks Aug.

Mosquito
€€

Carders 46, 08003 **Tel** *93 268 75 69*   **Map** *5 C2*

A laidback bar peopled by a healthy mix of Catalans and resident expats. Friendly staff, cheap drinks and a solid array of Asian tapas, like home-made Hong Kong dim sum. A full range of Chinese dumplings make this a pleasant change from the usual tapas joints. Closed Tue and lunchtime.

Pla de la Garsa
€€

C/Assaonadors 13, 08003 **Tel** *93 315 24 13*   **Map** *5 B2*

Situated in the stables of a 17th-century palace, the cosy atmosphere of this pretty, split-level restaurant makes it a good place for romantic evenings. For cheese lovers the 40-strong list is a winner. There's also an interesting selection of red wines. Closed for lunch daily.

Key to Symbols *see back cover flap*

Taller de Tapas

C/Argenteria 51, 08003 **Tel** 93 268 85 59   *Map 5 B2*

Exposed brick and sleek steel fittings give this restaurant a contemporary urban feel. Staff are professional and friendly, and the extensive tapas dishes are all freshly made on the spot. You can also try regional dishes such as the Costa Brava's cherished Palamos prawns. Peak times can be busy.

Agua

Passeig Marítim de la Barceloneta 30, 08003 **Tel** 93 225 12 72   *Map 6 D4*

Classy seafront restaurant with floor-to-ceiling windows and abstract fish sculptures. It is popular with a young, up-beat crowd and serves excellent tapas, fish and rice dishes. Specials include steamed mussels, *butan* potatoes, Norway lobsters au gratin and grilled fish. There's an appealing terrace on the beach as well.

Biblioteca

C/Junta de Comerç 28, 08001 **Tel** 93 412 62 21   *Map 2 F3*

Elegant, cream-coloured restaurant-cum-cookbook shop with Modernista tiles and open kitchen. The high-class cooking focuses on seasonal ingredients. Specialities include rice with pigeon and black pudding; and black spaghetti with *calçots* (Catalan onions) and poached egg. Closed Sun and daily for lunch; 2 wks Aug.

Café de l'Academia

C/Lledó 1, 08002 **Tel** 93 319 82 53   *Map 5 B3*

An intimate, candle-lit restaurant with exposed brick walls and a pretty terrace in the lovely Plaça Sant Just, in the centre of Barri Gòti. The menu offers superb Catalan fare, interesting salads and home-made pasta. The desserts are top-notch. Closed Sat, Sun; 3 wks Aug.

Cal Pep

Plaça de les Olles 8, 08003 **Tel** 93 310 79 61   *Map 5 B3*

Arguably the best bar in town for fresh fish and seafood, right off the boats. Cal Pep has an excellent selection of tapas. The long, narrow, standing bar means it gets crowded at peak times. Arrive early for one of five tables out back. Closed Sat dinner, Sun, Mon lunch; Easter; Aug.

Can Majó

C/Almirall Aixada 23, 08003 **Tel** 93 221 54 55   *Map 5 B5*

As places for *paella* go, this is one of the best especially when eaten on a warm summer's day on a terrace with sea views. If you start getting into the shellfish, prices hike right up, but it's worth it for freshness and quality of produce cooked to perfection. Closed Sun dinner, Mon.

El Salón

C/Hostal d'en Sol 6–8, 08002 **Tel** 93 315 21 59   *Map 5 B3*

The Baroque-style interior, plump velvet chairs and grand chandeliers give this establishment the feel of an 18th-century boudoir. The menu changes constantly but promises sumptuous ingredients and inventive dishes, often featuring French and Catalan specialities. Closed lunch, Sun.

Els Quatre Gats

C/Montsió 3 bis, 08002 **Tel** 93 302 41 40   *Map 5 A1*

This emblematic Barcelona institution was the first place ever to show Picasso's work. It is decorated by original works of early 20th-century artists and oozes history. The opulent dining room verges on cheesy but is great fun, and the Mediterranean fare is reasonable too. There is a good-value fixed price lunch menu.

Euskal Etxea

Placeta Montcada 1–3, 08003 **Tel** 93 310 21 85   *Map 5 B3*

Home to the Basque Cultural Institute, the Euskal Etxea is one of the best places in town for Basque *pintxos* (small rounds of bread with a myriad toppings). It also serves exceptionally good *a la carte* meals. The tapas bar is cheaper than the main restaurant.

Set Portes

Passeig Isabel II, 14, 08003 **Tel** 93 319 30 33   *Map 5 B3*

A long-standing Barcelona institution since 1836 with a who's who of past guests, including Winston Churchill and Che Guevara. It is famed for its classic marble tiles and wood-panelled dining room, and most of all for *paella*, which comes in ten different varieties. Open all day and until late.

Taxidermista

Plaça Reial 8, 08002 **Tel** 93 412 45 36   *Map 5 A3*

Soft colour schemes and high ceilings give this trendy restaurant an edge over the touristy competition on the bustling Plaza Reial. Inventive market cooking offers a range of dishes from around the Mediterranean rim including *babaganush*, sardine tarts and duck *confit*. They also serve tapas. Closed Mon; 2 wks Jan.

Carballeira

C/Reina Cristina 3, 08003 **Tel** 93 310 10 06   *Map 5 B3*

This was the first Galician seafood restaurant in Barcelona. Carballeira has become well known for its simply grilled fish and seafood, perfect *paellas* and the house special, which consists of Galician-style tender octopus sprinkled with paprika. Closed Sun dinner, Mon.

Comerç 24
C/Comerç 24, 08003 **Tel** *93 319 21 02*   **Map** *5 C3*

Designer tapas bar with charcoal grey walls and primary colour accents, serving some of the most inventive tapas in town. A "Festival" of tapas is served for groups of six or more. Try the *arròs a banda* (paella without the morsels) or the *tortilla de patatas* (potato omelette). Reservations necessary. Closed Sun, Mon.

Neri Restaurante
Carrer Sant Sever 5, 08002 **Tel** *93 304 06 55*   **Map** *5 A2*

Decorated in soft hues and sympathetically lit, the dining room at the Neri hotel is a great spot to take a break from sightseeing in the Barri Gòtic, even if you are not a guest at the hotel. Classic Mediterranean fare with a modern twist is the order of the day. A good-value fixed-price lunch menu is available during the week.

EIXAMPLE

Crêperie Bretonne
C/Balmes 274, 08006 **Tel** *93 217 30 48*   **Map** *3 A1*

This kitsch French pancake house has been around for more than 30 years. It serves 250 types of thin, light Brittany-style *crêpes*. They offer sweet or salted *crêpes* and with all kinds of French cheese fillings. Also try their herbal teas. Closed lunch, Mon; Aug.

Cata 1.81
C/València 181, 08011 **Tel** *93 323 68 18*   **Map** *3 A4*

Long, thin and blindingly white, this modern tapas bar was one of the pioneers of Post-Modernist tapas, turning classics like Spanish potato omelette into state-of-the-art taste explosions. The excellent wine list offers many by the glass. A top choice for those interested in the wonders of New Catalan cuisine. Closed lunch, Sun; 3 wks Aug.

Madrid-Barcelona
C/Aragó 282, 08007 **Tel** *93 215 70 27*   **Map** *3 A4*

This smart, split-level restaurant with its cast-iron balustrades and polished wood looks more expensive than it is. It is hugely popular, often with long queues coming out the door, for Málaga-style *pescaditos fritos* (fried fish) and other good value tapas. It can get very busy here; booking is recommended.

Shibui
C/Comte d'Urgell 272–274, 08036 **Tel** *93 321 90 04*

With its sleek blonde wood fittings, cardboard-brick walls and trim waiting staff, this excellent Japanese restaurant has Tokyo written all over it. The basement dining room also has custom-made tatami areas and sliding screens making them a brilliant choice for parties. A gluten-free menu and take-away are also available. Closed Sun.

Alkimia
C/Indústria 79, 08025 **Tel** *93 207 61 15*   **Map** *3 C2*

One of the rising stars, this small, designer restaurant revitalizes traditional Catalan dishes with new techniques and foreign flavours. Signature dishes include creamy rice with crayfish and *nyora* peppers, sticky slow-roasted bull tail and mandarin essence with *horchata* (tiger-nut) foam. Good value set lunch menu. Closed Sat, Sun; Easter, 3 wks Aug.

Casa Calvet
C/Casp 48, 08010 **Tel** *93 412 40 12*   **Map** *3 B5*

A beautiful restaurant that was originally designed by Gaudí as a private home and offices for a wealthy textile merchant. The cozy seating booths, formal table settings and old-school service harken back to another era, however the cooking is modern and executed with panache. A more economical fixed-price lunch menu is offered. Closed Sun and bank hols.

Cinc Sentits
C/Aribau 58, 08011 **Tel** *93 323 94 90*   **Map** *2 F1*

This warm yet minimal Michelin-starred restaurant offers impeccable service and a menu that is both unusual and accessible. Meticulously sourced products are cooked with flair. The *Sensaciones,* chef's choice tasting menu, is recommended. Kids are welcome during the week and at lunchtime. Closed Sun, Mon; Easter, 2 wks Aug.

Moo
C/Rosselló 265, 08008 **Tel** *93 445 40 00*   **Map** *3 A3*

Moo has walked away with a string of accolades, thanks to the inspired cooking of the Roca brothers who manage the restaurant. The tasting menu with matching wines is magical: Dublin bay prawns with rose and licorice, sea bass with lemon thyme and desserts inspired by perfumes. Very fashionable; reservations are essential. Closed Sun; Aug.

Noti
Carrer de Roger de Llúria 35–37, 08009 **Tel** *93 342 66 73*   **Map** *3 B4*

In a city where style often triumphs over substance, Noti stands out as a glorious exception. The decor is as sophisticated and glamorous as the crowd, but doesn't detract from the exceptional food – Mediterranean and French cuisine prepared with flair and originality. A reasonable fixed-price lunch menu is available. Closed Sat lunch, Sun.

Key to Price Guide *see p146* **Key to Symbols** *see back cover flap*

MONTJUÏC

Rosal 34   ⧉   €€
Carrer Roser 34, 08004 **Tel** *93 324 90 46*   **Map** *2 D3*

An upmarket tapas bar with a smart, bright dining room. Well-heeled diners are attracted by Rosal 34's innovative take on classic tapas, alongside original creations of the chef's own making. There is also an extensive wine list with some great recommendations. Closed Mon lunch, Sun.

La Font del Gat   ⧉ ⧉   €€€
Passeig Santa Madrona 28, 08038 **Tel** *93 289 04 04*   **Map** *1 B3*

High up on a hill, La Font del Gat is a short hop from the Fundació Joan Miró and Montjuïc's other museums. Fare includes good salads, soups and tapas and there is a reasonably-priced set lunch menu. The greatest attraction here, however, is the restaurant's terrace surrounded by trees, that offers great views over the city. Closed dinner; Mon; Aug.

Xemei   ⧉   €€€
Passeig de la Exposició 85, 08004 **Tel** *93 553 51 40*   **Map** *1 C3*

A small and convivial authentic Italian restaurant run by two brothers. Xemei specialises in dishes from the Venetian region – the *antipasti* are particularly good. The restaurant can get quite noisy inside, but there are tables on the pavement and the customer service is excellent. Closed Tue.

FURTHER AFIELD

GRÀCIA Chido One   ⧉ ⧉   €
C/Torrijos 30, 08012 **Tel** *93 285 03 35*   **Map** *3 C2*

Lined floor to ceiling with Mexican Day of the Dead artifacts and trophies, as well as retro *jalapeño* chilli cans, this trendy eatery serves excellent regional fare including steaming bowls of heart warming *posole*, soft fat *enchiladas* slathered with chilli sauce, tacos and lethal margaritas.

GRÀCIA Envalira   ⧉ ⧉ ⧉ ⧉   €€
Plaça del Sol 13, 08012 **Tel** *93 218 58 13*   **Map** *3 B1*

A real neighbourhood joint in the spirited Plaça del Sol in Barcelona, it's noisy, raucous and fun with a laidback anything-goes ambience. Intimate it is not, but it's a great place for hearty, no-nonsense fare with rice dishes topping the bill. Closed Sun dinner; Mon; Aug.

GRÀCIA San Kil   €€
Carrer Legalitat 22, 08024 **Tel** *93 284 41 79*

The Gràcia area is famous for its range of ethnic restaurants and San Kil is one of the best. The decor is low on frills and the TV is frequently left on but the Korean food more than makes up for it. A recommended speciality is the beef cooked on a red-hot iron plate at your table. Closed Sun.

GRÀCIA La Rosa del Desierto   ⧉ ⧉ ⧉   €€€
Plaça Narcís Oller 7, 08006 **Tel** *93 237 45 90*   **Map** *3 A2*

This was Barcelona's first ever Moroccan restaurant and is still widely regarded to be the best. With its atmospheric decor and cushion-covered benches it's a fun place for *couscous* and delicious tagines. They have interesting meat dishes, soups and salads on their menu. Also try one of their typical Arab teas. Closed Sun dinner; Mon; mid-Aug–mid-Sep.

GRÀCIA Botafumeiro   ⧉ ⧉ ⧉ ⧉ ⧉   €€€€
C/Gran de Gràcia 81, 08012 **Tel** *93 218 42 30*   **Map** *3 A2*

A legendary seafood restaurant with ice-banks piled high with boat-fresh fish and seafood at the entrance. A-listers from Woody Allen to Madonna have all made this a favourite haunt whilst in town thanks to discreet management and luxury surroundings. Try the tender *pulpo Gallego* (Galician octopus). Eating at the bar is cheaper. Reservations essential.

GRÀCIA Hofmann   ⧉ ⧉   €€€€
C/Granada del Penedès 16 **Tel** *93 218 71 65*   **Map** *5 B2*

The talented chef Mey Hofmann has been at the forefront of Barcelona's restaurant scene for many years, so it is no surprise that her own establishment is the recipient of a Michelin star. Expect high-quality, creative cuisine served in a sophisticated environment. Hofmann also runs a pastry shop at C/Flassaders 44 in the Born. Closed Sat, Sun; Easter, Aug.

GRÀCIA Roig Robí   ⧉ ⧉ ⧉ ⧉   €€€€
C/Sèneca 20, 08006 **Tel** *93 218 92 22*   **Map** *3 A2*

Small and intimate with a pretty interior courtyard for summer dining, this restaurant is a classic for genuine Catalan cuisine. The menu boasts a good selection of *bacalà* (salt-cod) dishes as well as typical vegetable dishes of broad beans and artichokes. Closed Sat lunch, Sun; 3 wks Aug.

HORTA Can Travi Nou
P 🏃 ♿ 🖼   €€€€

C/Jorge Manrique, 08035 **Tel** *93 428 03 01*

Few people venture so far from the centre for their supper, but this 14th-century farmhouse is well worth the trek to soak up the atmosphere of yesteryear, and the rolling terraces are wonderful for alfresco dining. Roast meats, rice dishes and fresh fish are on the menu. Closed Sun dinner.

POBLENOU Els Pescadors
P 🏃 ☰ ♿ 🖼   €€€

Plaça Prim 1, 08005 **Tel** *93 225 20 18*

The multiple-spaced restaurant – terrace, formal dining room and old-fashioned, tiled cafeteria – is named after the fishermen that used to frequent it. It's an excellent place for a catch-of-the-day special, zingy-fresh mussels and other fishy delights. Try the *anxoves* (anchovies). Excellent wine list. Closed Easter and Christmas.

SANT GERVASI La Balsa
P 🏃 🖼   €€€

C/Infanta Isabel 4, 08022 **Tel** *93 211 50 48*

Much-loved by Barcelona's glitterati: sportspersons, artists, actors and politicians are all in attendance at this uptown eatery. Service is discreet, the decor tasteful and the terraces among the best in town for enjoying Basque, Catalan and Mediterranean food at its finest. Closed Sun dinner, Mon lunch; lunch Aug.

TIBIDABO El Asador de Aranda
P 🏃 ☰ ♿ 🖼   €€€

Avinguda del Tibidabo 31, 08022 **Tel** *93 417 01 15*

A meat-lovers' paradise, this mansion-house restaurant at the top of the hill specializes in roasts, melt-in-the-mouth suckling pig and lamb; rich, juicy steaks, chops and ribs; and a fine line in *burgos morcillas* (black pudding). They also serve red wines from La Ribera. Closed Sun dinner.

CATALONIA

ALTAFULLA Faristol
🏃 🖼   €€

C/Sant Martí 5 (Tarragona), 43893 **Tel** *977 65 00 77*

Experience traditional Catalan fare at this charming 18th-century farmhouse. The English-Catalan couple that run it create a romantic getaway from the bustle of Barcelona. Rooms are also available. They usually have music on weekend nights. Mid-Sep–mid-Jun: open only Fri dinner–Sun lunch; mid-Jun–mid-Sep: open daily for dinner and Sat-Sun lunch.

ARENYS DE MAR Hispania
P 🏃 ☰ 🖼 ♿   €€€€

Carretera Reial, 54, 08350 **Tel** *93 791 04 57*

A famous bistro that has earned numerous awards for the quality of its cooking. People travel from far and wide for its clam *suquet* (fish stew) and home-made *crema catalana* (traditional vanilla custard with a burnt, caramel crust). Closed Sun dinner, Tue; Oct.

BERGA Sala
🏃 ☰   €€€€

Passeig de la Pau 27, 08600 **Tel** *93 821 11 85*

A good choice for hearty winter dishes that feature freshly picked wild mushrooms from the nearby forests, Berga is mushroom country, and wild game is available in season. Very innovative cuisine. They also have a set tasting menu. Closed Sun dinner, Mon.

BOLVIR DE CERDANYA Torre del Remei
P 🏃 ☰ ♿ 🖼   €€€€

Camí Reial (Girona), 17539 **Tel** *972 14 01 82*

One of the region's finest hotels and restaurants set in a summer palace and surrounded by verdant countryside. The chef de cuisine uses regional products to create meals such as melting veal cheeks with sweet and sour berry fruits, fresh scallops in Priorat sauce, desserts and local cheeses.

CAMBRILS Can Bosch
🏃 ☰   €€€€

Rambla Jaume I, 19, 43850 **Tel** *977 36 00 19*

This is a classic and highly-respected restaurant serving superb fish, seafood and rice dishes. Their *arroz negro* (rice cooked in squid ink) is justly famous. Patrons rave about their wine list almost as much as the food. Closed Sun dinner, Mon; 22 Dec–Jan.

CORÇA Botic
☰ ♿   €€€€

Ctra. C-66 Girona-Palamós Km 11.5, 17121 **Tel** *972 63 08 69*

This restuarant opened by Chef Albert 'Tito' Sastregener has a Michelin star and serves creative Catalan fare in elegant and modern surroundings. There is a very reasonable tasting menu, which consists of two tapas, four starters, two main dishes and two desserts. The wine list is excellent. Closed Mon and Tue (except Aug); mid-Oct–mid-Nov.

FIGUERES Hotel Empordà
P 🏃 ☰ 🖼   €€€€

Av. Salvador Dalí 170, 17600 **Tel** *972 50 05 62*

This is a legendary restaurant that played a great part in putting Catalan cuisine on the map for travelling gourmands. Established in 1961, folks still gather here to enjoy the legacy of chef Jaime Subirós' cuisine. An excellent fixed-price menu is available.

Key to Price Guide *see p146* **Key to Symbols** *see back cover flap*

GIRONA El Celler de Can Roca

Can Sunyer 46, 17007 **Tel** *972 22 21 57*

Celler de Can Roca offers a fusion of Catalan and French "nouvelle cuisine" cooking. A must on the list of dedicated food enthusiasts, the brothers Roca turn out innovative, technically brilliant dishes at terrifying speed. With three Michelin stars, this is a place to wow and be wowed. Closed Sun, Mon, 2 wks Jul; Christmas.

GRATALLOPS Cellers de Gratallops

Piró 32 (Priorat), 43737 **Tel** *977 83 90 36*

This smart village restaurant is owned by the *bodega's* Clos l'Obac, one of the pioneers of new Priorat wines and serves their entire range, along with local olive oils and an excellent Moroccan influenced menu. Well worth seeking out during a trip to wine country. Open Tue–Sun lunch only.

LA SEU D'URGELL El Castell

Carretera N260 km 229 (Lleida), 25700 **Tel** *973 35 00 00*

At the foot of La Seu d'Urgell castle, surrounded by stunning scenery, lies this idyllic hotel-restaurant. El Castell serves topflight modern Catalan cuisine and superlative wines. Many of the dishes include local wild mushrooms from the Pyrenees and meat from the region. A cheaper menu is served to outside tables. Closed Mon, Tue; 3 wks Jan, 3 wks Nov.

LLEIDA Gardeny

C/ Salmerón 10, 25004 **Tel** *973 23 45 10*

Excellent regional cooking with a modern twist, including snails Gardeny-style (oven baked), is served at this city centre restaurant. Specialities include ceps (mushrooms) and cod and *Esqueixada* with cod and elvers. Offers a good value set price lunch during the week and a gourmet menu at weekends. Closed Sun and Mon for dinner; Tue.

MANRESA Sibar

C/Carrasco i Formiguera 18 (Barcelona), 08242 **Tel** *93 874 81 71*

This modern establishment has a cafeteria on the ground floor for coffee and cakes, and a sleek elegant restaurant in the basement for formal dining. The *chuletón* (T-bone steak for a minimum of two people) is superlative, as are the unlikely sounding fried eggs and potatoes. Regional wines are a must. Closed Christmas.

MARTINET Boix

Carretera N260 km 204,5 (Lleida), 25724 **Tel** *973 51 51 01*

A famous Catalan hotel-restaurant located on the banks of the Riu Segre. It serves slow-roasted leg of lamb so tender you could eat it with a spoon, complimented perfectly by a bottle of soft luscious local wine from the Costers del Segre. Closed Sun dinner, Mon, 2 wks Feb.

PERALADA Castell de Peralada

Hotel Castell de Peralada, C/Sant Joan (Girona), 17491 **Tel** *972 53 81 25*

This medieval castle makes for a truly special lunch or dinner. It specializes in traditional Empordàn cuisine while the castle's own *bodegas* provide the wine. As the restaurant is inside a casino, under-18s are not allowed. Kids are allowed in Jul–Aug when a buffet is served on outside tables. Closed daily for lunch; Sep–May: closed Mon, Tue.

ROSES El Bulli

Cala Montjoi, Ap 30 (Girona), 17480 **Tel** *972 15 04 57*

With three Michelin stars, critics and foodies alike believe this bistro to be not only the best in Spain but one of the best in the world. Super-chef Ferran Adrià is certainly one of the most radical, producing state-of-the-art dishes in a pretty beachside setting. Reservations required one year in advance. Closed 21 Dec–mid-Jun; closed during 2012 & 2013.

SANT CELONI El Racó de Can Fabes

C/ de Sant Joan 6 (Barcelona), 08470 **Tel** *93 867 28 51*

Santi Santamaría (three Michelin stars) is one of Spain's most emblematic chefs and this delightful country restaurant is in the house where he was born. The seasonal menu is full of delights, based on local fare like wild mushrooms and lamb from Montseny, rice from the Ebro delta and truffles from Osona. Reservations essential. Closed Sun dinner, Mon and Tue; Jan.

SANT POL DE MAR Sant Pau

C/Nou 10 (Barcelona), 08395 **Tel** *93 760 06 62*

This Michelin-starred restaurant is an hour-long train ride from Barcelona. The bounty of earth and sea make for some wonderful dishes created from delicate courgette flowers, *espardenyes* (sea cucumbers) and wild boar. Closed Mon, Sun, Thu lunch; 3 wks May, 3 wks Nov.

SITGES El Velero

Passeig de la Ribera 38 (Barcelona), 08870 **Tel** *93 894 20 51*

A seaside restaurant whose imaginative creations are a cut above more standard offerings of *paella* and grilled fish. Here sole comes on a bed of wild mushrooms and is drizzled with unctuous crab sauce and lobster comes with chickpea cream. Closed Sun; 22 Dec–22 Jan.

TARRAGONA Degusta

C/Cavallers 6, 43003 **Tel** *977 25 24 28*

Situated in the old part of town, this restaurant serves innovative Mediterranean dishes and tapas. House specials include game in season, fresh fish and addictive home-made desserts. There is a pleasant terrace for outside dining, and a good wine list. Closed Sun; 22 Feb–8 Mar.

Cafés and Bars

This section lists the best and most colourful cafés and bars in Barcelona, including both the traditional and the new and fashionable. Most cafés serve a small selection of alcoholic drinks as well as soft drinks, and most bars offer coffee, so customers will nearly always find something to their liking in any establishment.

PRICE CATEGORIES
For a light bite, where available, for one, including a half-bottle of house wine, tax and service.

€ under €20
€€ €20–€35

OLD TOWN

Barcelona Rouge
€

C/Poeta Cabanyes 21, 08004 **Tel** *93 442 49 85*　　　　　　　　　　　　　**Map** *2 D3*

Few people know about this late-night bar, but, it is cherished by those that do. You have to ring a bell to get in, whereupon a small entrance way opens into a long, velvet-lined corridor guarded by angels to reveal a wide open space filled with sofas. They do not serve food. Closed Mon, Tue.

Boadas
€

C/dels Tallers 1, 08001 **Tel** *93 318 88 26*　　　　　　　　　　　　　　**Map** *2 F1*

Sophia Loren and other celebrities liked to drink here, and the wall of black and white photographs is testament to their loyalty. The liveried bar-tenders mix the meanest martinis in town for a grown-up crowd of well-heeled Catalans and discerning tourists. They do not serve food. Closed Sun.

Bodega La Palma
€

C/Palma de Sant Just 7, 08002 **Tel** *93 315 06 56*　　　　　　　　　　　**Map** *5 B3*

This is an old fashioned, rustic *bodega* (wine cellar) which resides in the heart of the old city. In keeping with tradition wine is poured from weathered barrels, and is served in ceramic pitchers. Their selection of tapas is also recommended. Closed Sun; Easter, Aug.

Caelum
€

C/de la Palla 8, 08002 **Tel** *93 302 69 93*　　　　　　　　　　　　　　**Map** *5 A2*

This elegant tearoom is housed in the former women's baths of the Jewish Quarter (El Call). The intimate, softly-lit dining room offers tea, infusions and cappuccinos as well as a good range of typical sweetmeats including *yemas* (sweet egg yolks), *roscos* (ring shaped biscuits) and chocolate truffles. Closed Mon morning.

Café Bliss
€

Plaça Sants Just i Pastor, 08002 **Tel** *93 268 10 22*　　　　　　　　　　**Map** *5 B2*

Hidden away down a tiny side street, on one of the loveliest Gothic squares in the old city, is this delightful café. Inside are comfy sofas and a range of international magazines and newspapers; outside there is a sunny terrace. It is perfect for coffee and cakes, light meals or just a romantic drink in the evening.

El Bosc de les Fades
€

Passatge de la Banca 5, 08002 **Tel** *93 317 26 49*　　　　　　　　　　　**Map** *5 A3*

Hollow tree trunks, twinkling fairy lights and trickling streams give this unusual bar a fairytale feel. More of a place for drinks than coffees, it is a must for barflies. Relax and enjoy their selection of cocktails, wine and beer, as well as delicious coffee concoctions.

El Xampanyet
€

C/Montcada 22, 08003 **Tel** *93 319 70 03*　　　　　　　　　　　　　　**Map** *5 B3*

This tiny, tiled bar is beloved by Barcelona residents for its cheap glasses of the Catalan champagne, as well as its excellent *montaditos* (little sandwiches) and tapas. Seating room is limited and the bar gets rammed, but no trip to Barcelona is complete without it. Closed Sun dinner, Mon; Aug.

Escribà
€

La Rambla 83, 08002 **Tel** *93 301 60 27*　　　　　　　　　　　　　　　**Map** *5 A3*

Situated in a whimsical, multi-coloured Modernista building on the southern edge of the Boquería market, this famed coffee shop is a Barcelona institution and one of the best patisseries in town (they made the wedding cake for a princess' wedding). It's a great place for an atmospheric pick-me-up after a morning spent exploring the stalls.

La Granja
€

C/Banys Nous 4, 08002 **Tel** *93 302 69 75*　　　　　　　　　　　　　　**Map** *5 A2*

A very bohemian place. Also called La Vaca Lechera (the dairy cow), this is a gorgeously old-fashioned dairy with cream coloured walls, faded photographs and antique dairy equipment. Thick, custardy hot chocolate is the speciality here. Perfect for chilly winter mornings. Closed Sun morning.

Key to Symbols *see back cover flap*

Marsella

C/Sant Pau 65, 08001 **Tel** 93 442 72 63   *Map 2 E3*

One of the oldest bars in the Barri Xino, the lower part of the Raval, once notorious for its unsavoury characters and prostitutes, it retains a ravaged charm. Dusty chandeliers and ancient wine bottles evoke a convivial atmosphere where the drink of choice is the little green fairy (absinthe). They do not serve food here. Open nights only.

Ginger

C/Palma de Sant Just 1, 08002 **Tel** 93 310 53 09   *Map 5 B3*

The folks at Ginger have hit on an inspired formula for their multi-levelled space. There's a wine bar at one end, cocktails at the other with banks of soft, squishy armchairs in between. Combined with low lighting, mellow jazz grooves and delectable tapas, it's easy to spend an entire evening here. Closed Sun, Mon.

Luz de Gas – Port Vell

Moll del Dipòsit s/n, 08039 **Tel** 93 209 77 11   *Map 5 B4*

This double-decked boat must be one of the most desirable summer haunts in all of Barcelona. Situated on the edge of the Port Vell harbour, alongside other gin palaces and luxury yachts, it's fabulous for people-watching over a cool, iced *cava*. They also serve tapas. Open Mar–Oct.

Va de Vi

C/Banys Vells 16, 08003 **Tel** 93 319 29 00   *Map 5 B2*

With its stone archways, slate-tiled floors and beaten wooden dining tables, this bar has buckets of atmosphere to add to a cellar that stocks more than 4,000 bottles of wine, *cava* and liqueurs. It's also a good place to try different Spanish cheeses and *charcuterie*. Perfect for a late-night supper. Opens daily at 6pm.

EIXAMPLE

Cacao Sampaka

C/Consell de Cent 292, 08007 **Tel** 93 272 08 33   *Map 3 A4*

The chocolate emporium of Albert Adrià (master-chef Ferran Adrià's brother), this is a must for chocolate addicts. Choose from bonbons made from cocoa beans from different parts of South America, flower, fruit or spice concoctions, and more bizarre flavours such as anchovy and black olive. (See p156). Closed Sun, Aug morning.

Laie Llibreria Cafè

C/Pau Claris 85, 08010 **Tel** 93 302 73 10   *Map 3 B3*

A stylish book shop-cum-café very close to the Plaça de Catalunya, this is a good spot to mull over your purchase with a cup of gourmet coffee. It also has a pretty interior terrace and offers a good fixed-price lunch menu and light meals until 9:30pm. Free Wi-fi. Closed Sun.

MONTJUÏC

Quimet i Quimet

C/Poeta Cabanyes 25, 08004 **Tel** 93 442 31 42   *Map 2 D3*

Widely regarded as Barcelona's finest tapas bar, Quimet i Quimet is a cramped and tiny bodega with bottles displayed up to the ceiling and heaps of charm. The speciality is *montaditos* – delicious combinations mounted on bread. Be warned there is nowhere to sit and queues can spill onto the pavement. Closed Sun; Aug.

FURTHER AFIELD

GRÀCIA Cafè del Sol

Plaça del Sol 16, 08012 **Tel** 93 415 56 63   *Map 3 B1*

One of Gràcia's most famous cafés, it used to be run by Señor Ramón, a passionate pianist. He died some years ago but his piano still dominates one corner of the room though it is never played. Instead, the stereo plays an eclectic mix of rock, punk, reggae and blues for music lovers. They also serve tapas.

TIBIDABO Mirabé

C/Manuel Arnús 2, 08035 **Tel** 93 434 00 35

An elegant lounge bar situated just where the funicular leaves for Tibidabo, the floor-to-ceiling windows offer fantastic views of the city, while the sprawling terraced gardens are idyllic for drinks in the spring and summer. They do not serve food.

SHOPPING IN BARCELONA

Barcelona is sophisticated, stylish and neatly divided into distinctive shopping districts – Passeig de Gràcia for chi-chi designer stores, the Barri Gòtic for more eclectic antiques and boutiques, El Born for serious fashion divas, and El Raval for markets and museum shops. Though these rules are by no means fixed, they do provide a useful rule of thumb and help define the city, when time is

A Modernista shop window

limited. All shops are closed on Sunday. There are food markets as well – 44 in all – for every *barrio*, and a scattering of flea markets such as the Parisian-style Els Encants and the antiques fair in Sant Cugat, which has a more Provençal flavour. A convenient way to tour Barcelona's shops and markets is by taxi or public transport. Even though there are many car parks in the city, there's little point in hiring a car.

Some of the beautifully displayed confectionery at Escribà

FOOD AND DRINK

Barcelona's pastry shops are sights in themselves and, with its displays of chocolate sculptures, no *pastisseria* is more enticing or spectacular than **Escribà**. Other food stores also have a great deal of character, none more so than **Colmado Quílez** in the Eixample. This wonderful old place stocks a huge range of hams, cheeses and preserves, in addition to a comprehensive selection of Spanish and foreign wines and spirits.

DEPARTMENT STORES AND 'GALERIES'

The branch of **El Corte Inglés**, Spain's largest department store chain, on Plaça Catalunya is a Barcelona landmark and a handy place to find everything under one roof, including plug adaptors and services like key-cutting. Other branches are located around the city. Barcelona's hypermarkets also sell a wide range of goods. As

they are on the outskirts of the city – south along the Gran Via towards the airport, and on the Avinguda Meridiana to the north – a car is the best way to reach them.

The *galeries* (fashion malls), built mostly during the affluent 1980s, are hugely popular. **Bulevard Rosa** has hundreds of stores selling clothes and accessories. **L'Illa** is a large, lively shopping mall containing chain stores as well as specialist retailers. **Maremagnum** has several shops and restaurants and is open daily including public holidays.

FASHION

International fashion labels are found alongside clothes by young designers on and around the Passeig de Gràcia. **Adolfo Domínguez** stocks classically styled clothes for men and women; **Armand Basi** sells quality leisure and sportswear; and discount designer fashion is available at

Betty B. Many stores offer traditional, fine-quality tailoring skills and **Calzados Solé**, which is situated in the Old Town, specializes in classic hand-made shoes and boots.

SPECIALITY STORES

A walk around Barcelona can reveal a wonderful choice of stores selling traditional craft items and handmade goods that in most places have now been largely replaced by the production line. **La Caixa de Fang** has a good variety of Catalan and Spanish ceramics, among them traditional Catalan cooking pots and colourful tiles. **L'Estanc** has everything for the smoker, including the best Havana cigars. **La Manual Alpargatera** is an old shoe store that specializes in Catalan-style espadrilles. These are handmade on the premises and come in all colours. The city's oldest store, **Cereria Subirà** (*see pp54–5*), sells candles in every imaginable form.

Menswear department in Adolfo Domínguez

DESIGN, ART AND ANTIQUES

If you are interested in modern design, or just looking for gifts, you should pay a visit to **Vinçon**, the city's famous design emporium. Situated in a Modernista townhouse on the Passeig de Gràcia, it has everything for the home, including beautiful fabrics and furniture. Another good place to find contemporary interior design is **Pilma**, which sells furniture, kitchen and bath-room accessories, upholstery, carpets, curtains, paintings and lighting from both local and international designers and architects.

Most of the commercial art and print galleries are found on Carrer Consell de Cent, in

Mouthwatering fruit stalls in La Boqueria market

The stylishly sparse display of furniture at Vinçon

the Eixample, while the Barri Gòtic – especially the Carrer de la Palla and Carrer del Pi – is the best place to browse around small but fascinating antiques shops. As well as fine furniture and old dolls, **L'Arca de l'Àvia** sells antique silks and lace, all of which are set out in pretty displays.

BOOKS AND NEWSPAPERS

Most city-centre newsstands sell English-language news-papers, but the best stocks of foreign papers and magazines are at FNAC at **L'Illa** and Plaça Catalunya. **Come In** is an English bookshop that also sells DVDs and board games.

MARKETS

No-one should miss the chance to look around **La Boqueria** on La Rambla, one of the most spectacular food markets in Europe. Antiques are sold in the Plaça Nova on Thursdays, and cheese, honey and sweets in the Plaça del Pi on the last Saturday and Sunday of each month from October to May. On Sunday mornings coin and stamp stalls are set up in the Plaça Reial. The city's tra-ditional flea market, **Encants Vells** *(see p99)*, takes place on Mondays, Wednesdays, Fridays and Saturdays just north of the Plaça de les Glòries Catalanes.

DIRECTORY

FOOD AND DRINK

Colmado Quílez
Rambla de Catalunya 63.
Map 3 A4.
Tel 93 215 23 56.

Escribà Pastisseries
La Rambla 83. **Map** 2 F4.
Tel 93 301 60 27.

Gran Via de les Corts
Catalanes 546.
Map 2 E1.
Tel 93 454 75 35.

DEPARTMENT STORES AND 'GALERIES'

Bulevard Rosa
Passeig de Gràcia 55.
Map 3 A4.
Tel 93 215 83 31.

El Corte Inglés
Avinguda Diagonal 617–19.
Tel 93 366 71 00.

L'Illa
Avinguda Diagonal 545–57.
Tel 93 444 00 00.

Maremagnum
Moll d'Espanya.
www.maremagnum.es

FASHION

Adolfo Domínguez
P de Gràcia 89. **Map** 3 A3.
Tel 93 487 98 01.

Armand Basi
Passeig de Gràcia 49. **Map**
3 A3. **Tel** 93 215 14 21.

Betty B
C/ Rec, 58. **Map** 5 C3.

Calçats Solé
Carrer Ample 7. **Map** 5 A3.
Tel 93 301 69 84.

SPECIALITY STORES

La Caixa de Fang
C/ Freneria 1. **Map** 5 B2.
Tel 93 315 17 04.

Cereria Subirà
Bajada Llibreteria 7. **Map**
5 B2. **Tel** 93 315 26 06.

L'Estanc
Via Laietana 4. **Map** 5 B3.
Tel 93 310 10 34.

La Manual Alpargatera
C/ d'Avinyó 7. **Map** 5 A3.
Tel 93 301 01 72.

DESIGN, ART AND ANTIQUES

L'Arca de l'Àvia
Carrer dels Banys Nous 20.
Map 5 A2.
Tel 93 302 15 98.

Pilma
Avinguda Diagonal 403.
Map 3 A2.
Tel 93 416 13 99.

Vinçon
P de Gràcia 96. **Map** 3 B3.
Tel 93 215 60 50.

BOOKS AND NEWSPAPERS

Come In
C/Balmes 129. **Map** 3 A3.
Tel 93 453 12 04.

MARKETS

La Boqueria
La Rambla 101. **Map** 5 A2.

Encants Vells
C/ Dos de Maig, P de les
Glòries. **Map** 4 F5.

Food and Drink

Barcelonans are proud of their culinary heritage and rightly so. The land produces superlative fruit and vegetables, flavourful meats and an astonishing array of cheeses; the bounty of the sea offers daily fresh fish and seafood and the wine-growing regions of the Penedès and the Priorat make some of the best value vintages in the world. Less well known are the candy-makers, chocolate shops and *patisseries*, all of which add up to a complete and sophisticated cuisine that is fast becoming the envy of the world.

CHARCUTERIE, CHEESE AND DELICATESSENS

If you can't join them you can at least take some delicious treats home. Barcelona has several wonderful stores for stocking up on general goodies. The Boqueria, the city's most famous food market on La Rambla, is the obvious place to start, but if you prefer to shop without the hustle and bustle, head for one of the city's many specialist food shops.

Origins 99.9% in El Born specialises in strictly Catalan products – jars of small, dusky Arbequina olives, Sant Joan truffle-scented salt, oils and vinegars, home-made preserves and artisan *charcuterie*. Just around the corner, **La Botifarrería de Santa María** is great for artisan *charcuterie* and a lip-smacking array of home-made sausages in many intriguing flavours, such as pork and cuttlefish, beef and beetroot, lamb and wild mushroom. Then there's **Casa Gispert** for top-grade dried fruit and nuts as well as coffee, which is toasted in-house, and the fabulous **Formatgeria La Seu** (closed August). This is the only cheese shop in Spain that stocks exclusively Spanish and Catalan cheeses. Prowl around the walk-in dairy and choose from a great seasonal collection of cheeses made by small producers. These range from creamy Catalan goat's cheese, six-month old Manchegos to beech-smoked San Simóns, that come in the shape of a dunce's cap. A tasting of three cheeses and a

tumbler of wine is available for the very reasonable price of €2.50. Formatgeria La Seu's owner, Katherine McLaughlin, also stocks a small range of artisan olive oils.

For more general food products and quintessentially Spanish canned goods (many of which come in wonderful packaging), **Colmado Quílez** is a fascinating old place that stocks just about everything from saffron to ham and sauerkraut. Another interesting store in the Eixample is **Mantequeria Ravell**, Barcelona's first proper delicatessen. Its merchandise isn't strictly Spanish – there are plenty of Italian and French goods as well – but it does boast the best and most expensive of everything from pink Himalayan salt to explosive pickled *guindilla* peppers from the Basque country. Its restaurant on the first floor, incidentally, is pricey but sublime.

The **Herboristeria del Rei** isn't actually a food store, but it does contain a formidable array of medicinal herbs, teas and honeys. When it opened in 1823, Queen Isabel II decreed that it be supplier to the royal household and the handsome marble fountain that contains a bust of Linneo, the botanist and famous herbalist, was where the leeches were kept.

CHOCOLATE AND CANDIES

Swanky chocolate and cake shops proliferate mainly in the Eixample, with the exception of **Xocoa**, which has branches all over the city,

including one in El Born and one in the Barri Gòtic. This is the trendiest of the chocolate-makers in the city, with its retro packaging and fun shapes, including chocolate CDs and giant keys. **Escribà Pastisseries** is more extravagant, sculpting magnificent cakes, pastries and life-size chocolate models of famous personalities. The most gourmet chocolate-maker however, is **Enric Rovira**. Although a little off the beaten path, it is worth the journey and effort to see his amazing chocolate re-creations of Gaudí's trademark *rajoles* paving stones and chocolate gift sets designed by well-known Catalan artists. **Cacao Sampaka** is the sweet shop owned by Albert Adrià (Ferran Adrià's brother) and offers amazing off-the-wall fillings of anchovy, black olive and blue cheese as well as the more traditional herb, spice and floral flavours.

Those looking to take home more traditionally Spanish sweets try **Antiga Casa Mauri** for thick bricks of *turrón* (Catalan nougat and almond pastes) and **Caelum** for convent-made sweetmeats such as *yemas* (sweetened egg yolks) and *mazapans* (marzipan treats). Award-winning patissier Carles Mampel creates spectacular cakes, desserts and *petit fours* at **Bubó**. They can be taken away or enjoyed at the adjoining café.

In **Papabubble**, a gorgeous wood-panelled, marble-tiled shop, you can still occasionally see the sweets being made.

BAKERIES AND PATISSERIES

Almost every street in the city features its very own *panadería*. Usually open all day, these shops are busiest early in the morning and at around 5pm, snack-time in Spain, when you will often find mothers indulging their kids with after-school treats.

Amongst the best of these shops is **Cusachs**, open since

1963 and still producing the traditional Catalan *coques*. These can either be sweet or savoury and are mostly eaten on 23 June, the Sant Joan festival *(see p35)* and the longest day of the year.

Another great *panadería* is **Foix de Sarriá** on Major de Sarriá, very well known for its excellent pastries and other baked goods. Amongst its specialities are "royal cake", *sachertorte panellets* (round marzipan cakes), *pasta de té* (fruit biscuits) and *saras* (sponge cake covered with butter cream and almonds).

For the best breads in town, visit **Barcelona Reykjavic**, which sells artisan, organic and wholegrain breads. Delicious homemade cakes and pizzas are also available, and all products are baked on the premises.

WINE AND CIGARS

For sheer scope you can't beat **Lavinia**, the biggest wine shop in Spain, with branches in Madrid as well as in Paris, which stocks thousands of labels from all over the world. Choice comes at a price, however, and you will get better deals downtown. In El Born, **Vila Viniteca** sells a formidable range of Spanish and Catalan wines ranging from cheap, cheerful table wines for around €3 a bottle, to decadently expensive Priorats and Riojas that retail in the region of €300. Last, but by no means least, to leave Barcelona without a bottle of the nation's beloved Catalan champagne *(cava)* would be verging on the sacrilegious. You can buy it everywhere, but for something truly special head for **Xampany**, which specialises in artisan *cavas* from the Penedès wine-producing region. The ultimate place for cigar-lovers and pipe smokers is **Gimeno**. This legendary purveyor of all things tobacco-related also stocks a fine range of Cuban havanas.

DIRECTORY

CHARCUTERIE, CHEESE AND DELICATESSENS

La Botifarrería de Santa María
Carrer Santa María 4. **Map** 5 B3.
Tel 93 319 97 84.

Casa Gispert
C/Sombrerers 23, Born.
Map 5 B3.
Tel 93 319 75 35.

Colmado Quílez
Rambla de Catalunya 63, Eixample.
Map 3 A3.
Tel 93 215 23 56.

Formatgeria La Seu
C/Dagueria 16, Barri Gòtic. **Map** 5 A2.
Tel 93 412 65 48.

Herboristeria del Rei
C/ del Vidre 1, Barri Gòtic. **Map** 5 A2.
Tel 93 318 05 12.

Mantequeria Ravell
C/Arago 313.
Map 3 A4.
Tel 93 457 51 14.

Origins 99.9%
C/Vidrieria 6-8, Born.
Tel 93 310 75 31.

CHOCOLATE AND CANDIES

Antiga Casa Mauri
C/Flassanders 32.
Map 5 C2.
Tel 93 310 04 58.

Bubó
C/Caputxes 10,
Map 5 A3.
Tel 93 268 72 24.

Cacao Sampaka
C/Consell de Cent 292, Eixample.
Map 3 A4.
Tel 93 272 08 33.

Caelum
C/Palla 8, Barri Gòtic.
Map 5 A2.
Tel 93 301 69 93.

Enric Rovira
Avinguda Josep Tarradellas 113, Eixample.
Tel 93 419 25 47.

Escribà Pastisseries
La Rambla 83, Barri Gòtic.
Map 5 A1.
Tel 93 301 60 27.

Papabubble
C/Ample 28, Barri Gòtic.
Map 5 A3.
Tel 93 268 86 25.

Xocoa
C/Vidreria 4, Born.
Map 5 B2.
Tel 93 319 79 05.
C/Princesa 10, Born.
Tel 93 319 66 40.
C/Petritxol 11–13.
Tel 93 301 11 97.

BAKERIES AND PATISSERIES

Barcelona Reykjavic
Doctor Dou 25.
Map 2 F2.
Tel 93 302 09 21.

Cusachs
Bailén 223, Eixample
Map 3 C2.
Tel 93 213 77 29.

Foix de Sarriá
Major de Sarriá 57.
Tel 93 203 07 14.
Fax 93 280 65 56.

WINES AND CIGARS

Gimeno
La Rambla 100.
Map 5 A1.
Tel 93 318 49 47.

Lavinia
Av. Diagonal 605, Eixample.
Map 3 A2.
Tel 93 363 44 45.

Vila Viniteca
C/Agullers 7–9, Born.
Map 5 B3.
Tel 93 268 32 27.

Xampany
C/Valencia 200, Eixample.
Map 3 A4.
Tel 93 453 93 38.

Clothes and Accessories

The streets of Barcelona are paved with clothing outlets and dedicated followers of fashion may be surprised to learn that the city can hold its own against any in New York, London or Paris. With cutting-edge, home-grown Catalan designers such as Antonio Miró and Custo, high-street fashion chains such as Mango and Zara, and literally thousands of unique boutiques, Spanish fashion is currently one of the most exciting in the world.

JEWELLERY, BAGS AND ACCESSORIES

Bags, jewellery, hats and other baubles are essential to serious style divas and Barcelona has plenty of tiny, Aladdin's Cave-type shops to help create the perfect outfit. **Fet amb Love** (Made with Love) is a tiny shop in the Passeig del Born that sells colourful, handmade jewellery and accessories that the owners Ana and Carmen source from all over the world. They also sell their own designs, which include Japanese silk hairpins and party handbags. **Rafa Teja Atelier** makes exquisite embroidered jackets, patchwork scarves, appliqué handbags and hand-painted silk kerchiefs in sumptuous fabrics, textures and colours.

Take your own piece of Barcelona streetlife home – literally – with a **Demano** handbag from stockists all over town, including **Vinçon** (see p155) and **Iguapop Gallery**. These innovative designs have been produced in conjunction with designers Marcela Manrique, Liliana Andrade, Eleonora Parachini and the City Hall in an endeavour to recycle the waste material (polyester PVC) from banners and placards used to announce the cultural events in the city.

0,925 is housed in the stables of the 13th-century Palau Cerbelló, which also comprises part of the Museu Picasso. It sells a good range of unusual, hand-made jewellery in silver, gold, titanium and palladium created by 20 or so different Spanish and Catalan designers. Another good bet for unique pieces is **Hipòtesi**. Started a couple of decades ago, today the store has around 650 different designers on

their books and stocks mainly jewellery as well as scarves and bags in materials as diverse as buttons, zips and beads to white gold, wood and platinum. This is also a good place to check out the latest talent from the Massana School of Art.

SPANISH AND INTERNATIONAL DESIGNER LABELS

Josep Font, one of the most awarded Catalan designers, offers truly unique skirts, dresses and long-pants for the elegant female customer. El Born has plenty of stores selling a top range of designer labels, including **M69** for the boys with seasonal collections from Paul Smith, Bikkembergs and Vivienne Westwood among others.

Avenida Diagonal and the Passeig de Gràcia, however, are the true homes of fashionistas, with all the big labels such as **Chanel, Carolina Herrera, Gucci** and **Yves Saint Laurent** as well as **Loewe** for luxury luggage and **Pelleteria La Sibèria** for prêt-a-porter and custom-made designers in suede, nappa and fur.

SECOND HAND AND VINTAGE FASHION

Diminutive Carrer Riera Baixa in El Raval is Barcelona's answer to London's Carnaby Street with its own Saturday market (opening times, however, can be erratic) and several wonderful shops. The theatre-turned vintage shop, **Lailo**, sells anything from collectable costumes from the Liceu opera house and vintage dresses to 1950s bathing suits. Across the road is **Mies & Felj** which

specialises in more recent fashions dating from the 1960s and 70s as well as brightly-patterned curtains, fur-lined leather jackets, Chinese dresses and other items such as vintage sportswear.

HIGH STREET AND SPORTS FASHION

Ubiquitous Spanish fashion houses **Zara** and **Mango** have stores all over town. Both flagships are on the Passeig de Gràcia and they are great for good value basics, workwear and fashionable party dresses. Both also offer a decent range of menswear. For slightly more upmarket tastes both **Massimo Dutti** and **Adolfo Domínguez** are reliable suppliers of more classical tailoring, smart casuals and practical items such as ties and belts.

More individual fashion is best sought out in the smaller, independent shops of El Born and the Barri Gòtic. Carrer d'Avinyo in the Old Town inspired the young Picasso to paint and today's hip young things to shop. A lively street with a market ambience, it is particularly good for independent clothing stores and essential sportswear – Adidas, Puma and Nike. For gorgeous, original women's clothes and footwear by Spanish designers, try **Como Agua de Mayo**. The designs are feminine and floaty yet supremely stylish and contemporary. **Desigual** is good for urban casuals, while **Doshaburi** stocks the largest selection of vintage Levis in Spain as well as the more quirky Japanese labels. **Custo**, the most famous of Barcelona's local designers, has two shops in the old city, both are piled high with his trademark brightly printed T-shirts and mismatched coats and skirts.

Finally, football fans can head for FC Barcelona's official stores, the **Botiga del Barça**. They stock all kinds of merchandise related to the sport, including stripes, carves, boots and balls.

HATS AND SHOES

Patterned leather shoes and decorative soles from the cult Mallorcan shoe-maker **Camper** can be purchased for around 25 per cent less in Barcelona than other places in Spain. **La Manual Alpargatera** is another cult classic, beloved by *sardana* dancers (Catalonia's national dance) and celebrities alike for his exquisite hand-made, individually fitted espadrilles and straw hats. Another shop, **Casas Sabaters**, has several branches around town, all offering a top quality range of leading Spanish footwear brands. They are also good for last-minute sale items and last-season's knock-offs. **Muxart** is a Barcelona-based local brand that only sells at its own stores. It sells some of the most amazing, original and pricey shoes, handcrafted from the finest materials and in a wide choice of colours. **Vialis** is another local brand, the first shop opening in El Born in 1998. The shoes are unusual, beautifully made and very comfortable. The collection of trainers is also popular. The old-fashioned hat shop **Sombrereria Obach** sells all the classics ranging from Basque berets to stetsons, trilbys and hand-woven Montecristi Panamas.

DIRECTORY

JEWELLERY, BAGS AND ACCESSORIES

0,925
C/ Montcada 25,
Born.
Map 5 B3.
Tel 93 319 43 18.
www.albertolobo.com

Demano
Pallars 94, 7, 1a.
Map 6 E2.
Tel 93 300 4807.
http://demano.net

Fet amb Love
Passeig del Born 2,
Born.
Map 5 B3.
Tel 93 319 66 42.

Hipòtesi
Rambla de
Catalunya 105,
Eixample.
Map 3 A3.
Tel 93 215 02 98.

Rafa Teja Atelier
C/Sta. Maria 18,
Born.
Map 5 B3.
Tel 93 310 27 85.

SPANISH AND INTERNATIONAL DESIGNER LABELS

Carolina Herrera
Passeig de Gràcia 87,
Eixample.
Map 3 A3.
Tel 93 272 15 84.

Chanel
Passeig de Gràcia 70,
Eixample.
Map 3 A4.
Tel 93 488 29 23.

Gucci
Passeig de Gràcia 76,
Eixample.
Map 3 A3.
Tel 93 416 06 20.

Josep Font
C/ Provença, 304,
Eixample.
Map 3 A3.
Tel 93 487 21 10.

Loewe
Passeig de Gràcia 35.
Map 3 A4.
Tel 93 216 04 00.

M69
C/Rec 28. **Map** 5 C3.
Tel 93 310 42 36.
www.m69barcelona.com

Pelleteria La Sibèria
Rambla de Catalunya 15,
Eixample.
Map 3 A5.
Tel 93 317 05 83.

Yves Saint-Laurent
Passeig de Gràcia 102.
Map 3 A3.
Tel 93 200 39 55.

SECOND HAND AND VINTAGE FASHION

Lailo
C/Riera Baixa 20, El Raval.
Map 2 F2.
Tel 93 441 37 49.

Mies & Felj
C/Riera Baixa 4, El Raval.
Map 2 F2.
Tel 93 442 07 55.

HIGH STREET AND SPORTS FASHION

Adolfo Dominguez
Passeg de Gràcia 32,
Eixample.
Map 3 A5.
Tel 93 487 41 70.

Botiga del Barça
Maremàgnum
(Moll d'Espanya).
Map 5 A4.
Tel 93 225 80 45.

Como Agua de Mayo
C/Argenteria 43.
Map 5 B3.
Tel 93 310 64 41.

Custo
Plaça de les Olles 7.
Map 5 B3.
Tel 93 268 78 93.

Desigual
C/Argenteria 65,
Born.
Map 5 B2.
Tel 93 310 30 15.

Doshaburi
C/Lledó 4-6,
Barri Gòtic.
Map 2 F2.
Tel 93 319 96 29.
www.doshaburi.com

Mango
Passeig de Gràcia 65.
Map 3 A4.
Tel 93 215 75 30.

Massimo Dutti
Passeig de Gràcia (corner Gran Via), Eixample.
Map 3 A5.
Tel 93 412 01 05.

Zara
Passeig de Gràcia 16,
Eixample.
Map 3 A5.
Tel 93 318 76 75.

HATS AND SHOES

Camper
Plaça Àngels con
C/Elizabets,
El Raval.
Map 2 F2.
Tel 93 342 41 41.

Casas Sabaters
C/Portaferrissa 25.
Map 5 A2.
Tel 93 302 11 32.

La Manual Alpargatera
C/D'Avinyó 7,
Barri Gòtic.
Map 5 A3.
Tel 93 301 01 72.

Muxart
Rambla de Catalunya 47.
Map 3 A5.
Tel 93 467 74 23.

Sombrereria Obach
Carrer del Call 2.
Barri Gòtic.
Map 5 A2.
Tel 93 318 40 94.

Vialis
C/Vidrieria 15.
Map 5 B3.
Tel 93 313 94 91.

Speciality Stores

Part of the fun of getting to know Barcelona is to meander through the Old Town's rabbit-warren-like streets, or to explore the wide boulevards of the Eixample. Both the areas have a wonderful choice of stores selling traditional crafts and hand-made goods that in many places have been replaced by the production line. The endless array of shops are a dazzling sight in themselves and even if you are just window-shopping, it's well worth taking a proper look around to see the merchandise on offer.

ART AND ANTIQUES

Antiques aficionados and collectors will be richly rewarded by what Barcelona has to offer. The equivalent of an antiques shopping mall, **Bulevard dels Antiquaris** is home to over 70 shops brimming over with relics from the past. These can range from ancient coins and alabaster statues to tin drums, Regency-period candelabras and assorted bric-a-brac. Carrer del Call, the old Jewish quarter in the Barri Gòtic, is another hub for collectors with plush shops, such as **L'Arca de l'Àvia**, which sells antique lace and linens, old dolls and fine furniture, **Heritage**, a purveyor of semi-precious stone jewellery, antique silks and textiles and the odd mink stole, and **Gemma Povo** for decorative antique iron work. Also check out several shops belonging to **Artur Ramon** on Carrer de la Palla (all bear his name) for 18th- and 19th-century glassware and ceramics and paintings dating back to the 14th century. **Tandem** specialises in a wonderful range of tawny, old globes.

Barcelona's oldest and most prestigious art gallery is **Sala Parés**, which exhibits serious Catalan artists, both past and present. For keepsake wall hangings that won't break the bank, try the **Boutique Galería Picasso** for prints, lithographs, posters and postcards by the great Spanish masters, Miró, Picasso and Dalí. **Espai Ras** is a gallery space that houses architecture, contemporary art, video installations and graphic design exhibitions. There is also a comprehensive bookshop to browse through.

BOOKS, MUSIC, DVDS AND STATIONERY

Barcelona is a wonderful city for unearthing intriguing knick-knacks and unique, one-of-a-kind gifts that people will treasure forever. **Papirvm** is an old fashioned stationery store, piled high with beautiful fountain pens, leather-bound and William Morris print notepads, and even feather quills as well as retro Boqueria waiters pads. **Altaïr** is arguably Spain's finest specialist travel bookshop stocking a stupendous range of armchair reads, maps, travel guides and coffee-table books for anyone who lives and loves to move. But if you're just looking for some holiday reading try the **Casa del Llibre**, Barcelona's biggest bookstore for English language novels, magazines, travel guides, maps and glossy coffee-table books.

Thanks to the wide influence of Barcelona's annual electronic music festival, Sónar (*see p163*), the city has become a hot spot for music collectors. **Wah Wah Records** and El Raval in general are good for stocking up on the latest club tunes and old vinyl, while **Herrera Guitars** is a safe bet for anyone in the market for a hand-made classical Spanish guitar. Commissions are accepted.

UNUSUAL GIFTS AND KNICK-KNACKS

El Born and the Barri Gòtic are treasure troves, at once delightful and inspiring. **Sabater Hnos. Fábrica de Jabones** sells homemade soaps, which come in all shapes and smells, from traditional lavender to delicious chocolate. **Natura** is ideal for cheap and chic presents such as groovy candy-striped socks, duvet slippers, Chinese-style notepads and other Oriental toys and trinkets. For the Don Juan in your life, **La Condonería** (the condom emporium) stocks all manner of rubber delights in every shape, size, colour and flavour imaginable. **Cereria Subirà** is a gorgeous shop, and the city's oldest, dating back to 1761. Today, it sells a phenomenal array of decorative and votive candles in numerous shapes and sizes, including some several feet tall for dramatic effect. **El Rei de la Màgia** is another golden-oldie, founded in 1881. It reveals a world of fairytale magic for budding magicians. Nearby, **Arlequí Màscares** creates traditional hand-painted folk masks out of papier-mâché, including Italian Commedia dell'arte masks, glossy French party masks, grotesque Catalan *gigantes* (giant heads used in local festivals), Greek tragedy and Japanese Noh masks.

LINGERIE AND PERFUMES

The French chain **Sephora** stocks a wide selection of brand-name perfumes and cosmetics, often cheaper than those at the airport. **La Galería de Santa María Novella** is the Barcelona outlet of the famous, luxury apothecary in Florence, which has produced artisan perfumes and colognes since 1400. Customers are captivated by the scent of flowers, spices and fruits as they enter the store. The shop also sells cosmetics and herbal remedies. This kind of luxury does not come cheap, however.

Le Boudoir is decked out like an 18th-century love nest complete with brass bed, gilded mirrors, velvet drapery and love poetry inscribed on the walls. It is also the sexiest shop in Barcelona for lace and silk lingerie, nightgowns, fluffy mules and furry handcuffs as well as tasteful sex toys and aphrodisiacs.

For more conventional underwear, the quality Spanish chain **Women's Secret** goes in for a funky line of candy-coloured bra and pants sets, swimwear and hip pyjamas.

INTERIORS

L'Appartement is an eclectic gallery and shop that exhibits and sells furniture ranging from funky lamps to cool folding armchairs. The Zara brand started **Zara Home** with four basic styles in its collection: classic, ethnic, contemporary and white, all at very reasonable prices. **Wa Was**, on the other hand, is more quirky, stocking neon-coloured lamps, decorative objects and cooking tools. They also sell original postcards of Barcelona. Fans of gizmos and gadgets will enjoy **Vinçon**. This is the mecca of Barcelona's design stores. Housed in a 1900 upper-class apartment, its vast space is filled with everything from French Le Creuset cookware to Basque *chiquito* straight-edged tumblers, silk bean bags and futons. The old-fashioned clientele is more inclined towards **Coses de Casa**. This is a superb place for handmade patchwork quilts, feminine rosebud prints and Laura Ashley-style floral designs for lovers of chintz.

DIRECTORY

ART AND ANTIQUES

L'Arca de L'Àvia
C/Banys Nous 20,
Barri Gòtic.
Map 5 A2.
Tel 93 302 15 98.

Artur Ramon Col. leccionisme
C/Palla 23, Barri Gòtic.
Map 5 A2.
Tel 93 302 59 70.

Artur Ramon Antiquari
C/Palla 25, Barri Gòtic.
Map 5 A2.
Tel 93 302 59 70.

Artur Ramon Mestres Antics
C/Palla 10, Barri Gòtic.
Map 5 A2.
Tel 93 301 16 48.

Boutique Galería Picasso
Tapineria 10.
Map 5 B2.
Tel 93 310 49 57.

Bulevard dels Antiquaris
Passeig de Gràcia.
Map 3 A2–A5.
Tel 93 215 44 99.

Espai Ras
Doctor Dou 10.
Map 2 F2.
Tel 93 412 71 99.
www.rasbcn.com

Gemma Povo
C/Banys Nous 5,
Barri Gòtic.
Map 5 A2.
Tel 93 301 34 76.

Heritage
C/Banys Nous 14, Barri
Gòtic. **Map** 5 A2.
Tel 93 317 85 15. http://
heritagebarcelona.com

Sala Parés
C/Petritxol 5,
Barri Gòtic.
Map 5 A2.
Tel 93 318 70 20.

Tandem
C/Banys Nous 19,
Barri Gòtic.
Map 5 A2.
Tel 93 317 44 91.

BOOKS, MUSIC, DVDS AND STATIONERY

Altaïr
Gran Via 616,
Eixample.
Tel 93 342 71 71.
www.altair.es

Casa del Llibre
Passeig de Gràcia 62,
Eixample.
Map 3 A4.
Tel 93 272 34 80.

Herrera Guitars
C/Marlet 6,
Barri Gòtic.
Map 5 A2.
Tel 93 302 66 66.
www.herreraguitars.com

Papirvm
C/Baixada de la
Llibreteria 2,
Barri Gòtic.
Map 5 A2.
Tel 93 310 52 42.
www.papirum-bcn.com

Wah Wah Records
Riera Baixa 14,
El Raval.
Map 2 F2.
Tel 93 442 37 03.

UNUSUAL GIFTS AND KNICK-KNACKS

Arlequí Màscares
C/ Princesa 7.
Map 5 B2.
Tel 93 268 27 52.
www.arlequimask.com

Cereria Subirà
Baixada Llibreteria 7.
Map 5 A2.
Tel 93 315 26 06.

La Condonería
Plaça Sant Josep Oriol 7,
Barri Gòtic.
Map 5 A2.
Tel 93 302 77 21.

Natura
C/Argenteria 78,
Born.
Map 5 B2.
Tel 93 268 25 25.

El Rei de la Màgia
Carrer de la Princessa 11.
Map 5 B2.
Tel 93 319 39 20.

Sabater Hnos. Fábrica de Jabones
Pl. Sant Felip Neri 1,
Barri Gòtic.
Map 5 B2.
Tel 93 301 98 32.

LINGERIE AND PERFUMES

Le Boudoir
C/Canuda 21.
Map 5 A1.
Tel 93 302 52 81.
www.leboudoir.net

La Galería de Santa María de Novella
C/Espaseria 4. **Map** 5 B3.
Tel 93 268 02 37.

Regia
Passeig de Gràcia 39.
Map 3 A2–A5.
Tel 93 216 01 21.

Women's Secret
C/Portaferrissa 7, Barri
Gòtic. **Map** 5 A2.
Tel 93 318 92 42.

INTERIORS

L'Appartement
C/Enric Granados 44.
Map 3 A4.
Tel 93 452 29 04.

Coses de Casa
Plaça Sant Josep Oriol 5,
Barri Gòtic. **Map** 2 F2.
Tel 93 302 73 28.

Vinçon
Passeig de Gràcia 96.
Map 3 A3.
Tel 93 215 60 50.

Wa Was
Carders 14,
Born. **Map** 5 B3.
Tel 93 319 79 92.

Zara Home
Rambla de Catalunya 71.
Map 3 A4.
Tel 93 487 49 72.

ENTERTAINMENT IN BARCELONA

Barcelona has one of the most colourful and alternative live arts scenes in Europe, offering a smörgasbord of entertainment, from the gilded Liceu opera house and the spectacular Modernista masterpiece Palau de la Música Catalana, to small independent theatres hosting obscure Catalan comedies and dark Spanish dramas. But

Busker in the Barri Gòtic

there's also much to see simply by walking around. Street performance ranges from the human statues on La Rambla to excellent classical, ragtime and jazz buskers in the plazas. In addition, there are a series of weekend-long musical and arts fiestas that run throughout the year, many of which now attract an international audience of people from all over the world.

The magnificent interior of the Palau de la Música Catalana

ENTERTAINMENT GUIDES

The most complete guide to what's going on each week in Barcelona is *Guía del Ocio*, out every Thursday. The Friday *La Vanguardia* also has a good entertainment supplement, *Què Fem?*, and there is a weekly Catalan edition of *Time Out*.

SEASONS AND TICKETS

Theatre and concert seasons for the main venues run from September to June, with limited programmes at other times. The city's varied menu of entertainment reflects its rich multi-cultural artistic heritage. In summer the city hosts the Grec Festival de Barcelona *(see p35)*, a showcase of international music, theatre and dance, held at open-air venues. There is also a wide variety of concerts to choose from during September's Festa de la Mercè *(see p36)*. The simplest way to get

theatre and concert tickets is to buy them at the box office, although tickets for many theatres can also be bought from branches of the Caixa de Catalunya and La Caixa savings banks, or from Servi Caixa machines. The Ticket Ramblas central point in the Virreina Palace (Rambla 99) also offers 50 per cent discounted theatre tickets from 3 hours before the show. Grec festival tickets are sold at tourist offices.

FILM AND THEATRE

The **Mercat de les Flors** *(see p164)* is an exciting theatre which focusses on contemporary dance and theatre. The adjoining **Teatre Lliure** presents high-quality productions of classic and modern plays in Catalan. The new **Teatre Nacional de Catalunya** *(see p99)*, next to the Auditori de Barcelona, is another fine showcase for Catalan drama. The main venue for classical ballet is the **Liceu** opera house.

MUSIC

Barcelona's Modernista **Palau de la Música Catalana** *(see p63)* is one of the world's most beautiful concert halls, with its stunning interior decor and world-renowned acoustic. Also inspiring is the **L'Auditori de Barcelona** *(see p166)*, which gives the city two modern halls for large-scale and chamber concerts. Its reputation was considerably bolstered when it became the home of the Orquestra Simfònica de Barcelona.

The Liceu opera house, known for operatic excellence, came back from a fire that destroyed the building in 1994 and has been operating at full octave level ever since.

Big names like David Byrne and Paul McCartney have performed at **Razzmatazz** *(see p166)*. Jazz venues include the **Harlem Jazz Club** *(see p166)* and **Jamboree** *(see p166)*, and salsa fans will enjoy a quick slink down to **Antilla Barcelona**.

Outrageous stage show at one of Barcelona's many clubs

Auditorium of the Teatre Nacional de Catalunya

NIGHTLIFE

Among Barcelona's most famous modern sights are the hi-tech designer bars built in the prosperous 1980s, for example the **Mirablau**, which looks over the city. The **Torres de Àvila**, in the Poble Espanyol (*see p89*), is the height of post-Modernism. **Otto Zutz** has regular DJs and the less chic but still fun **Apolo** has live music. **Elephant** is located in a beautiful Modernista villa and attracts a fashionable crowd.

Two of the best-known bars are in the old city: **Boadas** for cocktails and **El Xampanyet**

(*see p152*) for sparkling wine and tapas. **El Bosc de les Fades** is the café of the wax museum and is imaginatively decorated like a fairy's woodland grotto.

FESTIVALS

During the summer, the streets are alive with outdoor festivals, performances and music. The **Festival del Sónar**, in June, began in an experimental manner as a place to showcase the latest musical talents of Southern European youth using new technologies. The **Clàssic als Parcs**, in June-July, is a good bet for a more serene entertainment.

AMUSEMENT PARK

In summer, Barcelona's giant amusement park on the summit of **Tibidabo** (*see p98*) is usually open till the early hours at weekends, but also busy on other days. It is even more fun if you travel there by tram, funicular or cable car.

SPORTS

The undoubted kings of sport in Catalonia are **FC Barcelona**, known as Barça. They have the largest football stadium in Europe, Camp Nou, and a fanatical following (*see p95*). Barcelona also has a high-ranking basketball team.

Packed house at the gigantic Camp Nou stadium

DIRECTORY

FILM AND THEATRE

Liceu
La Rambla 51–59. **Map 2**
F3. **Tel** 93 485 99 00.

Teatre Lliure
Passeig de Santa Madrona,
40–46. **Map 1** B3.
Tel 93 289 27 70.

Teatre Nacional de Catalunya
Plaça de les Arts 1. **Map 4**
F5. **Tel** 93 306 57 00.

MUSIC

L'Auditori de Barcelona
Carrer de Lepant 150. **Map**
6 E1. **Tel** 93 247 93 00.

Antilla Barcelona
Carrer de Aragó 141–143.
Tel 93 451 45 64.
www.antillasalsa.com

Palau de la Música Catalana
Carrer de Sant Pere Mès
Alt s/n. **Map 5** B1.
Tel 90 244 28 82.

NIGHTLIFE

Apolo
Carrer Nou de la
Rambla 113. **Map 2** E3.
Tel 93 441 40 01.
www.sala-apolo.com

Boadas
Carrer dels Tallers 1.
Map 5 A1.
Tel 93 318 88 26.

El Bosc de les Fades
Pasatge de la Banca.
Tel 93 317 26 49.

Elephant
Passeig dels Til.lers 1,
Tibidabo.
Tel 93 334 02 58.
www.elephantbcn.com

Mirablau
Plaça Doctor Andreu.
Tel 93 418 58 79.

Otto Zutz
Carrer de Lincoln 15.
Map 3 A1.
Tel 93 238 07 22.

Torres de Àvila
Poble Espanyol, Avinguda
del Marqués de Comillas.
Map 1 A1.
Tel 93 424 93 09.

El Xampanyet
Carrer Montcada 22.
Map 5 B2.
Tel 93 319 70 03.

FESTIVALS

Grec Festival de Barcelona
www.barcelonafestival.
com

Classic als Parcs
Information Parcs i Jardins
Tel 010 (from Barcelona).

Festival del Sónar
Palau de la Virreina.
www.sonar.es

ServiCaixa
Tel 90 233 22 11.
www.servicaixa.com

Telentrada
Tel 90 210 12 12.
www.telentrada.com

AMUSEMENT PARK

Tibidabo
Tel 93 211 79 42.

SPORTS

FC Barcelona
Camp Nou, Avinguda
Aristides Maillol.
Tel 93 496 36 00.

Film and Theatre

Large, multiscreen complexes as well as smaller, more intimate venues today screen a variety of films, catering to all tastes. As a result, Barcelona now hosts several film festivals through the year. Theatre, on the other hand, dates back to medieval times and the city's productions have evolved to become the most cutting-edge in Spain. Although language may be a problem, it's well worth seeing a theatrical production. If not, there are always many dinner-shows to interest non-purists.

FILM

Directors such as Alejandro Amenábar (*The Others*), Catalan writer and director Isabel Coixet (*My Life Without You*) and, of course, Spain's bad boy of film, Pedro Almodóvar (*All About My Mother, Bad Education, Volver*) have revitalised Spanish cinema. Today Barcelona itself has become the venue for independent film festivals and the biggest event of the year is the **Festival Internacional de Cinema de Catalunya**, held in Sitges in October.

Most Spanish cinemas dub films into Spanish or Catalan, but there are an increasing number of VO (original version) venues that screen not only Hollywood block-busters, but also film *noir* and independent art house movies. The **Centre de Cultura Contemporània (CCCB)** has provided a focal point for modern Barcelona since its opening in 1995, and, has played an integral part in the rejuvenation of El Raval. The CCCB serves as a crossroads of contemporary culture with cutting-edge art exhibits, lectures and film screenings.

Icària Yelmo Cineplex is the town's biggest multiscreen VO complex, built around an American-style mall with a number of fast-food eateries on the ground floor and shops on the first. Barcelona's biggest cinema, with a capacity of 1,832, is **Urgel** (all films here are shown in Spanish only, regardless of the original language). Featuring one of Europe's largest screens at over 200 sq m (518 sq km),

this is a great place to watch the latest releases. For something a bit more risqué, try the **Renoir Floridablanca**, a relatively new cinema on the edge of El Raval and the Eixample. It screens a range of European and international movies (subtitles are usually in Spanish or Catalan). In Gràcia, **Verdi** and **Verdi Park** are also good for more independent movie-making as well as an interesting selection of foreign films. They also occasionally have small, themed film festivals that include shorts by new local talent. During the summer, both the **Castell de Montjuïc** (*see p89*) and the **Piscina Bernat Picornell**, the Olympic swimming pool in Montjuïc, host a number of open-air cinema screenings.

The Catalan government's repertory cinema, the **Filmoteca de la Generalitat de Catalunya** (closed August), screens an excellent range of films over a period of two or three weeks before the schedule changes. The line-up encompasses anything from obscure, bleak Eastern European epics to up-beat modern musicals such as Baz Luhrmann's *Moulin Rouge*. The two-screen **Méliès** is a gem offering art-house mov-ies, Hollywood classics, B&W horrors and anything by Fellini or Alfred Hitchcock. **Casablanca** is a small cinema in Passeig de Gràcia showing new independent films from around the world in the original language and is quite a favourite with the local film buffs.

There are also an increasing number of small "bar-cinemas,"

where for the price of a beer you can watch a film on a small screen on a hardbacked school play-ground chair. For children, there is the **IMAX Port Vell**, which shows the usual 3-D roller-coaster knuckle-biters, Everest expeditions and squid entangled journeys to the bottom of the sea.

It's worth knowing that all cinemas have a *dia de l'espectador*, usually Monday night, when tickets are reduced. Weekend matinées are also usually cheaper.

THEATRE AND DANCE

Although English language productions are still in short supply, there are some rather good independent groups that perform at the **Llantiol Teatre** in El Raval. However, many Catalan and Spanish productions are well worth seeing, regardless of the language constraints. Theatre groups **Els Comediants** and **La Cubana**, in particular, offer a thrilling mélange of theatre, music, mime and elements from traditional Mediterranean fiestas. The tiny **Llantiol** stages a repertoire, that changes weekly, of alternative shows, comedy, magic and other off-the-cuff performances designed to attract a mixed crowd from the city's growing expatriate community to local arts lovers. Similarly, the **L'Antic Teatre**, on the other side of town, is a cultural centre and bar with a scruffy but pleasant summer roof-terrace and small vegetarian restaurant that hosts a number of alternative production companies, such as the Argentinian Company 4D Òptic. Also good for avant-garde performances and music is the **Mercat de les Flors**, a converted flower market in the Montjuïc. It is also host to a handful of different themed film festivals including a celebration of Asian film in the autumn.

La Rambla and Paral.lel are the main hubs of the city's bigger, more mainstream theatres. The **Teatre Tivoli** is a gargantuan theatre where high quality productions, dance and musical recitals by Catalan, Spanish and international stars are held. The **Teatre Poliorama** on La Rambla meanwhile goes more for musicals, occasional operas and flamenco performances three times a week. For serious theatre-lovers however, the **Teatre Nacional de Catalunya (TNC)** is an imposing columned affair designed by the Catalan architect Ricard Bofill, with state-of-the-art facilities and a weighty line-up of

Spanish and Catalan directors. The **Teatre Apolo** is good for big-bang musicals such as Queen's *We Will Rock You* and ABBA's *Mamma Mia*. Modern dance is much loved in Barcelona and there's no shortage of productions, often staged at the city's main theatres. The **Teatre Victòria** on Avinguda del Paral.lel is a reasonable bet for ballet and more classical dance productions, as is the Liceu opera house *(see p166)*.

Visitors who want to see flamenco *(see p167)* while in Barcelona can experience reasonably authentic renditions of the sexy, footstomping excitement of the *peñas* (folk bars) of Andalusia. However, if you do get a chance to see the

Catalan flamenco singer Mayte Martín, it's well worth snapping up tickets.

There are also a handful of places that put on a reasonable dinner and show for non-purists including **El Tablao de Carmen** *(see p167)*. **Los Tarantos** in Plaça Reial has daily flamenco concerts at affordable prices (usually less than €10).

Salsa, merengue and other sizzling Caribbean moves have a solid following with various clubs playing host to big name bands from New York, Puerto Rico and Cuba. Join the party (and take part in regular, free dance lessons) at **Antilla BCN Latin Club**, or, the **Buenavista Salsa Club** in Eixample.

DIRECTORY

FILM

Casablanca
Passeig de Gràcia 115, Eixample.
Map 3 A3.
Tel 93 218 43 45.

CCCB
C/Montalegre 5.
Map 2 F2.
Tel 93 306 41 00.
www.cccb.org

Festival Internacional de Cinema de Catalunya
Sitges.
Tel 938 94 99 90.
www.cinemasitges.com

Filmoteca de la Generalitat de Catalunya
Avda Sarrià 31–33, Eixample.
Tel 93 410 75 90.

Icària Yelmo Cineplex
C/Salvador Espriu 61, vila Olímpica.
Map 6 E4.
Tel 93 221 75 85.
www.yelmocineplex.es

IMAX Port Vell
Moll d'Espanya, Port Vell.
Tel 93 225 11 11.
www.imaxportvell.com

Méliès
C/Villarroel 102, Eixample. **Map** 2 E1.
Tel 93 451 00 51.

Piscina Bernat Picornell
Av. de l'Estadi 30–38.
Map 1 A3.
Tel 93 423 40 41.
www.picornell.cat

Renoir Floridablanca
C/Floridablanca 135, Eixample.
Map 1 C1.
Tel 93 426 33 37.
www.cinesrenoir.com

Urgel
Comte d'Urgell 29.
Map 2 E1.
Tel 90 242 42 43.

Verdi
C/Verdi 32, Gràcia.
Map 3 B1.
Tel 93 238 79 90.
www.cines-verdi.com

Verdi Park
C/Torrijos 49, Gràcia.
Map 3 C2.
Tel 93 238 79 90.

THEATRE AND DANCE

L'Antic Teatre
C/Verdaguer i Callís 12, La Ribera. **Map** 5 A1.
Tel 93 315 23 54.
www.lanticteatre.com

Antilla BCN Latin Club
C/Aragó 141, Eixample.
Map 3 A4. *Tel 93 451 45 64.* **www**.antillasalsa.com

Buenavista Salsa Club
C/Rosselló 217, Eixample.
Map 3 A3.
Tel 93 237 65 28.
www.salsabuenavista.com

Gran Teatre del Liceu (Opera House)
La Rambla 51–59.
Map 5 A1.
Tel 93 485 99 00.
www.liceubarcelona.com

Llantiol
C/Riereta 7, El Raval.
Map 2 E2.
Tel 93 329 90 09.
www.llantiol.com

Los Tarantos
Plaça Reial 17.
Map 5 A3.
Tel 93 319 17 89.

Mercat de les Flors
C/de Lleida 59.
Map 1 B2.
Tel 93 426 18 75.
www.mercatflors.org

Teatre Apolo
Av del Paral.lel 59.
Map 1 B1.
Tel 93 441 90 07.

Teatre Nacional de Catalunya (TNC)
Plaça de les Arts 1.
Map 6 F1.
Tel 93 306 57 00.
www.tnc.cat

Teatre Poliorama
La Rambla 115, Barri Gòtic. **Map** 5 A1.
Tel 93 317 75 99.
www.teatrepoliorama.com

Teatre Tívoli
C/Casp 10–12, Eixample.
Map 3 B5.
Tel 93 412 20 63.

Teatre Victòria
Av del Paral.lel 67–69.
Map 1 B1.
Tel 93 329 91 89.
www.teatrevictoria.com

Music

Few cities in the world can match the eclectic range of Barcelona's music scene. Stunning world-class venues such as Palau de la Música and L'Auditori de Barcelona play host to mega-stars, while smaller jazz rooms attract smouldering songsters. Then there are also the underground dives for the best in experimental electronica as well as the dusty, dimly-lit flamenco folk clubs. Traditional Catalan music and dancing (*sardanes*) can be heard in the Cathedral square most weekends.

OPERA AND CLASSICAL MUSIC

Opera and classical music are beloved by Catalans who lap it up with near religious reverence. Indeed, many of the great artists of the 20th century were locals, including the cellist Pablo Casals and opera singers José Carreras and Montserrat Caballé, who performed *Barcelona*, the dramatic operatic duet with the late Freddy Mercury.

The city is also home to some of the most spectacular venues in the world, including the glamorous, gilded **Gran Teatre del Liceu**, which first opened its doors in 1847. The opera house has been a continuing beacon of Catalan arts for more than a century and a half, with a rich and dramatic history of fire and bomb attacks. It burned down for the third time in 1994, but careful renovations have restored it to its former glory. Despite its misfortunes, it has sustained a stellar line-up of the greatest composers in the world, among them Puccini, Tchaikovsky and Diaghilev's Russian Ballets, as well as Catalan composers such as Pedrell, Vives and Enric Granados.

The whimsical fancy of the **Palau de la Música** is another of Barcelona's architectural triumphs. A jewel-bright vision by the Modernista master Lluís Domènech i Montaner, this sublime concert hall has a dedicated public, and performers who vie to play here. The Palau is the main venue for the city's jazz and guitar festivals and national and international symphony orchestras perform here regularly. Both of these venues can be visited on daytime guided tours, but booking tickets for a production is the best way to experience the atmosphere.

Modern, but no less important as a shrine to the Catalan arts scene, **L'Auditori de Barcelona** was built to accommodate growing demand for better facilities and to attract ever greater numbers of world class musicians. It began primarily as a place for classical concerts and orchestral recitals, but has since begun to embrace giants of jazz, pop and rock. It is also worth keeping your eyes peeled for regular choral music being performed at the city's churches and cathedrals, most notably the Iglesia Santa Maria del Pi, the main cathedral on Plaça del Pi, and the Iglesia Santa Maria del Mar, particularly around Christmas time and Easter.

LIVE MUSIC: ROCK, JAZZ AND BLUES

In terms of popular music Barcelona may not have the endless clubs, pubs, stadiums and music emporiums that make London the best place on the planet for live music, but it doesn't do too badly considering its size. The city attracts a star-studded cast that range from pop stars such as Kylie Minogue and Madonna to contemporary jazz prodigies such as the Brad Mehldau Quartet, hip-hoppers, rappers and world groove mixers, country and good old-fashioned rock and roll.

Barcelona still has a clutch of tiny, intimate venues. **Jamboree**, a cellar-like venue on Plaça Reial, attracts a number of jazz heavyweights as well as more experimental outfits and solo artists such as the saxophonist Billy McHenry. Another good bet is the **JazzSí Club Taller de Músics**, a more obscure destination but much beloved by aficionados of the genre. It doubles up as a jam session space for students from the nearby music school. The famous Cova del Drac closed down in 2004 and reopened a couple of years later as the **Jazz Room**. It functions largely as a dance club but there are usually a couple of live gigs every month. **Heligogàbal**, a small underground bar in Gràcia, also hosts jazz concerts.

Concerts are generally free, or very cheap. The **Harlem Jazz Club** is narrow, crowded and smoky but it's one of the city's longest surviving clubs for alternative and lesser-known jazz troupes. **Little Italy** is a boon for those who like the tinkle of the piano keyboard and the soft pluck of the double bass. Enjoy an eclectic mix of blues, jazz and bossa nova over dinner on Wednesdays and Thursdays. The most formal of the jazz venues, however, is Barcelona's "free" theatre – the **Teatre Lliure** in Montjuïc is an excellent source for contemporary jazz masters, modern orchestras and experimental grooves, playing host to a diverse number of musicians from Eric Mingus to The Sun Ra Arkestra directed by Marshall Allen. For lovers of the genre, this is the best of the lot.

One of the two major players for pop and rock maestros is **Bikini**, Barcelona's very own Studio 54 – in fact, it opened in 1953, preceding the New York icon by a year. This veteran of the scene, which opens from midnight onwards, is still going strong with a robust line-up of big name bands and a cocktail of different club nights. The other, **Razzmatazz**, arguably the city's most important live music venue, plays host to the likes of

Róisín Murphy, Arctic Monkeys, Air and Jarvis Cocker. Club sessions go until dawn in Lolita, The Loft and three other clubs next door. The Loft is a trendy club that also holds rock and jazz concerts several nights a week.

For a touch of unbeatable glam **Luz de Gas** is a glitzy ballroom that oozes old-fashioned atmosphere with its lamp-lit tables, chandeliers and a list of bands and shows that enjoyed their heyday in the 1970s and '80s. The biggest international stars – including Eric Clapton, Madonna, Beyoncé and Coldplay – take over the huge arenas on Montjuïc, the **Estadi Olímpic** and the **Palau Sant Jordi** *(see p89)*.

If your taste is for the small and subtle, the **Bar Pastis** is a miniscule bar, decorated with dusty bottles and yellowing posters from French musicals. Live French love ballads, tango and coplas can be heard here most nights of the week.

FLAMENCO

Although flamenco is traditionally an Andalusian artform, originally created by the gypsies of Southern Spain to depict their sufferings and hardship, it has for many years been a popular form of entertainment in Barcelona and throughout Spain. One of the best places to see a live show is **El Tablao de Carmen**, a stylish restaurant serving both Catalan and Andalucian dishes in the Poble Espanyol. The venue is named after Carmen Amaya, a famous dancer who performed for King Alfonso XIII in 1929, in the very spot where it now stands. Various dinner/show packages are available.

For a less formal ambience, **Los Tarantos**, situated in the Plaça Reial, is a lively atmospheric nightspot with live flamenco and Latin music every night of the week. Although it caters to the tourist trade, the performances are very reasonably priced.

JazzSí Club Taller de Músics *(see p166)* offers traditional flamenco concerts on Fridays, often accompanied by well-known guest musicians.

DIRECTORY

OPERA AND CLASSICAL MUSIC

L'Auditori de Barcelona
C/Lepant 150, Eixample.
Map 4 E1.
Tel 93 247 93 00.
www.auditori.com

Gran Teatre del Liceu
La Rambla 51,
Barri Gòtic.
Map 5 A1.
Tel 93 485 99 00.
www.liceubarcelona.com

Palau de la Música Catalana
C/Sant Pere Més Alt s/n,
La Ribera.
Map 5 B1.
Tel 902 442 882.
www.palaumusica.org

LIVE MUSIC: ROCK, JAZZ AND BLUES

Bar Pastis
C/Santa Mònica 4,
El Raval. **Map** 2 F4.
Tel 93 318 79 80.
www.barpastis.com

Bikini
Deu I Mata 105,
Les Corts.
Tel 93 322 08 00.
www.bikinibcn.com

Harlem Jazz Club
C/Comtessa de
Sobradiel 8,
Barri Gòtic.
Tel 93 310 07 55.
www.harlemjazzclub.es

Heliogàbal
Ramón y Cajal 80,
Gràcia.
Map 3 C2.
www.heliogabal.com

Jamboree
Plaça Reial 17,
Barri Gòtic.
Map 5 A3.
Tel 93 319 17 89.
www.masimas.com

Jazz Room
C/Vallmajor 33.
Tel 93 319 17 89.
www.masimas.com

JazzSí Club Taller de Músics
C/Requesens 2,
El Raval.
Tel 93 329 00 20.
www.tallerdemusics.com

Little Italy
C/Rec 30,
Born.
Map 5 C3.
Tel 93 319 79 73.

Luz de Gas
C/Muntaner 246,
Eixample.
Map 2 F1.
Tel 93 209 77 11.
www.luzdegas.com

Razzmatazz
C/Pamplona 88,
Poblenou.
Map 4 F5.
Tel 93 320 82 00.
www.salarazzmatazz.com

Teatre Lliure
Plaça Margarida Xirgu 1,
Tel 93 289 27 70.
www.teatrelliure.com

FLAMENCO

El Tablao de Carmen
Arcs, 9.
Poble Espanyol.
Map 1 B1.
Tel 933 25 68 95.
www.tablaodecarmen.com

Los Tarantos
Plaça Reial 17.
Map 5 A3.
Tel 933 19 17 89.

CONCERT VENUES

L'Auditori
C/Lepant 150.
Tel 93 247 93 00.
www.auditori.com

Espai Lliure
Plaça Margarida Xirgu 1,
Montjuïc.
Tel 93 289 27 70.

Sala Fabià Puigserver
Passeig Santa Madrona
40-46, Montjuïc.
Map 1 B3.
Tel 93 289 27 70.

Nightlife

If New York is the city that never sleeps, then Barcelona is the one that never goes to bed and those with energy can party around the clock, all week. It has one of the most varied scenes, with something for everybody. Old-fashioned dance halls rub shoulders with underground drum and bass clubs and trashy techno discos, and club-goers are either glammed-up or grunged-out. Each *barrio* (neighbourhood) offers a different flavour.

NIGHTLIFE

In the summer the beaches become party havens when the *xiringuitos* (beach bars) spring back into life. Wander from Platja de Sant Sebastià in Barceloneta, all the way to Bogatell (a few kilometres beyond the Hotel Arts) and you'll find people dancing barefoot on the sand to the tune of Barcelona's innumerable DJs. Way uptown (above the Diagonal), the city's most glamorous terraces morph into social hubs while the Barri Gòtic – lively at the best of times – becomes one massive street party throughout the summer. If you want to hang with the locals, the demolition of some of El Raval's less salubrious streets has meant that the neighbourhood has become much safer and easier to move about. The underground vibe, however, remains steadfastly intact with tiny hole-in-the-wall-style bars where folks drink and boogie till the early hours. Similarly, Gràcia has a bohemian, studenty ambience. If it's an alternative scene you seek Poble Sec has a handful of "ring-to-enter" joints and the city's only serious drum and bass club, **Plataforma**. The city also has a thriving and friendly gay scene, most notably within the Eixample Esquerra, also known as the Gay Eixample, boasting numerous late-night drinking holes, discothèques, saunas and cabarets.

BARRI GÒTIC

The Plaça Reial is overrun with tourists banging on tin drums and whooping it up, but if you're looking for more grown-up fun, check out the

Fantástico Club. Pop and electro music combined with candy-coloured decor make this club a hit with the fashionable crowd. Underground and cosmopolitan are words that best describe the atmosphere and clientele of **Club Fellini**, where eccentricity merges into the freakishly original. It has three rooms with different music and decor in each. The nightclub **New York**, in contrast, has come over all loungey and these days is inclined towards more commercially gratifying tunes. The vibe here is more disco.

EL RAVAL

Designer clubs proliferate in Barcelona these days, but check out the old-school ambience of **Marsella**, founded in 1820 and still famous for its wicked green absinthe *(absenta)*. The likes of Picasso, Hemingway and Miró are said to have drunk here and the 19th-century-styled interior, with marble tables, chandeliers and battered old mirrors evokes a bygone era. With its red, black and white decor and a specially-designed underlit bar, **Zentraus** is one of the best looking clubs in the neighbourhood. Doubling up as a restaurant until midnight or so, the tables are cleared away once the DJ sessions get underway. For the more adventurous, **Moog** is more extreme with blaring, heart-pumping techno for aficionados of the genre. The stark industrial interior gives it the character of a New York nightclub in the mid-1990s. Likewise, the state-of-the-art sound system ensures a thumping, ear-bleedingly good night out.

PORT VELL AND PORT OLÍMPIC

Beach parties aside, this area continues to be a hub for creatures of the night. The Port Olímpic itself is nothing but bars and boats, while the leisure and shopping complex **Maremagnum** has a clutch of elegant clubs. Under the Hotel Arts, **Catwalk** is still one of the only places in the city for hip hop and R'n'B. **C.D.L.C.** and nearby restaurant and lounge bar **Shôko**, in front of the Hotel Arts, however, still manage to draw the celebrities staying nearby.

EIXAMPLE

One of the city's best loved discos, **City Hall** is a multiple space and terrace, where you can pick and choose your groove according to your mood. It has different themes every night from Saturday night-fever discos to Sunday chill-outs. **Buda Barcelona** is quite literally oozing with glitz and glamour, beloved by models and their entourages. It is a place where anything goes, from dancing on the bar tops to dancing with your top off. For a more understated type of glamour, **Opium** is housed in a converted cinema and therefore bags the title for the best projections in town. **Dow Jones** has a unique "Stock Exchange" system for setting the prices of drinks, which rise and fall with demand. For sports fans they also offer Sky coverage.

POBLE SEC

The most alternative night-life has come to roost in the "dry village," though in name only. The bars are wet and the music is happening. **Apolo** is another old-fashioned music hall, though it attracts a more independent breed of DJ and performer. Expect anything here, from soulful gypsy folk singers from Marseille, to the legendary purveyor of deep funk, Keb Darge.

Further into the village, **Mau Mau** is an alternative club and cultural centre with a firm eye on what's new and happening. This could mean local DJs, Japanese musicians such as the cultish Cinema Dub Monks, alternative cinema, and multimedia art installations. If it's of the here and now, chances are Mau Mau's on it. For the seriously hardcore and lovers of high-speed garage, **Plataforma** is Barcelona's only serious drum and bass club, hosting DJs from far and wide in a huge concrete warehouse.

GRÀCIA AND TIBIDABO

Tiny and always packed, the **Mond Bar** attracts music-lovers from all over wishing to dip into tunes from the past. The resident DJs delight a 20-something crowd with 1970s sessions of northern soul and Motown. And high up above the rest, **Elephant** offers the best in mansion-house clubbing experiences, with chill-out lounges, two dance floors, a VIP area, sprawling terraces and prices to suit the altitude.

OUT OF TOWN

The mega-clubs are located well away from the city centre and from anyone trying to sleep, and most of them are only open on Friday and Saturday nights. The big boys are based in Poble Espanyol, where folks can party until the sunrise. **La Terrrazza,** is only open in the summer, but is well-known for its all-night rave parties under the stars, and takes its name from the giant terrace it occupies. Nearby, on Plaça Espanya, the Ibiza-style **Discothèque** is extremely popular. Don't even think about getting in without an appropriately glamorous outfit, and remember, less is most definitely more.

Further out of town you will find **Oshum**, the most sophisticated and innovative night club in the area. It also houses a restaurant and a lounge terrace, with an exquisite design. It tries to reproduce the Ibiza spirit. Alternatively, **Liquid** is the city's only summer club with a swimming pool. The only drawback is that should you wish to leave before the party's over, finding a taxi back into town can be a big problem.

DIRECTORY

BARRI GÒTIC

Club Fellini
La Rambla 27,
Barri Gòtic.
Map 2 F3.
Tel 93 272 49 80.
www.clubfellini.com

Fantástico Club
Passatge Escudellers 3,
Barri Gòtic.
Map 5 A3.
Tel 93 317 54 11.

New York
C/Escudellers 5,
Barri Gòtic.
Map 5 A3.
Tel 93 318 87 30.

EL RAVAL

Marsella
C/Sant Pau 65
El Raval.
Map 2 F3.
Tel 93 442 72 63.

Moog
C/Arc del Teatre 3,
El Raval. **Map** 2 F4.
Tel 93 319 17 89.
www.masimas.com

Zentraus
Rambla de Raval 41,
El Raval.
Map 2 F3.
Tel 93 443 80 78.
www.zentraus.com

PORT VELL AND PORT OLÌMPIC

Catwalk
Ramon Trias Fargas 2–4,
Port Olímpic. **Map** 6 E4.
Tel 93 224 07 40.
www.clubcatwalk.net

C.D.L.C.
Passeig Marítim 32,
Port Olímpic. **Map** 6 E4.
Tel 93 224 04 70.
www.cdlcbarcelona.com

Shôko
Passeig Marítim 36,
Port Olímpic. **Map** 6 E4.
Tel 93 225 92 00.
www.shoko.biz

EIXAMPLE

Buda Barcelona
C/Pau Claris 92, Eixample.
Map 3 B3. *Tel 93 318 42 52.* **www**.buda restaurante.com

City Hall
Rambla Catalunya 2–4,
Eixample. **Map** 3 A3.
Tel 93 317 21 77.
www.ottozutz.es

Dow Jones
Bruc 97, Eixample.
Map 3 B4.
Tel 93 207 60 45.

Opium
C/Paris 193, Eixample.
Tel 93 414 63 62. **www**.grupocostaeste.com

POBLE SEC

Apolo
C/Nou de la Rambla 113,
Poble Sec.
Map 2 D4.
Tel 93 441 40 01.
www.sala-apolo.com

Mau Mau
C/Fontrodona 33,
Poble Sec.
Map 2 D3.
Tel 93 441 80 15.
www.maumaunderground.com

Plataforma
C/Nou de la Rambla 145,
Poble Sec.
Map 2 D4.
Tel 93 329 00 29.

GRÀCIA AND TIBIDABO

Elephant
Passeig dels Til.lers 1,
Tibidabo.
Tel 93 203 75 46.
www.elephantbcn.com

Mond Bar
Plaza del Sol 21, Gràcia.
Map 3 B1.
Tel 93 272 09 10.

OUT OF TOWN

Discothèque
C/Tarragona 141–147.
Tel 90 202 38 65.
www.discotheque.info

La Terrrazza
Poble Espanyol, Avda
Marquès de Comillas.
Map 1 B1.
Tel 93 272 49 80.
http://laterrrazza.com

Liquid
Complex Esportiu
Hospitalet Nord, Av.
Manuel Azaña, Hospitalet.
www.liquidbcn.com

Oshum
Av. Doctor
Marañón 17.
Tel 93 118 86 01.
www.oshumclub.com

Sports and Outdoor Activities

From the mountains to the sea, Catalonia provides all manner of terrain for enjoying the outdoor life. The hot summer months can be filled with water activities, from fishing to white-water rafting, while skiers head for the hills with the first snowfalls of winter. Nature lovers will find spectacular wildlife habitats, while Barcelona city offers beaches and numerous sports facilities.

CITY FACILITIES

Barcelona has around 30 municipal pools *(piscines municipales)*, including the **Piscines Bernat Picornell** next to the **Estadi Olímpic** and **Palau Sant Jordi** sports stadia on Montjuïc. The pools were the venue for the 1992 Olympic swimming events. The Estadi Olímpic is an athletics stadium and is often used for concerts. The Palau Sant Jordi is used for indoor sports, as well as musical and recreational activities. Tennis fans are well provided for and the **Centre Municipal de Tennis Vall d'Hebron** caters for younger players too. Ice-skating can be fun and the **Pista de Gel del FC Barcelona** offers skate rental and runs an ice hockey school. Golf courses within easy reach of Barcelona are **Golf Sant Cugat** and **Golf El Prat**. There are several riding stables, and the **Escola Hípica** at Sant Cugat allows day outings over the Collserola hills. Cycle shops hire by the hour, half day and full day. **Bike Tours Barcelona** organizes cycle tours around Barcelona.

Griffon vulture

AIRBORNE ACTIVITIES

Catalonia has several small airports where planes can be hired and parachute jumps made. One of the best known flying clubs is **Aeroclub** in Sabadell. Paragliding is popular from any high spot and **Esports 10** offers all kinds of adventure sports, including bungee jumping and ballooning, as an exciting alternative way to see the sights.

BIRD WATCHING

Bird life in Catalonia is a huge attraction for dedicated bird-watchers. Northern European visitors in particular will be thrilled by the sight of hoopoes, bee-eaters, golden orioles and pratincoles. Two major wetland areas, where migratory birds include flamingoes, are **Delta de l'Ebre** *(see p129)*, south of Tarragona, with a visitor centre in Deltebre, and **Aiguamolls de l'Empordà** around Sant Pere Pescador in the Bay of Roses. Both are easy to get to, and their visitor centres supply binoculars and guide services.

The best times to visit are early morning and evening. The Pyrenees are home to many raptors, including short-toed, golden and Bonelli eagles, and Egyptian, griffon and bearded vultures. The **Parc Natural del Cadí-Moixeró** *(see p114)*, in the foothills of the Pyrenees, has a visitor centre in Bagà. Look out for alpine choughs, wallcreepers and peregrine falcons, as well as black woodpeckers in the wooded areas.

An angler's paradise – fishing for trout amid spectacular scenery

FIELD SPORTS

Sea fishing is free, but a permit *(un permís)* is required for river fishing. Permits can usually be obtained through local tourist offices.

The Noguera Pallaresa and Segre are fine trout fishing rivers and the season runs from mid-March to the end of August. The game-hunting season is generally from October to March. Short leases and permits can be obtained from the **Federació Catalana de Caça** in Barcelona or from a local hunting association *(associació de caça)*. Travel agents specializing in hunting and fishing breaks will also readily organize licences.

HIKING

All the national parks and reserves publish maps and walking suggestions. Good areas close to Barcelona are the Collserola hills and the chestnut woods of Montseny. Long-distance GR (*Gran Recorrido*) footpaths criss-cross Catalonia and the walking

Paragliding above the Vall d'Aran in the eastern Pyrenees

Shooting the rapids on the white waters of the Noguera Pallaresa

possibilities in the **Parc Nacional d'Aigüestortes** *(see p113)* and the Pyrenees are particularly good, with mountain refuges *(see p133)* for serious hikers. Walkers can obtain information from the **Centre Excursionista de Catalunya** *(see p133)*. The **Llibreria Quera**, in Carrer de Petritxol (No. 2) in Barcelona's Barri Gòtic, is the best bookshop for maps and guide books.

All the usual rules apply to those setting off to explore the wilderness – check weather forecasts, wear appropriate clothing, take adequate provisions and let someone know where you are going.

WATER SPORTS

There are around 40 marinas along Catalonia's 580 km (360 miles) of coast, and a very wide range of watersports and activities is available. In Barcelona itself, the **Centre Municipal de Vela Port Olímpic** gives sailing lessons and has a variety of craft. The Costa Brava has long been a good

spot for scuba diving. The best place is around the protected Illes Medes *(see p121)*, from the resort of L'Estartit. There are also diving schools around Cadaqués and Cap Begur, notably at Calella de Palafrugell, launching point for the Illes Ullastres.

The town of Sort on the Riu Noguera Pallaresa is a centre for exciting water sports such as white-water rafting, canoeing, kayaking and cave diving. Bookings for these and other adventure activities can be made through **Yetiemotions**.

WINTER SPORTS

The Pyrenees offer great winter skiing just two or three hours' drive from Barcelona and at weekends the resorts fill up with city crowds. There are some 20 ski areas. La Molina is good for beginners and Baqueira-Beret *(see p113)* is where Spain's royal family skis. Puigcerdà *(see p114)* in the Cerdanya is a good base for downhill and nordic skiing within reach of 15 ski stations in Catalonia, Andorra and France. The **Associació Catalana d'Estacions d'Esquí i Activitats de Muntanya (ACEM)** supplies resort details, while **Teletiempo**, a weather hotline, provides information on current weather conditions. In Barcelona, a dry ski slope has been installed beside the Piscines Bernat Picornell on Montjuïc.

Skiing at one of the many ski stations in the Pyrenees within easy reach of Barcelona

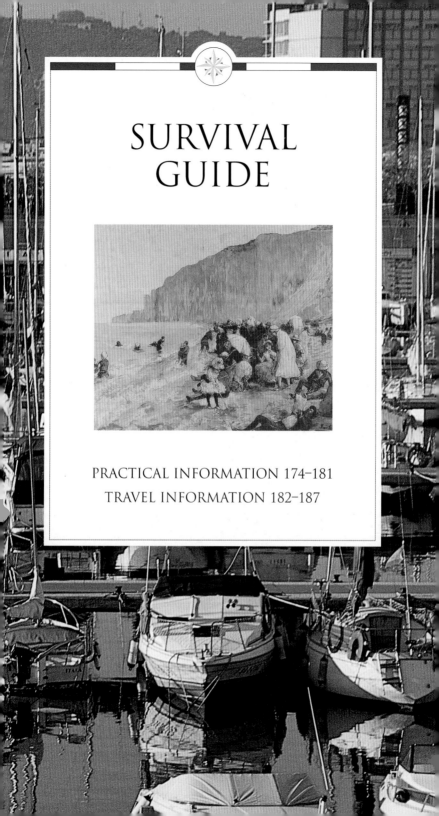

SURVIVAL
GUIDE

PRACTICAL INFORMATION

Catalonia has an excellent tourist infrastructure and offers visitors a wealth of options, from soaking in the sun on a sandy beach to hiking on a remote mountain trail. There are tourist offices in every town, which can assist in finding accommodation, restaurants and

Sign for a tourist office

activities. Larger offices usually have leaflets in several different languages. Be aware that August is Spain's main vacation month, and many businesses close for the whole month. Try to find out in advance if your visit coincides with local *festes* (fiestas), as these can entail widespread closures.

VISAS AND PASSPORTS

Spain is part of the Schengen common European border treaty. Visas are not currently required for citizens of the EU, Iceland, Liechtenstein, Norway, the USA, Canada, Australia or New Zealand. However it is best to check visa requirements before travelling. Spanish embassies supply a list of other countries in the non-visa category. Tourists from these countries may stay for 90 days within a continuous 180-day period. The *Oficina d'estrangers de Barcelona*, a local government office, handles visa extensions.

TAX-FREE GOODS AND CUSTOMS INFORMATION

Non-EU residents can reclaim IVA (VAT) on single items worth over €90 bought in shops displaying a "Tax-free Shopping" sign, within six months of purchase. (Food, drink, cars, motorbikes, tobacco and medicines are exempt.) You pay the full price and ask the sales assistant for a tax free cheque, which you then present to customs to be stamped as you leave Spain (do this before checking your bags). The refund is issued either on your credit card or in cash at La Caxia bank branches at Terminals 1 and 2 of Barcelona airport.

TOURIST INFORMATION

Barcelona has three main *oficines de turisme* providing information on city, its attractions, transport and places to stay and eat, all run by **Turisme de Barcelona**. A fourth office, in the Passeig de Gràcia and run by **Turisme de Catalunya**, a department of

the Generalitat (Catalonia's government), provides information on the rest of the region. Other major towns have their own tourist offices providing information published by the Generalitat and the province's local administration *(patronat)*. There are Spanish National Tourist Offices in the following English-speaking cities: New York, Chicago, Miami, Los Angeles, London and Toronto.

In Barcelona during the summer, pairs of young information officers, known as Red Jackets and generally English-speaking, provide tourist information in the streets of the Barri Gòtic, La Rambla and the Passeig de Gràcia.

Tourists consulting a map in Barcelona

SOCIAL CUSTOMS AND ETIQUETTE

Catalans are generally more reserved than other Spaniards, but they will greet strangers at bus stops, in lifts, in shops and in other public places. They shake hands and often kiss on both cheeks when introduced to strangers or when seeing friends or family.

LANGUAGE

Though Catalan is the language spoken by native Catalans, Catalonia is a bilingual country where people also speak *Castellano* (Spanish). If you respond in Spanish to a question or greeting made in Catalan, the speaker will usually switch to Spanish. Official signs and documents are in both languages. However, as Barcelona in particular regards itself as truly cosmopolitan, most tourist literature is also in English and French.

OPENING HOURS

Most museums and monuments close on Mondays. On other days they generally open from 10am to 2pm and, usually reopen from 4 or 5pm to 8pm. It is worth checking specific opening times in advance as larger museums often stay open throughout the day. Churches may only be opened for services. In smaller towns it is common for churches, castles and other sights to be kept locked. The key *(la clau)*, available on request, will be with a caretaker, kept at the town hall *(ajuntament)*, or perhaps at the local bar. Admission is charged for most museums and monuments, although museums are often free on some specific days and on certain national holidays.

TRAVELLING ON A BUDGET

Nearly all restaurants offer a three-course midday *Menú del día* with wine for as little as €9. You may have to ask to see it.

There are three official types of accommodation, with a

hostal or a *pensión* being significantly cheaper than a hotel. The quality varies widely, so ask to see a room if you haven't booked in advance.

Holders of the International Student Identity Card (ISIC) are entitled to benefits such as discounts on travel and entrance fees to museums and galleries. **Viatgeteca** sells these as well as youth hostel cards. **Unlimited Youth Student Travel** specializes in student travel.

Many museums offer free or discounted entry to retired visitors. Be prepared to show your passport to prove your age.

MACBA *(see p62)* offers reduced admission to students

TRAVELLERS WITH SPECIAL NEEDS

Catalonia's association for the disabled, the Federació ECOM *(see p133)*, has hotel lists and travel advice for the whole region. **Disabled**

Sign for disabled access

Accessible Travel can organize tours and excursions, and will also give free advice on accessible hotels in the city. Tourist offices and the social services departments of town halls supply information on local facilities. A travel agency, **Viajes 2000**, specializes in vacations for disabled people.

TRAVELLING WITH CHILDREN

Barcelona is one of the most child-friendly major cities in Europe, given its numerous parks, play-areas, beaches and activities. As in the rest of Spain, people in Catalonia are very family oriented and children are generally

welcome in all restaurants and bars until late in the evening. It is also usual for people to try and interact with your children, offering them sweets in shops or striking up a conversation with them.

All children under 1.35 m (4 ft 5 inches) are required by law to use a specially adapted car seat, except when travelling by taxi. Children under the age of four travel for free on the Metro and on trains there is a reduced fare for those aged between 4 and 13.

GAY AND LESBIAN TRAVELLERS

Barcelona is a famously tolerant and open-minded city. The gay centre of Barcelona is in the Eixample district (sometimes referred to as "Gayxample"), where most of the gay bars, hotels, restaurants and shops are concentrated.

The busy gay beach resort of Sitges is a short journey by train or car, but there are also some smaller beaches within Barcelona: Platja Mar Bella has a gay beach, and Platja de Sant Sebastià has a mixed, clothing optional, nude beach at the end of the Barceloneta district.

ELECTRICAL ADAPTORS

Spain's electricity supply is 220 volts. Plugs have two round pins. A three-tier standard travel converter enables you to use appliances from abroad. You can also find adaptors in department stores *(see p154)* across the city and in hardware stores *(ferreteries)*.

SPANISH TIME

Spain is 1 hour ahead of Greenwich Mean Time (GMT) during the winter *(l'hivern)* and 2 hours during the summer *(l'estiu)*, and uses the 24-hour clock. *La matinada* is the small hours, *el matí* (morning) lasts until about 1pm, while *migdia* (midday) is from 1 to 4pm. *La tarda* is the afternoon, *el vespre* the evening and *la nit* the night.

RESPONSIBLE TOURISM

There has been a growth in sustainable tourism in Catalonia over recent years, concentrated on the excellent network of *Casas rurales*. These are small, traditional, family-owned farmhouses that offer room and board in traditional, rural areas. **ASETUR** is the association of rural tourism in Spain and has substantial information on its website. There are also many local green tourism initiatives and activities in different regions; information can be found through local tourist offices. Catalonia still has many small shops selling local produce and it is possible to support the local economies through shopping in these rather than in chain stores.

DIRECTORY

TOURIST OFFICES

Turisme de Barcelona
Plaça de Catalunya 17, subterrani.
Map 5 A1. **Tel** 93 285 38 34.
C/Ciutat 2 (Ajuntament).
Map 5 A2. **Tel** 93 285 38 34.
Estació Sants, Pl Països Catalans.
Tel 93 285 38 34.

Turisme de Catalunya
Palau Robert, Pg de Gràcia 107.
Map 3 A3. **Tel** 93 238 80 91/2/3.

SPECIAL NEEDS

Disabled Accessible Travel
Tel 60 591 87 69.
www.disabledaccessible
travel.com

Viajes 2000
C/Aribau 123. **Map** 2 F1.
Tel 93 323 96 60.

STUDENTS AND YOUTH

Unlimited Youth Student Travel & Viatgeteca
Carrer Calàbria 147.
Map 2 D1. **Tel** 93 483 83 41.

RESPONSIBLE TOURISM

ASETUR
Travessera de les Corts 131–159.
www.ecoturismorural.com

Personal Security and Health

Spanish pharmacy sign

In Catalonia, as in most parts of Western Europe, rural areas are quite safe, while towns and cities warrant more care. Keep cards and money in a belt, don't leave valuables in your car and avoid poorly lit areas at night. If you feel ill, there will always be a local *farmàcia* (pharmacy) open. In Spain, pharmacists can prescribe some drugs as well as advise. Report lost documents to your consulate *(see p177)* and to the *Mossos d'Esquadra* at the local *comissaria* (police station). Emergency numbers are listed opposite.

POLICE IN CATALONIA

In Catalonia, police services are organized into three forces. The *Guàrdia Civil* (paramilitary Civil Guard), dressed in olive-green, polices only borders and airports. In black and red uniforms, the *Mossos d'Escuadra*, the autonomous government's police service, deals with major crime in larger towns and national security, as well as immigration. The *Guàrdia Urbana*, dressed in blue, deals with traffic regulation and the policing of local communities.

If you are a victim of crime, report to the local *comissaria*. There are several dotted around the city, including at Carrer Nou de la Rambla 76–8 (between Montjuïc and the Old Town), at Gran Via 456 (in the Eixample) and at Carrer de l'Almirall Cervera 34 (in Barceloneta). There is also a small office located in the Plaça Catalunya Metro station.

Crowds strolling on the busy street of La Rambla

WHAT TO BE AWARE OF

As in most European cities, pickpocketing in Barcelona is common so it is wise to take sensible precautions when out and about, especially if travelling during peak season. Always be vigilant with handbags, wallets and cameras, especially in crowds, at major tourist attractions, and cafés and bars. In particular, keep an eye on your bag at outdoor cafés, as possessions have been known to disappear.

The more common tricks include someone distracting your attention by alerting you to a "stain" on your clothing (this happens a lot in the Metro) or carnation sellers who deftly empty your wallet when you are trying to pay

them. Never leave valuables in your car and be aware of people hanging around ATMs since credit card frauds are also on the increase, especially along the coast.

Barcelona is generally safe for walking, although it is advisable to avoid the Barri Xinès area at night. It should be remembered, however, that violent crime and muggings in Barcelona are rare.

Always take care when using pedestrian crossings, particularly those without lights. Wait until there is a large enough gap to cross safely.

IN AN EMERGENCY

The national telephone number throughout Spain for all emergency services is 112. After dialling, ask for *policia* (police), *bombers* (fire brigade) or *ambulància* (ambulance). There are also local numbers for the individual emergency services *(opposite)*.

Outside of Barcelona, the largely voluntary *Creu Roja* (Red Cross) often responds to 112 emergency calls for ambulances.

Ambulances transport patients straight to hospital *urgències* (accident and emergency departments).

Red Cross ambulance sign

URGÈNCIES

Accident and Emergency sign

LOST AND STOLEN PROPERTY

Report a loss or theft straight away to the *Guàrdia Urbana*, as many insurance companies give you only 24 hours to make the report. You must make a *denúncia* (written statement) to the police and get a copy for your insurers.

Your consulate can replace a missing passport or issue you with an emergency passport to return to your country of residence, but cannot provide financial assistance, even in emergencies.

Mosso d'Esquadra   **Guàrdia Urbana**

OUTDOOR HAZARDS

Catalonia's hot summers create the prime conditions for forest fires; extinguish cigarettes and take empty bottles away with you as sun shining on the glass can cause flames. If you go climbing or hill-walking, be properly equipped and let someone know your route. Do not enter a *vedat de caça* (hunting reserve) or *camí particular* (private driveway).

In late spring and throughout the summer, make sure you have some good insect repellent with you to deal with Tiger Mosquitoes, a more virulent strain of irritating, biting insects from Asia that have become prevalent in the area surrounding Barcelona.

LEGAL ASSISTANCE

If you are arrested, you have the right to telephone your consulate which can provide a list of bilingual lawyers. The *Collegi d'Advocats* (Lawyers' Association) can guide you on getting legal advice or representation.

Some holiday insurance policies cover legal costs and provide a helpline you can call for assistance.

The most common incidents where the law is broken involve alcohol or drugs. It is illegal to drink alcohol in the street, or to purchase alcohol from unlicensed street vendors. If you are caught you may incur a large fine. Driving offences such as speeding and drink driving also result in heavy fines and the possible loss of your licence.

Front of a high-street *farmàcia* (pharmacy) in Catalonia

MEDICAL TREATMENT

Any EU national who falls ill in Spain is entitled to social security cover. The Spanish health service is generally efficient and care is of a high standard. To claim medical treatment, UK citizens must apply for a European Health Insurance Card online or at a post office prior to travelling. All basic and emergency treatments are covered by the card at public hospitals, but additional medical insurance is needed for treatment in private hospitals.

For private medical care in Spain ask at a tourist office, or at your consulate or hotel for the name of a doctor. Visitors from the US should make sure their insurance covers medical care abroad. If payment is needed at the time of treatment, ask for an itemized bill. Some insurance companies will ask for an official translation.

For non-emergencies, a *farmacèutic* (pharmacist) can advise and, at times, prescribe without a doctor's consultation for minor infections, but if you have a fever they will direct you to *urgències* (emergencies) at a hospital or, in smaller towns, to an *ambulatori* (medical centre). The *farmàcia* sign is an illuminated red or green cross. The addresses of those open at night or at weekends are listed in all pharmacy windows.

PUBLIC CONVENIENCES

There are a number of pay-per-use automatic public toilets in the city centre. If you can't find one, simply walk into a bar, café, department store or hotel and ask for *els serveis* or *el lavabo* (in Catalan), or *los servicios* or *los aseos* (in Spanish). On motorways, there are toilets at service stations. Women may have to request *la clau* (the key).

Patrol car of the *Guàrdia Urbana*

Ambulance displaying the Barcelona 061 emergency number

Fire engine displaying the national emergency number

DIRECTORY

EMERGENCY SERVICES

Police *(Policía)*
Fire Brigade *(Bombers)*
Ambulance *(Ambulància)*
Tel 112 (national number).

Police
Policía Nacional ***Tel*** *091.*
Guàrdia Urbana ***Tel*** *092.*
Mossos d'Esquadra ***Tel*** *088.*

Fire Brigade *(local numbers)*
Tel 080 (Barcelona), 085 (Lleida, Girona, Tarragona).

Ambulance *(local numbers)*
Tel 061 (Barcelona), use 112 (national number) elsewhere.

CONSULATES

Australia
Plaza Gala Placídia 1.
Map 3 A1. *Tel 93 490 90 13.*

Canada
Calle Elisenda de Pinós 10, 08034 Barcelona. *Tel 93 204 27 00.*

United Kingdom
Avinguda Diagonal 477, 13°
08036 Barcelona.
Tel 93 366 62 00.

United States
Passeig de la Reina Elisenda 23, 08034 Barcelona.
Tel 93 280 22 27.

Banking and Local Currency

You may enter Spain with an unlimited amount of money, but if you intend to export more than €6,000, you should declare it. Traveller's cheques may be exchanged at banks, bureaux de change (*canvi* in Catalan, *cambio* in Spanish), some hotels and some shops. Banks generally offer the best exchange rates. The cheapest exchange rate may be offered on your credit or direct debit card, which may be used in cash dispensers displaying the appropriate sign.

A branch of La Caixa, the largest savings bank in Spain

BANKS AND BUREAUX DE CHANGE

As a rule of thumb, banks in Catalonia are open from 8am to 2pm on weekdays. Some open until 1pm on Saturdays, but most are closed on Saturdays from July through September. Branches of some of the larger banks in the centre of Barcelona are beginning to extend their weekday opening hours, but this is not yet a widespread practice.

Most banks have a foreign exchange desk signed *Canvi/ Cambio* or *Moneda estrangera/ extranjera*. Always take your passport as proof of ID to effect any transaction.

You can draw cash on major credit and debit cards at a bank. Several US and UK banks have branches in Barcelona, including **Citibank**, **Barclays** and **Lloyds TSB**. If you bank with them, you can cash a cheque there.

A bureau de change, which is indicated by the sign *Canvi/ Cambio*, or the sign "Change", will invariably charge a higher rate of commission than a bank, but will often remain open after hours. *Caixes d'estalvi/Cajas de ahorro* (savings banks) also exchange money. They open from 8:30am to 2pm on weekdays, and also on Thursdays from 4:30 to 7:45pm.

ATMS

If your card is linked to your home bank account, you can use it with your PIN to withdraw money from cash dispensers/ATMs. Nearly all dispensers take **VISA** or **MasterCard**. Cards with a Cirrus or Maestro logo can also be widely used to withdraw

money from cash machines. When you enter your PIN, instructions are displayed in Catalan, Spanish, English, French and German. Many dispensers are inside buildings these days, and to gain access customers must run their cards through a door-entry system.

ServiCaixa cash dispensers can also be used to purchase theatre, concert and cinema tickets, a convenient way to beat the queues for the most popular shows. Credit for mobile phones can also be topped up using one of these dispensers.

TRAVELLER'S CHEQUES AND CARDS

Traveller's cheques issued by **American Express** (AmEx), **Travelex**, and Thomas Cook are all accepted in Spain. If you exchange AmEx cheques at an AmEx office, commission is not charged.

The most widely accepted card in Spain is the VISA card, although MasterCard and American Express are also taken in most parts of the city. Credit cards are usually the cheapest method of payment, as you are not charged commission and are given the official rate of the day. All cash dispensers accept most foreign cards, although the commission charged depends on your own bank. You may be given the choice to pay the commission in either Euros or in your home currency. More and more cash machines are now closed at night, particularly in the old city, due to crime.

Before you travel, it is a good idea to phone your card provider and bank to inform them that you will be abroad,

otherwise you may find that your card gets blocked when you start using it in Barcelona.

When you pay with a card, cashiers will usually pass it through a card reading machine. In shops you will always be asked for additional photo ID. As leaving your passport in the hotel safe is preferable, make sure that you have an alternative original document on hand (photocopies will rarely do) such as a driver's licence. Cards are not readily accepted in many smaller bars and restaurants, so it is advisable to check first or carry some cash with you.

THE EURO

The Euro (€) is the common currency of the European Union. It went into general circulation on 1 January 2002, initially for 12 participating countries. Spain was one of those countries, with the Spanish peseta phased out in 2002. EU members using the Euro as sole official currency are known as the Eurozone. Several EU members have opted out of joining this common currency. Euro notes are identical throughout the Eurozone countries, each one including designs of fictional architectural structures and monuments. The coins, however, have one side identical (the value side), and one side with an image unique to each country. Notes and coins are exchangeable in all participating countries.

Euro Banknotes

Euro banknotes have seven denominations. The €5 note (grey in colour) is the smallest, followed by the €10 note (pink), €20 note (blue), €50 note (orange), €100 note (green), €200 note (yellow) and €500 note (purple).

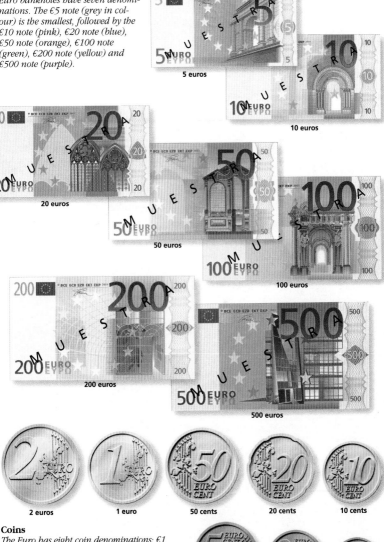

5 euros

10 euros

20 euros

50 euros

100 euros

200 euros

500 euros

Coins

The Euro has eight coin denominations: €1 and €2; 50 cents, 20 cents, 10 cents, 5 cents, 2 cents and 1 cent. The €2 and €1 coins are both silver and gold in colour. The 50-, 20- and 10-cent coins are gold. The 5-, 2- and 1-cent coins are bronze.

2 euros

1 euro

50 cents

20 cents

10 cents

5 cents

2 cents

1 cent

Communications and Media

Public telephones, run by the Spanish telecommunications company Telefónica, are easy to find and operate with a card or coins, but international calls have a high charge. Depending on your service provider, you may find it is cheaper to use your mobile phone at roaming rates. The postal service, Correos, is identified by a crown insignia in blue or white on a yellow background. Registered mail can be sent from all Correos offices. These also sell stamps, but it is more usual, and quicker, to buy them from *estancs* (tobacconists). There are a number of Internet cafés based in the city centre.

Telefónica

Logo of the Spanish telecom system

INTERNATIONAL AND LOCAL TELEPHONE CALLS

Public telephone boxes *(cabines)* are available throughout the city, and payphones can also be found in some bars and post offices. Both types take coins. There is a high minimum connection charge, especially for international calls, so it is best to ensure that you have plenty of change ready. Phonecards are a more convenient option and can be bought at *estancs* and newsstands. Some phones have electronic multilingual instruction displays.

Calls can also be made from *locutoris* (public telephone offices) and paid for afterwards. The cheapest offices are those away from the city centre. Private ones, which are often located in shops, are usually much pricier.

The charges for international calls are divided into four bands: EU countries; non-EU European countries and Northwest Africa; North and South America; and rest of the world. With the exception of

local calls, using the telephone system can be expensive. Calls from a hotel may also incur a high surcharge.

Reversed-charge (collect) calls made to EU countries may be dialled directly, but most others must be made through the operator.

Spain abolished provincial area codes in 1998, so the full number, including the initial 9, must always be dialled, even from within the area.

MOBILE PHONES

Spain currently has four mobile phone operators: MoviStar (run by Telefónica), Vodafone, Orange and Yoigo. Roaming rates vary widely depending on agreements between your service provider and the local Spanish provider. Some operators offer special deals for travelling in EU countries. Check with your service provider before leaving. If

you plan to make a lot of calls, another good option is to buy a Spanish top-up phone with SIM card and number. A basic phone can be bought for about €30 and SIM cards are sold at most El Cortes Inglés and FNAC stores.

When using a mobile phone in Spain, remember to dial 00 followed by your national dialling code (44 for the UK, 1 for the USA) before the number. Most mobile phone operators will charge you to receive calls when using the service outside of your home country.

POSTAL SERVICE

Correos, Spain's postal service, is rather slow. It is better to send any urgent or important post by *urgente* (express) or

Typical mailbox

certificado (registered) mail, or to use a private courier service.

Post can be registered and sent from all Correos offices. However, it is more convenient to buy stamps for postcards and letters from an *estanc* (tobacconists). Postal rates fall into

---

USEFUL SPANISH DIALLING CODES

- When calling within a city, within a province, or to call another province, dial the entire number. The province is indicated by the initial digits: Barcelona numbers start with 93, Lleida 973, Girona 972 and Tarragona 977.
- To make an international call, dial 00, followed by the country code, the area code and the number.
- Country codes are: UK 44; Eire 353; France 33; US and Canada 1; Australia 61; New Zealand 64. When dialling overseas numbers it may be necessary to omit

the initial digit of the destination's area code.
- For directory service, dial 11888.
- For international operator service, dial 1408 (English- and French-speaking operators).
- To make a reversed-charge (collect) call to the UK only, dial 900 961682 (from a private landline or telephone box) and you will then be instructed to dial the number required.
- To report technical faults, dial 1002.
- The speaking clock and wake-up calls can be accessed by dialling 1212.

three price bands: Spain, Europe and the rest of the world. Parcels must be weighed and stamped by Correos and must be securely tied with string, or a charge may be made at the counter to have them sealed by a clerk. Smaller packages, like books, can be sent through the yellow post boxes with stamps bought from the *estanc* after weighing.

Main Correos offices open from 8:30am to 8:30pm Monday to Friday and from 9:30am to 2pm on Saturday. Branches in the suburbs and in villages open from 9am to 2pm Monday to Friday and from 9:30am to 1pm on Saturday.

ADDRESSES

In Catalan addresses the street name is written first, followed by the building number, the floor number, and the number or letter of the apartment. For example, C/ Mir 7, 5è-A means apartment A on floor 5 of building number 7 in Carrer Mir. *Carrer* is often shortened to C/. Floor designations are: *Baixos* (ground floor), *Entresol*, *Principal*, *1r*, *2n* and so on, meaning that *2n* is in fact the 4th level above the ground. Some newer buildings use the less complicated designation of *Baixos* followed by *1r*, *2n* and so on upwards. The postcodes have five digits; the first two are the province number.

Sign for an Internet hotspot

INTERNET AND EMAIL

All hotels, airports and many bars in the centre have Internet hotspots, although often they will charge you a small fee for access and you will usually need to ask for a password. Barcelona has a free, non-user registration Wi-Fi service with 185 municipal hotspots in civic centres, museums, sports clubs and libraries. A full list of municipal hotspots can be found on the local government website. Internet cafés are mainly based in the city centre and nearly all hotels have a computer, or computers, for guests to send emails. Phone centres *(locutorios)* also offer Internet access at a cheaper rate.

TELEVISION AND RADIO

TV3 television station logo

Catalans have a choice of watching TV3 in Catalan run by the regional government, or TVE1 and TVE2, Spain's two state television channels. There is a Catalan channel, Canal 33, and five main Spanish independents: Antena 3, Tele-5, Canal+ (Canal Plus), Cuatro and La Sexta. A regular foreign language news service is provided by Barcelona Televisio (BTV). Most foreign films on television (and in cinemas) are dubbed. Subtitled films are listed as *V.O. (versión original)*. There are a number of good cinemas in Barcelona that show their films exclusively in *V.O.* Satellite channels such as CNN, Cinemanía and Eurosport and many other European channels are commonly provided in hotels.

The main radio stations are Catalunya Ràdio (102.8FM) and COM Ràdio (100.4FM), the Spanish state Radio Nacional de España (738FM), and the independent stations Radio 2 (93.0FM), broadcasting classical music, and Ser (96.9FM), a Spanish general-interest station.

NEWSPAPERS AND MAGAZINES

Some newsagents and kiosks in the city centre stock periodicals in English. Newspapers in English available on the day of publication are the *International Herald Tribune*, the *Guardian International* and the *Financial Times*. Others can be found a day after publication. *The European* newspaper and weekly news magazines such as *Time*, *Newsweek* and *The Economist* are readily available. *Catalonia Today*, a monthly newspaper in English, is available at central kiosks and newsstands.

The main Catalan-language newspapers are *Avui* and *El Periódico*. *La Vanguardia*, in Spanish, is published in Barcelona and is widely respected. The Spanish newspapers *El País*, *El Mundo* and *ABC* are also reliable.

Barcelona's best weekly listings magazine in Spanish is *Guía del Ocio*. The monthly *Metropolitan* and *BCN Week* (every two months) are published in English and found in pubs, cinemas and bars. Also available is the Catalan-language *Time Out*.

A newsstand on La Rambla in Barcelona

DIRECTORY

POST OFFICES

Central Post Office
Plaça Antonio López s/n.
Map 5 B3. **Tel** 934 868050.

INTERNET CAFES AND OFFICE CENTRES

Ciber Virreina
c/ Asturies 78 (Gracia).
Map 3 B1. **Tel** 93 368 5770.

Work Centers
Ronda Universitat 13.
Map 2 F1. **Tel** 93 481 41 48.
Roger de Lluria 2.
Map 5 B1. **Tel** 93 390 83 54.
www.workcenter.es

TRAVEL INFORMATION

Catalonia's three main airports – El Prat, Girona and Reus – receive international flights from all over the globe. While Barcelona's El Prat mainly handles scheduled services, Girona and Reus deal with package holiday flights. Rail networks and toll highways radiate from Barcelona to serve the region's major towns. Barcelona has a well-developed ringroad *(ronda)* system, and a tunnel through the Collserola Hills brings the inland highways right into the city. Both its Metro and suburban train links are good, and most rural areas are served by intermittent bus services. For remote areas, a car may be required.

Spain's national airline

GREEN TRAVEL

As a tourist-intensive area, Catalonia faces environmental challenges, especially around the busy coastal areas. Trains are an easy alternative to flying or taking the car, and international and national services are both efficient and economical *(see p184)*.

The local Catalan train network – called *Rodalies* – provides access to most of the region, although to reach some rural areas without direct links, such as the Montseny, the Pyrenean mountain villages, and La Garrotxa, you may have to arrange a taxi connection.

Barcelona has a number of cycle-hire shops and a growing network of cycle lanes that provide access to all the major sights of the city. *Bicing*, the municipal government-run free cycle service, can be used with a Bicing card and supplies maps of the city's cycle lanes. Though this is currently open to residents only, commercial operators offer rentals to visitors from around €10 for 2 hours, to €60 for a week.

A waiting area in Barcelona's El Prat airport

ARRIVING BY AIR

Barcelona's El Prat airport is divided into two main terminals: T1 and T2. Most international flights now arrive at T1 (including all flights operated by **Iberia** and **British Airways**). EasyJet is currently operating from T2. If you need to transfer between terminals, use the free bus shuttle service, which leaves from outside each terminal.

Barcelona is served by many international airlines. The Spanish national carrier, Iberia, offers daily scheduled flights to Barcelona from all west European capitals. It also offers direct flights from several eastern European capitals.

British Airways offers daily flights to Barcelona from Heathrow, Gatwick and East Midlands airports. EasyJet flies to Barcelona from Gatwick, Stansted, Luton, Bristol, Newcastle and

Pont Aeri
Puente Aéreo

Sign for the shuttle service linking Barcelona and Madrid

Liverpool. **Ryanair** flies to Girona and Reus airports from Birmingham, Bristol, Durham, Liverpool, Manchester, Newcastle, Stansted, Luton, Bournemouth, East Midlands, Blackpool and Glasgow.

Delta Air Lines and **United Airlines** offer direct flights to Barcelona from the US. Iberia operates a comprehensive service from both the United States and Canada.

Catalonia's other two airports mainly handle charter flights: Girona serves the Costa Brava, and Reus, near Tarragona, the Costa Daurada. There are regular buses from Reus and Girona to Barcelona. For passengers arriving from Madrid or other Spanish cities, Spain's domestic flights are operated by Iberia and its associated airlines **Air Nostrum**, **Air Europa** and **Spanair**. Iberia's low-cost carrier **Vueling** offers a good service from many Spanish and European destinations to Barcelona.

The most frequent shuttle service between Madrid and Barcelona (El Prat only) is Iberia's **Pont Aeri (Puente Aéreo)**. It flies every quarter of an hour at peak times and passengers can buy tickets just 15 minutes in advance using a self-ticketing machine. The flight takes 50 minutes.

Other services between Madrid and Barcelona are less frequent but, on the whole, their prices tend to be lower. The major international car rental companies *(see p187)* have desks at both terminals of El Prat airport. Girona also has some rental companies on site and cars can be delivered to Reus from nearby Tarragona. There will also be local firms offering tempting deals, but check the small print carefully.

GETTING TO BARCELONA

Barcelona airport is only 16 km (10 miles) away from the city. There is a regular bus service to the city centre from both terminals, operating from 6am until 1:05am and costing about €5. It takes 25–30 mins from T2 and 35 mins from T1. The final stop is in Plaça Catalunya, but there are also stops in Plaça Espanya and along Gran Vía.

The cheapest way to get to the city is by train. There is a train every 20 minutes. A shuttle bus will take you to the airport train station from T1 and it is a 10-minute walk across the pedestrian flyover from T2. The city centre train stops are at Passeig de Gràcia and Sants.

There are plenty of taxis available from outside of both terminals – join the queue at the taxi rank. Taxis to central Barcelona are metered cost between €20 and €30, depending on traffic, the time of day and which terminal you are using. There is a small supplement added for journeys to and from the airport and for each piece of luggage.

A new Metro line, L-9, which is due to open in 2014, will run from Plaça Catalunya to both airport terminals.

TICKETS AND FARES

Air fares to Barcelona and the coastal resorts vary through the year, depending on demand. They are generally highest during the summer months. Special deals, particularly for weekend city breaks, are often available in the winter and may include a number of nights at a hotel. Christmas and Easter flights are almost always booked up well in advance.

Charter flights from the UK to Girona and Reus can be very cheap, but tend to be less reliable, and often fly at unsociable hours.

Good deals can be found online to fly to Barcelona from other cities in Spain through Vueling, Air Europa, Spanair or Iberia.

SEA TRAVEL

The **Grimaldi Group** has a ferry service between Civitavecchia (near Rome) or Livorno (near Florence) and Barcelona. **Atlas Cruises and Tours** offers

transatlantic cruises between the US and Barcelona, as well as cruises around the Mediterranean. **Costa Cruises** offers Mediterranean cruises starting in Barcelona, while **Thomson Cruises**, in the UK, has cruises calling at Barcelona, but starting out from Mallorca.

TRAVEL TO THE BALEARIC ISLANDS

Barcelona is the main city on the Spanish mainland from which to reach the Balearic Islands. Flights are run by Iberia, Air Europa, Spanair and Vueling. **Balearia** runs a hydrofoil (a kind of catamaran) service to Ibiza, which takes 8 hours. It also goes to Majorca, taking 7 hours, and Menorca, taking 4 hours. They also offer car ferry crossings, which take about 8 hours, by **Acciona Trasmediterránea** to Ibiza, Majorca and Menorca. To travel to Formentera you need to take a ferry service from Ibiza. It is wise to book in advance, especially in summer.

Balearia car ferry to the Balearic Islands

DIRECTORY

AIRPORTS

Barcelona El Prat
Tel 902 40 47 04.

Girona
Tel 902 40 47 04.

Reus
Tel 902 40 47 04.

AIRLINES

Air Europa
Tel 902 401 501 (Spain).
www.air-europa.com

British Airways
Tel 902 11 13 33 (Spain).
Tel 0844 493 0787 (UK).
www.britishairways.com

United Airlines
www.united.com

Delta Air Lines
Tel 900 80 07 43 (Spain).
Tel (800) 241 41 41 (US).
www.delta.com

EasyJet
Tel 807 07 00 70 (Spain).
Tel 0871 244 2366 (UK).
www.easyjet.com

Iberia, Air Nostrum
Tel 902 400 500 (Spain).
Tel 0870 609 0500 (UK).
Tel (800) 772 4642 (US).

Ryanair
Tel 08712 460000 (UK).
www.ryanair.com

Spanair
Tel 902 13 14 15 (Spain).
www.spanair.com

Vueling
Tel 807 200 200 (Spain).
www.vueling.com

SEA TRAVEL

Atlas Cruises & Tours
Tel (800) 942 3301 (US).
www.atlastravelweb.com

Costa Cruises
Tel 902 23 12 31 (Spain).
www.costacruceros.es

Grimaldi Group
Tel 902 531 333 (Spain).

Thomson Cruises
Tel 0871 230 2800 (UK).
www.thomson.co.uk/cruises

TRAVEL TO THE BALEARIC ISLANDS

Acciona Trasmediterránea
Tel 902 45 46 45 (Spain). www.transmediterranea.es

Balearia
Tel 902 16 01 80 (Spain).
www.balearia.com

Travelling by Train and Metro

Metro and FGC rail services sign

There are two providers of rail services in Catalonia. The Spanish national **RENFE** *(Red Nacional de Ferrocarriles Españoles)* operates Spain's inter-city services, including first-class fast Talgo and AVE trains and some of Barcelona's commuter services *(Rodalies)*. The Catalan government's **FGC** *(Ferrocarrils de la Generalitat de Catalunya)* runs some suburban trains in Barcelona and some special-interest services in Catalonia's provinces. Barcelona also has the Metro, an efficient city-wide network of underground (subway) trains.

Trains on the platform at one of Barcelona's major railway stations

ARRIVING BY TRAIN

There are direct international train services to Barcelona from several European cities including Paris, Montpellier, Geneva, Zurich and Milan. Sleeping compartments can be booked on direct service overnight trains. All trains entering the eastern side of Spain from France go through Port Bou/Cerbère or La Tour de Carol on the Franco-Spanish border. Travelling to Barcelona from departure points not offering a direct service may mean picking up a connection here. International trains arrive at Sants mainline station, located in the centre of Barcelona.

renfe

Logo of the Spanish national rail service

Services from Barcelona to other cities in Spain are fast and frequent. Overnight trains are offered by Estrella (a basic service) to Madrid, A Coruña and Vigo, and by Trenhotel (a more sophisticated service) to Seville and Málaga. AVE runs a high-speed train between Barcelona and Madrid, the journey takes 3 hours, and there are 17 services a day.

EXPLORING CATALONIA BY TRAIN

Catalonia has a network of regional trains *(regionals)* covering the whole of Catalunya and run by **RENFE**. There are three types – the *Media Distancia* and Talgo linking the main towns with few stops in between, and the *Regional* trains which take longer and stop frequently. A high-speed Euromed service from Barcelona to Tarragona (continuing south to Castelló, València and Alacant/ Alicante) leaves from Estació de Sants. **FGC** *(Ferrocarrils de la Generalitat de Catalunya)* is a network of suburban trains run by the Catalan government in and around Barcelona. FGC also runs some special services, such as the rack railway (cog railroad) from Ribes de Freser *(see inside back cover)* to Núria in the Pyrenees and La Cremallera, which runs up to Montserrat. It also runs the cable cars and funiculars at the Monastery of Montserrat *(see pp122–3)* and at Vallvidrera, as well as several historic steam trains and an electric train for tourists. Details are available at the FGC station at Plaça de Catalunya or by calling the FGC number listed in the Directory.

Most trains are accessible for the disabled – it is worth checking at the time of booking.

TICKETS AND RESERVATIONS

Tickets for Talgo, AVE, Alvia, international trains and all other long-distance travel by train may be bought at any of the major RENFE railway stations from the *taquilla* (ticket office). They are also sold by travel agents, plus a booking fee. Tickets can be purchased on the RENFE website, and long-distance train tickets have a 60 per cent discount if bought online at least 15 days in advance. During the peak months (July to September), many of the most popular inter-city routes, particularly to the coasts, are booked up weeks in advance, so it is worth planning ahead. You can also reserve tickets by phone *(see directory)*. They are held for 48 hours (up to 2 hours before the train leaves) and can be collected at main stations.

Tickets for local and regional services can be purchased from station booking offices. In some larger stations, they can also be bought from ticket machines. Tickets for *Rodalies* (local services) cannot be reserved. A one-way journey in Catalan is *anada* and a round trip is *anada i tornada*.

DIRECTORY

PUBLIC TRANSPORT

RENFE Information and Credit Card Bookings
Tel 902 320 320.
www.renfe.es

Secretaria General de Juventud (Young People's Tourist Office)
Carrer de Calàbria, 147.
Tel 93 483 83 83.

FGC Information
Tel 93 205 15 15.
www.fgc.es

TMB Information
Tel 93 318 70 74 or 012.
www.tmb.cat

Ticket machines in use at one of Barcelona's Metro stations

TRAIN FARES

Fares for rail travel depend on the speed and quality of the service. Talgo and AVE trains are more expensive than local and regional trains. RENFE offers discounts to children and people over 60, groups of ten and through travel cards on local, regional and long-distance trains.

Interrail tickets are available for people of all ages from EU member states and Switzerland. Eurail tickets are for residents of non-European countries (note that you will need to prove your residence status to train staff). These tickets offer discounts on rail travel and can be purchased at Estació de Sants and Estació de França stations. Young Person's cards are available through the **Secretaria General de Juventud** and are intended for people under 26, of any nationality. They offer a discount of up to 20 per cent on journeys from any point in Spain to Europe. To purchase these, you will need to have proof of your age and identity.

THE BARCELONA METRO

There are seven underground Metro lines in Barcelona, run by **TMB** (*Transports Metropolitans de Barcelona*). Lines are identified by number and colour. Platform signs distinguish between trains and their direction by displaying the last station on the line. In the street it is easy to spot a Metro station – look for a sign bearing a red "M" on a white diamond background.

The Metro is usually the quickest way to get around

the city, especially as all multi-journey tickets are valid for the Metro and FGC lines (in Zone 1), as well as on the bus and local RENFE services. A RENFE or FGC sign at a Metro station indicates that it has a RENFE or FGC connection.

Metro trains run from 5am to midnight from Monday to Thursday, to midnight on Sunday and weekday public holidays, from 5am to 2am on Friday and the day before a public holiday, and all night on Saturdays.

Barcelona is in the process of building a new Metro line, the L9, which will eventually reach the airport and pass

A one-way (single) Metro ticket for Barcelona's subway

through the heart of the city. There are currently five new stops on the L9 on the outskirts of the city, with more

being added over the coming years. When completed in 2014, the L9 will be the longest Metro line in Europe.

BARCELONA TICKETS AND TRAVELCARDS

A range of tickets and money-saving travel cards are available to tourists. Some cover train, bus and Metro. Combined tickets allow travellers to hop from Metro to FGC to bus lines without leaving the station to pay again.

Tickets are as follows: *T-dia* and *T-mes* are for unlimited daily and monthly travel respectively; the *senzill* ticket, for one single journey, can be used on Metro, bus and FGC; the *T-10*, which can be shared and is the most useful for tourists, allows ten trips and combines journeys on Metro, bus and FGC in one trip (with a time limit of an hour and a half); the *T-50/30* is for 50 journeys in 30 days on Metro, bus and FGC.

Details of special tourist travel cards are on the inside back cover of this guide. There are 2-, 3-, 4- and 5-day travelcards available which offer unlimited journeys on the Metro, FGC and bus.

USING A METRO TICKET MACHINE

Insert tickets that don't work to make a duplicate.

Press to ask for information.

4 Collect your ticket and change due.

3c Insert coins.

3b Insert banknote(s).

3a Insert credit card.

2 Select ticket: *senzill* (single trip), *T-10* (10 trips), *T-50/30* (50 trips in 30 days), then choose the area and quantity.

1 Select language: Catalan/Spanish, English, French.

Travelling by Car and Bus

Barcelona road signs

Driving conditions in Catalonia vary enormously, from the dense road network and heavy traffic in and around Barcelona to almost empty country roads in the provinces, where villages – and in particular petrol (gas) stations – can be far apart. Toll highways *(autopistes)* are fast and free-flowing, but the ordinary main roads along the coast are usually very busy at all times of day. For tourists without private cars, joining an organized bus tour is a good way to visit well-known, but rather more remote, places of interest.

A toll motorway, a popular way of travelling across the region

ARRIVING BY CAR

Many people drive to Spain via the French motorways (highways). The most direct routes across the Pyrenees are the motorways through Hendaye in the west and La Jonquera in the east. Port Bou is on a scenic coastal route, while other routes snake over the top, entering Catalonia via the Vall d'Aran, Andorra, and Puigcerdà in the Cerdanya. From the UK, car ferries run from Plymouth to Santander and from Portsmouth to Bilbao in northern Spain.

CAR RENTAL

International car rental companies, such as **Hertz**, **Avis** and **Europcar**, as well as some Spanish ones, such as **National ATESA**, operate all over Catalonia. You are likely to get better deals with international companies if you arrange a car from home. A hire car is *un cotxe de lloguer*. Catalonia's three main airports *(see p182)* have car rental desks. However, those at Girona and Reus have irregular opening hours, so if you need a car

there, it is best to book in advance and they will meet your requirements. Avis offers deals in chauffeur-driven cars from major cities.

Logo of the National ATESA car-rental company

TAKING YOUR OWN CAR

A green card from a car insurance company is needed to extend your comprehensive cover to Spain. In the UK, the RAC, AA and Europ Assistance have rescue and recovery policies with European cover.

Vehicle registration, insurance documents and your driver's licence must be carried at all times. Non-EU citizens should obtain an international driver's licence; in the US, these are available through the AAA. You may also be asked for a passport or national identity card as extra proof of identification.

A country of origin sticker must be displayed on the rear of foreign vehicles. All drivers must carry a red warning triangle, spare light bulbs, a visibility vest and a first-aid kit. Failure to do so will incur an on-the-spot fine.

DRIVING IN CATALONIA

At junctions give way to the right unless directed otherwise. Left turns across the flow of traffic are indicated by a *canvi de sentit* sign.

Speed limits for cars without trailers are: 120 km h (75 mph) on *autopistes* and *autovies* (toll and non-toll motorways/highways); 90 km h (56 mph) on *carreteres nacionals* (main roads), *carreteres comarcals* (secondary roads); 80 km h (50 mph) on Barcelona's ring roads and 30 or 40 km h (19 or 25 mph) in urban areas. There are on-the-spot speeding fines of up to €520.

The blood alcohol legal limit is 0.5 g per litre (0.25 mg per litre in a breath test) – tests are frequently given and drivers over the limit are fined. Front and rear seat belts must be worn. Ordinary unleaded fuel *(Súper 95)*, superior unleaded fuel *(Súper 98)* and diesel *(gas oil)* are all available everywhere and sold by the litre.

AUTOPISTES

On toll motorways *(autopistes)*, tolls are calculated per kilometre driven. Over some stretches near cities a fixed toll is charged. You collect a ticket from the *peagte* (toll booth/plaza) when you join the *autopiste*, and pay when you leave. You must join one of three channels at the *peatge*: *Automàtic* has machines for credit cards; in *Manual* an attendant takes your ticket and money; for *Teletac* you need an electronic chip on your vehicle's windscreen (windshield).

Autopistes have emergency telephones every 2 km (1.25 miles) and service stations every 40 km (25 miles).

PARKING

Central Barcelona has a pay-and-display system from 9am to 2pm and 4 to 8pm Monday to Friday and all day Saturday. You can park in blue spaces for about €2–3 per hour. Tickets are valid for 2 hours but can be renewed. Green spaces are reserved for residents but can be used, if available, at a higher rate and are free at off-peak hours.

At underground car parks (parking lots), *lliure* means there is space, *complet* means full. Most are attended, but in automatic ones, you pay before returning to your car. Do not park where the pavement edge is yellow or where there is a private exit *(gual)*. Blue and red signs saying "1–15" or "16–30" mean you cannot park in the areas indicated on those dates of the month.

TAXIS

Barcelona's taxis are yellow and black, and display a green light when they are free. All taxis are metered and show a minimum fee at the start of a journey. Rates increase after 10pm and at weekends, although the minimum fee stays the same. In unmetered taxis, such as those in villages, it is best to negotiate a price for the trip before setting off. Supplements are charged for going to and from the airport and for suitcases. **Radio Taxis** have cars adapted for disabled people, but they need to be booked a day ahead. They also have some cars that will take up to seven people.

An Alsa long-distance bus

LONG-DISTANCE BUSES

Spain's largest inter-city bus company, **Alsa**, is an agent for **Eurolines**. This runs regular services from all over Europe to Sants bus station in Barcelona. Buses from towns and cities in Spain arrive at Estació del Nord and Sants.

No parking at any time of day

Several companies run day trips or longer tours to places of interest in Catalonia. **Turisme de Catalunya** *(see p175)* has details of trips to Catalonia; in other towns, tourist offices can help with tours in their provinces.

BUSES IN BARCELONA

The main city buses are white and red. You can buy a single ticket on the bus, or a *T-10* ten-trip ticket at Metro stations, valid for bus, Metro and FGC *(see p185)*. Other combined tickets are described inside the back cover. The *Nitbus* runs nightly from around 10pm to 5am, and the *Aerobus* offers a service between Plaça de Catalunya and El Prat airport. A good way to sightsee is by **Bus Turístic**. It runs all year on three routes from Plaça de Catalunya. A ticket, bought on board, is valid for all three routes and lets you get on and off as you please. **Julià Tours** and **Pullmantur** also offer tours of Barcelona.

(see p175) *(see p185)*

DIRECTORY

CAR RENTAL

Avis
Tel 93 298 36 00
(Barcelona airport).
Tel 902 18 08 54.
www.avis.es

Europcar
Tel 902 10 50 30.
www.europcar.es

Hertz
Tel 902 402 405.
www.hertz.es

National ATESA
Tel 93 521 90 95.
(Barcelona airport).
Tel 902 100 101.
www.atesa.es

TAXIS

Radio Taxis
Tel 93 303 30 33.
Tel 93 225 00 00.
Tel 93 420 80 88 (taxis for the disabled).

TOUR BUS OPERATORS

Alsa
Tel 90 242 22 42.

Bus Turístic
www.barcelonabusturistic.cat

Eurolines
Tel 08717 81 81 81 in UK.
Tel 90 240 50 40 in Spain.

Julià Tours
Tel 93 317 64 54.

Pullmantur
Tel 93 317 12 97.

BUS STATIONS

Estació del Nord
Carrer d'Alí Bei 80.
Tel 90 226 06 06.
www.barcelonanord.com

Estació de Sants
Plaça del Països Catalans.
Tel 90 226 06 06.

A busy taxi rank in Barcelona

BARCELONA STREET FINDER

he map references given with the sights, shops and entertainment venues described in the Barcelona section of the guide refer to the street maps on the following pages. Map references are also given for Barcelona's hotels *(see pp134–41)*, restaurants *(see pp146–51)* and cafés and bars *(see pp152–3)*. The schematic map below shows the areas of the city covered by the *Street Finder*. The symbols for sights, features and services are listed in the key at the foot of the page.

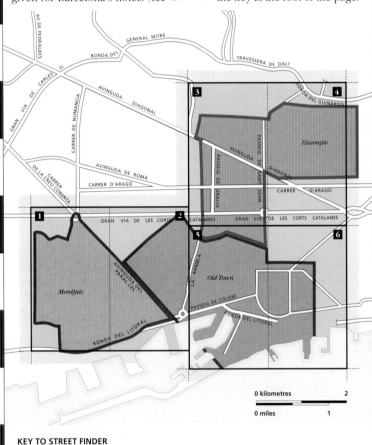

KEY TO STREET FINDER

▩ Major sight	🚢 Golondrina boarding point	🚓 Police station
▢ Place of interest	🚠 Cable car	✝ Church
▢ Other building	🚡 Funicular station	⊠ Post office
⮂ Main train station	🚋 Tramway stop	= Railway line (railroad)
Ⓕ Local (FGC) train station	🚕 Taxi rank	– Pedestrianized street
Ⓜ Metro station	🅿 Parking	
🚌 Main bus stop	ℹ Tourist information	**SCALE OF MAP PAGES**
🚍 Bus station	✚ Hospital with A&E unit	0 metres 250
		0 yards 250

Labels on map:

AV DE PEDRALBES
GENERAL MITRE
RONDA DEL
TRAVESSERA DE DALT
GRAN VIA DE CARLES III
AVINGUDA DIAGONAL
CARRER DE NUMANCIA
RONDA DEL GUINARDO
3   **4**
PASSEIG DE
Eixample
AVINGUDA DE SANT JOAN
DE LA CREU COBERTA
AVINGUDA DE ROMA
PASSEIG DE GRACIA
DIAGONAL
CARRER D'ARAGO
CARRER D'ARAGO
1   **2**
GRAN VIA DE LES CORTS CATALANES   GRAN VIA DE LES CORTS CATALANES
5   **6**
AVINGUDA DEL PARAL.LEL
LA RAMBLA
Old Town
Montjuïc
PASSEIG DE COLOM
RONDA DEL LITORAL
RONDA DEL LITORAL

0 kilometres   2
0 miles   1

Street Finder Index

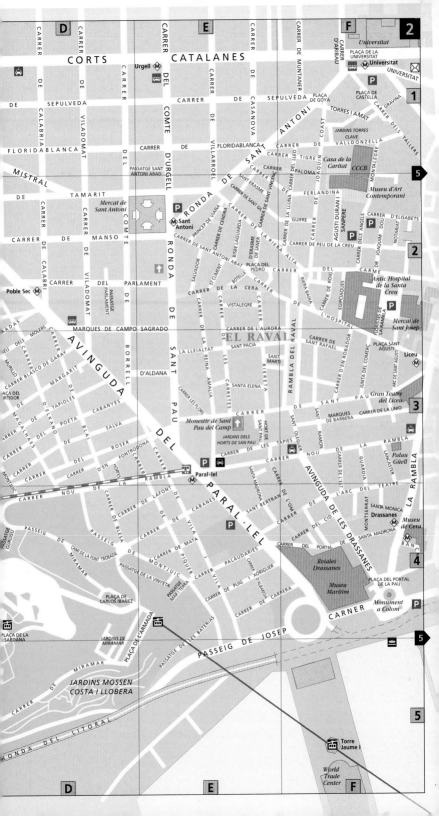

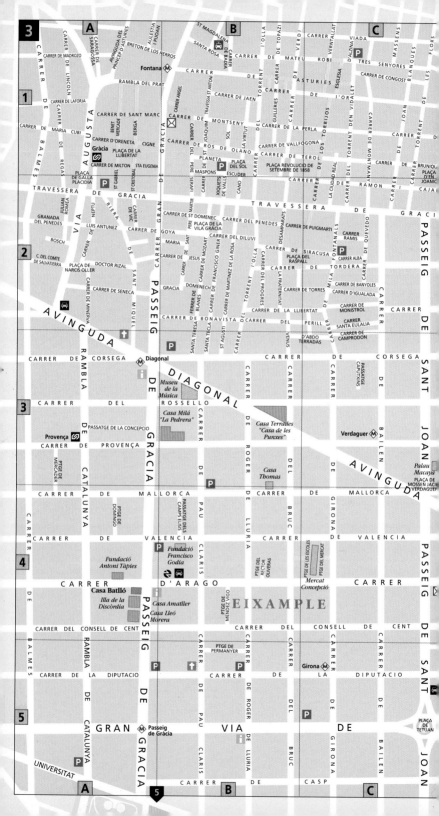

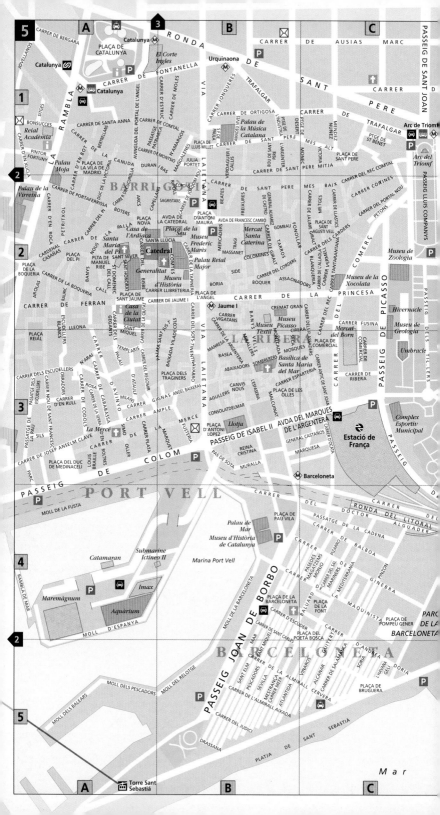

General Index

Acknowledgments

Dorling Kindersley would like to thank the following people whose contributions and assistance have made the preparation of this book possible.

Main Contributor

Roger Williams contributed to the *Eyewitness Travel Guide to Spain* and has written Barcelona and Catalonia titles for Insight Guides. He was also the main contributor to the *Eyewitness Travel Guide to Provence*. *Lunch with Elizabeth David*, set around the Mediterranean, is his latest novel.

Additional Contributors

Mary Jane Aladren, Pepita Arias, Emma Dent Coad, Sally Davies, Rebecca Doulton, Josefina Fernández, Nick Rider, David Stone, Judy Thomson, Clara Villanueva, Suzanne Wales (Word on Spain).

Design and Editorial Assitance

Amaia Allende, Queralt Amella Miró, Gillian Andrews, Imma Espuñes i Amorós, Claire Baranowski, Marta Bescos, Daniel Campi (Word on Spain), Paula Canal (Word on Spain), Anna Freiberger, Mary-Ann Gallagher, Alrica Green, Lydia Halliday, Jessica Hughes, Claire Jones, Juliet Kenny, Elly King, Priya Kukadia, Kathryn Lane, Caroline Mead, Sam Merrell, Barbara Minton, Marianne Petrou, Mani Ramaswamy, Ellen Root, Collette Sadler, Meredith Smith, Susie Smith, Alícia Ribas Sos, Helen Townsend, Hugo Wilkinson, Lola Carbonell Zaragoza.

Proofreader

Stewart J Wild, Huw Hennessey.

Indexer

Hilary Bird.

Special Photography

Max Alexander, Departure Lounge/Ella Milroy, D. Murray/J. Selmes, Dave King, Ian O'Leary, Alessandra Santarelli, Susannah Sayler, Clive Streeter

Photography permissions

© Obispado de VIC; © Cabildo de la Catedral de Girona; Teatre Nacional de Catalunya (Barcelona); Institut Mpal. del Paisatge Urba i la Qualitat de Vida, Ajuntament de Barcelona.

Dorling Kindersley would like to thank all the churches, museums, restaurants, hotels, shops, galleries and other sights too numerous to thank individually.

Picture credits

KEY: t=top; tl=top left; tlc=top left centre; tc=top centre; trc=top right centre; tr=top right; cla=centre left above; ca=centre above; cra=centre right above; cl=centre left; c=centre; cr=centre right; clb=centre left below; cb=centre below; crb=centre right below; bl=bottom left; b=bottom; bc=bottom centre; bcl=bottom centre left; br=bottom right; bcr=bottom centre right; d=detail.

Works of art have been reproduced with the permission of the following copyright holders:

Salvador Dalí *Rainy Taxi* and *ceiling fresco in the Wind Palace Room, Teatre - Museu Dalí* © Kingdom of Spain, Gala - Salvador Dalí Foundation, DACS, London 2006; George Kolbe *Morning* © DACS, London 2006; IOC/Olympic Museum Collections; Joan Miró *Dona i Ocell* 1983 and Tapestry of the Foundation Joan Miró 1975 © Succession Miró/ADAGP, Paris and DACS, London 2006.

The publisher would like to thank the following individuals, companies and picture libraries for their kind permission to reproduce their photographs:

ACE PHOTO LIBRARY: Mauritius 19t; AENA AEROPUERTOS ESPANOLES Y NAVEGACIÓN AEREA: 182bl; AISA, Barcelona: 14b, 18b, 23bl, Jaume Huguet *San Jorge* 28c, 40, 41c, 44cb, 46c, 46bl, 176bl; ALAMY IMAGES: Douglas Armand 97cra; Jon Arnold Images 76tr; Andrew Bargery 62br, 76bl; Neil Barks 77tl; Peter Barritt 82tr; Oliver Bee 76clb, 77br; Dalgleish Images 96bl; Danita Delimont 174cb; Iain Davidson Photographic 102tcl, 103tl; Chad Ehlers 97tl; Mike Finn-Kelcey 185bc; Richard Foot 96tr; Kevin Foy 185tl; B J Gadie 62tc; Guido 186cla; Carlos Rios 181clb; Stephen Saks Photography 68t; Neil Setchfield 60br; Ruben Vicente 187bl; Ken Welsh 175tl; ALSA GROUP S.L.L.C: 187tr; AQUILA PHOTOGRAPHICS: Adrian Hoskins 112bla; 112bl; James Pearce 21b; NATIONAL ATESA: 186cr.

JAUME BALANYA: 81crb; BALEARIA: 183cr; MIKE BUSSELLE: 111b, 112t.

COCEMFE: 154c; CODORNIU: 33t, 33c; BRUCE COLEMAN COLLECTION: Erich Crichton 20tr; José Luis González Grande 21tr; Norbert Schwirtz 21tl; Colin Varwdell 21cra; Comerç 24: 142cl; CORBIS: Peter Aprahamian 62bl, 105br; Carlos Dominguez 11clb; Owen Franken 124tl, 125c; Dave G.

Houser 10cla; Andrea Jemolo 82cla; Jose Fuste Raga 11tl; James Sparshatt 82tl; Mark L. Stephenson 83tr; Sandro Vannini 82bc; Vanni Archive 83br. COVER, Madrid: Pepe Franco 154c; Matias Nieto 191b.

EUROPEAN COMMISSION: 179.

FIRO FOTO: 69cl; FLICKR.COM: www.flickr.com/photos/del15xavii_xavo/4123975385/177tr; FRIEIXENET: 32c, 33b; FUNDACION COLLECTION THYSSEN-BORNEMISZA: Fra Angelico *Madonna of Humility* 95t; FUNDACIO JOAN MIRO, Barcelona: Joan Miró *Flama en l'espai i dona nua* 1932 © Succession Miró/ ADAGP, Paris and DACS, London 2006 88t.

GENERALITAT DE CATALUNYA: 177tr; GODO PHOTO: 124bl, 129t, José Luis Dorada 125t.

ROBERT HARDING PICTURE LIBRARY: 25tr, 59ca, 72ca, 88b, 89b.

THE ILLUSTRATED LONDON NEWS PICTURE LIBRARY: 47t; INDEX, Barcelona: CJJ.19b, 44t, 47c; IMAGE BANK: 24b, 73b; Andrea Pistolesi 92; IMAGES COLOUR LIBRARY: 24c; AGE Fotostock 76, 113b, 118–119, 155t, 155c, 170cr; NICK INMAN: 20b, 96br.

LA CAXIA: 178tr; LIFE FILE PHOTOGRAPHIC: Xabier Catalan 25c; Emma Lee 25cra.

MARKA, Milan: Sergio Pitamitz 62tl; MAS SALVANERA: Ramón Ruscalleda 133t; MARY EVANS PICTURE LIBRARY: 27 (inset); JOHN MILLER: 108; MUSEU NACIONAL D'ART DE CATALUNYA: J. Calveras J. Sagrista 90-91; Ramon Marti Alsina *La Compañia de Santa Barbara* 1891 45t; MUSEU PICASSO: Pablo Ruiz Picasso *Auto Retrato* 1899–1900 © Succession Picasso/ DACS, London 2006 64bl; ABADIA DE MONTSERRAT (BARCELONA) 122br.

NATURAL SCIENCE PHOTOS: C Dani & I Jeske 170c; NATURPRESS, Madrid: 17b; Oriol Alamany 34c, 37b; Walter Kvaternik 37c, 26–27, 177cra; Carlos Vegas 178t, 180tr; Jose A Martinez 109b.

ORONOZ, Madrid: 41b, 42t, 42c, 45bl, 46t.

PHOTOGRAPHERSDIRECT.COM: Michael Dobson/ Echo Imagery 107c, 107br; Fran Fernandez Photography 102b, 105c, 106tl, 107tl; Jan van der Hoeven 101t, 103b, 104cla, 106br. PICTURES COLOUR LIBRARY: 74–75; FRANCISCO FERNANDEZ PRIETO:104BC; PRISMA, Barcelona: 4t, 9 (inset), 18t, 38–9, 45cb, 46cra, 131 (inset), 154b, 163c, 173 (inset); Carles Aymerich 22bl, 36c; A. Bofill 19c; Roger Bosch *El Paralelo* 1930 8–9; Barbara Call 17t; Jordi Cami 34b; Ramon Cases Carbo *Procession outside Santa María del Mar* c. 1898 28t; Albert Heras 2–3, 36b; Kuwenal 43t, 43c; Mateu 35c; Joaquim Mir Trinxet *La Catedral de los Pobres* 29c; Isidro Nunell Monturiol *Esperando la Sopa* 1899 29t; Santiago Rusiñol y Prats *Jardines de Aranjuez* 1907 28b; Antoni Tàpies *Litografía* 1948 © Foundation Tàpies, Barcelona/ADAGP, Paris & DACS, London 2006 29b.

RAIMAT: 32cb; red-head: 52; RENFE: 184cb; REX FEATURES: 117cb; ELLEN ROONEY: 1.

M ANGELES SANCHEZ: 35b; SCIENCE PHOTO LIBRARY: Geospace 12; SPECTRUM COLOUR LIBRARY: 24tr; STOCKPHOTOS, Madrid: 170b; Campillo 171t; SUPERSTOCK: Age Fotostock 184cla.

TV3 TELEVISION DE CATALUNYA: 181cra: TEXTIL CAFÉ: 142c

MAP COVER - PHOTOLIBRARY: age fotostock/Javier Larrea.

JACKET: Front – PHOTOLIBRARY: age fotostock/ Javier Larrea. Back - AWL IMAGES: Jon Arnold bl; Danita Delimont Stock tl; DORLING KINDERSLEY: Ella Milroy cla; Naomi Peck clb. Spine - PHOTOLIBRARY: age fotostock/Javier Larrea t. FRONT END PAPER: clockwise John Miller; Image Bank Andrea Pistolesi; Red-Head; Images Colour Library/ Age Fotostock.

All other images © Dorling Kindersley. For further information see www.DKimages.com.

SPECIAL EDITIONS OF DK TRAVEL GUIDES

English–Catalan Phrase Book

In Emergency

Help!	Auxili!	ow-**gzee**-lee
Stop!	Pareu!	pah-**reh**-oo
Call a doctor!	Telefoneu un metge!	teh-leh-fon-**eh**-oo oon **meh**-djuh
Call an ambulance!	Telefoneu una ambulància!	teh-leh-fon-**eh**-oo oo-nah ahm-boo-**lahn**-see-ah
Call the police!	Telefoneu la policia!	teh-leh-fon-**eh**-oo lah poh-lee-**see**-ah
Call the fire brigade!	Telefoneu els bombers!	teh-leh-fon-**eh**-oo uhlz boom-**behs**
Where is the nearest telephone?	On és el telèfon més proper?	on-ehs uhl tuh-leh-fon mehs proo-**peh**
Where is the nearest hospital?	On és l'hospital més proper?	on-ehs looss-pee-tahl mehs proo-**peh**

Communication Essentials

Yes	Sí	see
No	No	noh
Please	Si us plau	sees **plah**-oo
Thank you	Gràcies	grah-**see**-uhs
Excuse me	Perdoni	puhr-**thoh**-nee
Hello	Hola	oh-**lah**
Goodbye	Adéu	ah-they-**oo**
Good night	Bona nit	bo-nah neet
Morning	El matí	uhl muh-**tee**
Afternoon	La tarda	lah **tahr**-thuh
Evening	El vespre	uhl vehs-pruh
Yesterday	Ahir	ah-ee
Today	Avui	uh-voo-ee
Tomorrow	Demà	duh-**mah**
Here	Aquí	uh-**kee**
There	Allà	uh-**lyah**
What?	Què?	keh
When?	Quan?	kwahn
Why?	Per què?	puhr **keh**
Where?	On?	ohn

Useful Phrases

How are you?	Com està?	kom uhs-**tah**
Very well, thank you	Molt bé, gràcies.	mol **beh** grah-**see**-uhs
Pleased to meet you.	Molt de gust.	mol duh **goost**
See you soon.	Fins aviat.	feenz uhv-**yat**
That's fine.	Està bé.	uhs-**tah** beh
Where is/are ...?	On és/són?	ohn ehs/**sohn**
How far is it to ...?	Quants metres/ kilòmetres hi ha d'aquí a ...?	kwahnz meh-truhs/kee-loh muh-truhs yah dah-**kee** uh
Which way to ...?	Per on es va a ...?	puhr on uhs **bah** ah
Do you speak English?	Parla anglès?	par-luh an-**glehs**
I don't understand	No l'entenc.	noh luhn-**teng**
Could you speak more slowly, please?	Pot parlar més a poc a poc, si us plau?	pot par-**lah** mehs pok uh pok sees **plah**-oo
I'm sorry.	Ho sento.	oo **sehn**-too

Useful Words

big	gran	gran
small	petit	puh-**teet**
hot	calent	kah-**len**
cold	fred	fred
good	bo	boh
bad	dolent	doo-**len**
enough	bastant	bahs-**tan**
well	bé	beh
open	obert	oo-**behr**
closed	tancat	tan-**kat**
left	esquerra	uhs-**kehr**-ruh
right	dreta	dreh-**tuh**
straight on	recte	rehk-**tuh**
near	a prop	uh prop
far	lluny	lyoon-**yuh**
up/over	a dalt	uh dahl
down/under	a baix	uh bah-eeshh
early	aviat	uhv-**yat**
late	tard	tahrt
entrance	entrada	uhn-**trah**-thuh
exit	sortida	soor-**tee**-thuh
toilet	lavabos/ serveis	luh-**vah**-boos sehr-**beh**-ees

more	més	mess
less	menys	menyees

Shopping

How much does this cost?	Quant costa això?	kwahn kost ehs-**shoh**
I would like ...	M'agradaria ...	muh-grad-uh-**ree**-ah
Do you have?	Tenen?	tehn-un
I'm just looking, thank you	Només estic mirant, gràcies.	noo-mess ehs-**teek** mee-**rahn** grah-see-uhs
Do you take credit cards?	Accepten targes de crèdit?	ak-**sehp**-tuhn tahr-**zhuhs** duh kreh-deet
What time do you open?	A quina hora obren?	ah **keen**-uh oh-ruh oh-bruhn
What time do you close?	A quina hora tanquen?	ah **keen**-uh oh-ruh tan-kuhn
This one.	Aquest	ah-**ket**
That one.	Aquell	ah-**kehl**
expensive	car	kahr
cheap	bé de preu/ barat	beh thuh **preh**-oo/bah-**rat**
size (clothes)	talla/mida	tah-lyah/mee-thuh
size (shoes)	número	noo-**mehr**-oo
white	blanc	blang
black	negre	neh-gruh
red	vermell	vuhr-**mel**
yellow	groc	grok
green	verd	behrt
blue	blau	blah-oo
antique store	antiquari/botiga d'antiguitats	an-tee-**kwah**-ree/boo-tee-gah/dan-tee-ghee-**tats**
bakery	el forn	uhl forn
bank	el banc	uhl bang
book store	la llibreria	lah lyee-bruh-**ree**-ah
butcher's	la carnisseria	lah kahr-nee-suh-**ree**-uh
pastry shop	la pastisseria	lah pahs-tee-suh-**ree**-uh
chemist's	la farmàcia	lah fuhr-**mah**-see-ah
fishmonger's	la peixateria	lah peh-shuh-tuh-**ree**-uh
greengrocer's	la fruiteria	lah froo-ee-tuh-**ree**-uh
grocer's	la botiga de queviures	lah boo-**tee**-guh duh keh-vee-oo-**oo**-ruhs
hairdresser's	la perruqueria	lah peh-roo-kuh-**ree**-uh
market	el mercat	uhl muhr-**kat**
newsagent's	el quiosc de premsa	uhl kee-**ohsk** duh **prem**-suh
post office	l'oficina de correus	loo-fee-see-nuh duh koo-**reh**-oos
shoe store	la sabateria	lah sah-bah-tuh-**ree**-uh
supermarket	el supermercat	uhl soo-puhr-muhr-**kat**
tobacconist's	l'estanc	luhs-**tang**
travel agency	l'agència de viatges	la-**jen**-see-uh duh vee-**ad**-juhs

Sightseeing

art gallery	la galeria d'art	lah gah-luh-**ree**-yuh dart
cathedral	la catedral	lah kuh-tuh-**thrahl**
church	l'església	luhz-**gleh**-zee-uh
	la basílica	lah buh-**zee**-lee-kuh
garden	el jardí	uhl zhahr-**dee**
library	la biblioteca	lah bee-blee-oo-**teh**-kuh
museum	el museu	uhl moo-**seh**-oo
tourist information office	l'oficina de turisme	loo-fee-**see**-nuh thuh too-**reez**-muh
town hall	l'ajuntament	luh-djoon-tuh-**men**
closed for holiday	tancat per vacances	tan-**kat** puh bah-**kan**-suhs
bus station	l'estació d'autobusos	luhs-tah-see-**oh** dow-toh-**boo**-zoos
railway station	l'estació de tren	luhs-tah-see-**oh** thuh **tren**

Staying in a Hotel

Do you have a vacant room?	¿Tenen una habitació lliure?	teh-nuhn oo-nuh ah-bee-tuh-see-**oh** lyuh-ruh

English	Catalan	Pronunciation
double room with double bed	habitació doble amb llit de matrimoni	ah-bee-tuh-see-oh doh-bluh am lyeet duh mah-tree-moh-nee
twin room	habitació amb dos llits/ amb llits individuals	ah-bee-tuh-see-oh am dohs lyeets/ am lyeets in-thee-vee-thoo-ahls
single room	habitació individual	ah-bee-tuh-see-oh een-dee-vee-thoo-ahl
room with a bath	habitació amb bany	ah-bee-tuh-see-oh am bahnyuh
shower	dutxa	doo-chuh
porter	el grum	uhl groom
key	la clau	lah klah-oo
I have a reservation	Tinc una habitació reservada	ting oo-nuh ah-bee-tuh-see-oh reh-sehr-vah-thah

Eating Out

English	Catalan	Pronunciation
Have you got a table for...	Tenen taula per...?	teh-nuhn tow-luh puhr
I would like to reserve a table	Voldria reservar una taula.	vool-dree-uh reh-sehr-vahr oo-nuh tow-luh
The bill please.	El compte, si us plau.	uhl kohm-tuh sees plah-oo
I am a vegetarian	Sóc vegetarià/ vegetariana	sok buh-zhuh-tuh-ree-ah buh-zhuh-tuh-ree-ah-nah
waitress	cambrera	kam-breh-ruh
waiter	cambrer	kam-breh
menu	la carta	lah kahr-tuh
fixed-price menu	menú del dia	muh-noo thuhl dee-uh
wine list	la carta de vins	lah kahr-tuh thuh veens
glass of water	un got d'aigua	oon got dah-ee-gwah
glass of wine	una copa de vi	oo-nuh ko-pah thuh vee
bottle	una ampolla	oo-nuh am-pol-yuh
knife	un ganivet	oon gun-ee-veht
fork	una forquilla	oo-nuh foor-keel-yuh
spoon	una cullera	oo-nuh kool-yeh-ruh
breakfast	l'esmorzar	les-moor-sah
lunch	el dinar	uhl dee-nah
dinner	el sopar	uhl soo-pah
main course	el primer plat	uhl pree-meh plat
starters	els entrants	uhlz ehn-tranz
dish of the day	el plat del dia	uhl plat duhl dee-uh
coffee	el cafè	uhl kah-feh
rare	poc fet	pok fet
medium	al punt	ahl poon
well done	molt fet	mol fet

Menu Decoder *(see also pp30–31 & 144–5)*

Catalan	Pronunciation	English
l'aigua mineral	lah-ee-gwuh mee-nuh-rahl	mineral water
sense gas/amb gas	sen-zuh gas/am gas	still/sparkling
al forn	ahl forn	baked
l'all	lahlyuh	garlic
l'arròs	lahr-roz	rice
les botifarres	lahs boo-tee-fah-rahs	sausages
la carn	lah karn	meat
la ceba	lah seh-buh	onion
la cervesa	lah-sehr-ve-sah	beer
l'embotit	lum-boo-teet	cold meat
el filet	uhl fee-let	sirloin
el formatge	uhl for-mah-djuh	cheese
fregit	freh-zheet	fried
la fruita	lah froo-ee-tah	fruit
els fruits secs	uhlz froo-eets seks	nuts
les gambes	lahs gam-bus	prawns
el gelat	uhl djuh-lat	ice cream
la llagosta	lah lyah-gos-tah	lobster
la llet	lah lyet	milk
la llimona	lah lyee-moh-nah	lemon
la llimonada	lah lyee-moh-nah-thuh	lemonade
la mantega	lah mahn-teh-gah	butter
el marisc	uhl muh-reesk	seafood
la menestra	lah muh-nehs-truh	vegetable stew
l'oli	loll-ee	oil
les olives	luhs oo-lee-vuhs	olives
l'ou	loh-oo	egg

Catalan	Pronunciation	English
el pa	uhl pah	bread
el pastís	uhl pahs-tees	pie/cake
les patates	lahs pah-tah-tuhs	potatoes
el pebre	uhl peh-bruh	pepper
el peix	uhl pehsh	fish
el pernil salat serrà	uhl puhr-neel suh-lat sehr-rah	cured ham
el plàtan	uhl plah-tun	banana
el pollastre	uhl poo-lyah-struh	chicken
la poma	la poh-mah	apple
el porc	uhl pohr	pork
les postres	lahs pohs-truhs	dessert
rostit	rohs-teet	roast
la sal	lah sahl	salt
la salsa	lah sahl-suh	sauce
les salsitxes	lahs sahl-see-chuhs	sausages
sec	sehk	dry
la sopa	lah soh-puh	soup
el sucre	uhl-soo-kruh	sugar
la taronja	lah tuh-rohn-djuh	orange
el te	uhl teh	tea
les torrades	lahs too-rah-thuhs	toast
la vedella	lah veh-theh-lyuh	beef
el vi blanc	uhl bee blang	white wine
el vi negre	uhl bee neh-gruh	red wine
el vi rosat	uhl bee roo-zaht	rosé wine
el vinagre	uhl bee-nah-gruh	vinegar
el xai/el be	uhl shahee/uhl beh	lamb
el xerès	uhl shuh-rehs	sherry
la xocolata	lah shoo-koo-lah-tuh	chocolate
el xoriç	uhl shoo-rees	red sausage

Numbers

0	zero	seh-roo
1	un (masc)	oon
	una (fem)	oon-uh
2	dos (masc)	dohs
	dues (fem)	doo-uhs
3	tres	trehs
4	quatre	kwa-truh
5	cinc	seeng
6	sis	sees
7	set	set
8	vuit	voo-eet
9	nou	noh-oo
10	deu	deh-oo
11	onze	on-zuh
12	doce	doh-dzuh
13	tretze	treh-dzuh
14	catorze	kah-tohr-dzuh
15	quinze	keen-zuh
16	setze	set-zuh
17	disset	dee-set
18	divuit	dee-voo-eet
19	dinou	dee-noh-oo
20	vint	been
21	vint-i-un	been-tee-oon
22	vint-i-dos	been-tee-dohs
30	trenta	tren-tah
31	trenta-un	tren-tah oon
40	quaranta	kwuh-ran-tuh
50	cinquanta	seen-kwahn-tah
60	seixanta	seh-ee-shan-tah
70	setanta	seh-tan-tah
80	vuitanta	voo-ee-tan-tah
90	noranta	noh-ran-tah
100	cent	sen
101	cent un	sent oon
102	cent dos	sen dohs
200	dos-cents (masc)	dohs-sens
	dues-centes (fem)	doo-uhs sen-tuhs
300	tres-cents	trehs-senz
400	quatre-cents	kwah-truh-senz
500	cinc-cents	seeng-senz
600	sis-cents	sees-senz
700	set-cents	set-senz
800	vuit-cents	voo-eet-senz
900	nou-cents	noh-oo-cenz
1,000	mil	meel
1,001	mil un	meel oon

Time

one minute	un minut	oon mee-noot
one hour	una hora	oo-nuh oh-ruh
half an hour	mitja hora	mee-juh oh-ruh
Monday	dilluns	dee-lyoonz
Tuesday	dimarts	dee-marts
Wednesday	dimecres	dee-meh-kruhs
Thursday	dijous	dee-zhoh-oos
Friday	divendres	dee-ven-druhs
Saturday	dissabte	dee-sab-tuh
Sunday	diumenge	dee-oo-men-juh

Rail Transport Maps

The main map shows the whole of Barcelona's Metro system, which has nine lines. It also shows the city's FGC suburban lines, funiculars and tram *(see pp184–5)*. Public transport in Barcelona is modern and efficient, and the integrated transport system allows for interchanging between different modes of transport if you have a multi-journey (for example a *T-10*) card. A special ticket for tourists is the *Barcelona Card*, available in one-day to five-day values, which offers unlimited travel on Metro and bus, and discounts at leading sights and museums. The inset map shows Catalonia's mainline rail network, which is run by RENFE, the Spanish state system. The stations selected for inclusion here are those closest to sights described in this guide.

KEY

L1	Metro line	Funicular
O	Interchange station	FGC line
	Tram line	Renfe line

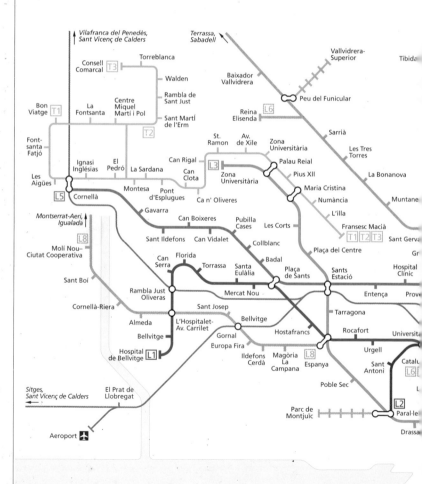